Said in Stone

Your Game, My Way

Steve Stone

TRIUMPH
BOOKS

This book is available in quantity at special discounts for your group or organization. For further information, contact:

Triumph Books
542 South Dearborn Street
Suite 750
Chicago, Illinois 60605
(312) 939-3330
Fax (312) 663-3557
www.triumphbooks.com

Printed in U.S.A.
ISBN: 978-1-60078-538-2
Design by Sue Knopf

To Paul H. Stone, my father,
who passed away in January of 2011
and who designed my pitching motion—
whose unwavering belief and support
of my every effort, both in and out of baseball,
helped make me who I am today.
He was a constant source of belief,
even when I lost some in myself,
and he was always there to help restore it.
I dedicate this particular book
to not only a wonderful father,
but a truly great human being.

Contents

Preface

If you want to learn about the game I love, you've come to the right place.

During my 14 professional seasons in baseball I always heard retired players saying, "The game was better during my era." I promised myself often I would never make that broad assessment.

I'm older and wiser now, and in this book, I state cases for both sides of the argument.

Entire books have been devoted to each position, each play, and each situation. Instead of getting too in depth, I want to give you the technical aspect of each position, along with a few things that you probably don't know, and that way I can touch on all of them.

Each chapter also includes funny stories and anecdotes. Past, present, and future predictions are encompassed in this book. I know you'll learn some things that you didn't know. I hope you'll laugh, too, because baseball is loaded with great characters who do strange things.

My goal is to help you to understand a very complicated game that, on the surface, looks quite simple. Baseball is similar to chess: once you learn how the pieces and players move, you can understand the game.

But like chess, baseball has many layers. Keep digging and you will see how this simple-looking game is infinitely complex. The greater your understanding of the game, the more you will appreciate the beauty of the most difficult of all sports.

To understand this great game, it helps to know about the man whose nickname was "the Genius." This manager was widely acclaimed as the smartest baseball man in the game. Some very smart players whom I've talked to over the years still think that his baseball mind was second to none. I don't know if he was the best, but he was always in the conversation.

Yet this lifelong baseball man presided over one of the greatest baseball collapses in history. The 1964 Philadelphia Phillies had it all wrapped up with a 6½-game lead with 12 games to go, only to lose 10 consecutive games and finish in second place in the National League by one game.

As manager of the California Angels, he allowed his right-handed pitcher, Luis Sanchez, to face Cecil Cooper in the seventh inning of the fifth and deciding game of the 1982 American League playoffs, even though he had Andy Hassler, who was unhittable against left-handed hitters, warming up in the bullpen. Hassler never faced Cooper, who hit a two-run single off Sanchez to give the Brewers a 4–3 lead and the AL title. Hassler, by the way, entered after Cooper's single and struck out Ted Simmons to end the inning.

The Genius never managed a team to the World Series, and he was under .500 lifetime.

The Genius was Gene Mauch. People still say he was a baseball savant. My question always has been, if the Genius couldn't get to the World Series and finished his managerial run under .500, what does that say about the rest of us baseball lifers?

Here's another story that tells you a lot about the game we love. After the 1972 season I played in a golf tournament on the Monterey Peninsula in California. My partner that day was Hank Sauer, a former home run hitter and baseball executive with the San Francisco Giants.

Hank was my Triple A Fresno manager, and we had a cocktail after the round. Hank said, "Kid, they tried to trade you last year, but I told the general manager that you were going to be good."

I thanked him for his confidence in me. "I want to assure you that as long as I'm here, you're here," he continued. "You'll have a good career, and it will be with the San Francisco Giants."

I felt relieved because I came up with the Giants and liked San Francisco.

Ten days later, I was golfing at the Silverado Resort in Napa Valley when I was informed there was a telephone call for me in the clubhouse from Nick Peters, a Giants beat writer now in the National Baseball Hall of Fame.

Nick informed me that I had been traded to the Chicago White Sox. Hank spent another 20 years with the Giants.

As my former partner Harry Caray would say, "That's baseball."

• • •

As I set out to understand about getting better as a baseball player, specifically as a pitcher, I made a conscious decision each day to do something when I came to the park to make me better. Whether it was something physical or mental or some type of observance during the course of a game, I decided that I was going to do something to make myself better. Watching the other team, for example, is going to make you better. You might even decide to watch batting practice or to watch the opposing outfielders throw. Or you might run a little extra, which will give you a little more endurance. Work out just a little bit harder on given days, depending on what your pitching schedule is.

That was my philosophy. Many people don't understand that players squander countless hours at the ballpark doing things that don't really make them better as a baseball player. I'm not saying you can't have any fun. I'm not saying that you shouldn't work on a crossword puzzle on occasion or play cards, as some people do in the locker room.

But if you try on a daily basis to make yourself better, it's not going to take a long time to get better. Not everyone is a superstar, nor do they have to be. If you consider that 10 percent of the players are superstars and 10 percent in the game are interchangeable with minor league players because they keep going up and down, it's the 80 percent in the middle who can get better on a daily basis by doing something small to get better.

Just the old-fashioned notion of having conversations with guys on your team, some of the great hitters on your team—and every team obviously has them—can make you better. Sit down and ask a player if you could have a couple of minutes of his time, and ask him his philosophy about what he's looking for.

Some guys aren't going to tell you all of their trade secrets because they realize in this game it often is a matter of you're here one day and gone the next. But most guys are more than willing to share with their teammates many of the philosophies that make them a great hitter.

If you're a hitter, you might want to have a conversation with one of the great pitchers on your team and ask, "How would you get me out?" Have him explain it to you. Hitting coaches are another valuable source of information, not just on the mechanics of hitting but also on the psychology of hitting. Pitching coaches are another valuable resource. Sure, they can all tell you how to improve your curveball, and there are several things mechanically that you can ask about. But those are things that you will talk about on a daily basis.

I'm suggesting going away from the norm, having that conversation with somebody you wouldn't usually talk to. Try talking to a coach, especially a baserunning coach for a pitcher, and asking what he looks for when trying to steal a base and how you can improve in holding runners close. An active mind can sit back and come up with 50 or 100 things that he's either weak at or doesn't know.

During the course of a game, you can sit and talk with your teammates. That's certainly a valuable source of information. But you can also learn just by looking at the field, because there's a tremendous amount to be gleaned from just observing what goes on on the field on an inning-by-inning and pitch-by-pitch basis.

Whenever I had the chance, I would try to talk to as many of the older baseball people as I could. They were veterans, guys who were retired, guys who were always around teams. I would always try to engage them in conversation and, if out of a 10-minute conversation I was able to learn one thing that I never had heard of, or one philosophy that I had never thought of, I was better for it.

That comes back to the original premise of getting a little better every day. As I started to figure out how to make myself better, it was the very simple thing of dedicating every day to getting just a little bit better—however that may be.

This is one of the things that I think is so important. It doesn't matter what your skill set is. What does matter is making yourself better, because there is no such thing in baseball as staying the same. You either go forward or you slip backward. It's as simple as that, whether it's as a team or as an individual. That's a way to make sure you're going to stay around in this game: constant improvement.

A significant portion of this book details why organizations don't assemble a winning baseball team, while explaining to you—the fan—each position, each front-office position, each roster, and the configuration of all of the above. But one of the easiest ways to explain a baseball season that doesn't go your way is commonly known as "the good luck and bad luck syndrome."

I will often hear a manager or general manager, or in some cases, an owner, say things like, "We will not blame anything on injuries. However, we had our second baseman go out in June, we had our shortstop go out in July, we had two starting pitchers out by August, and our bullpen disintegrated." They go on and on complaining about things they just said they weren't going to complain about, or things they weren't going to use as excuses.

But at the end of the day, after 162 games, there are no excuses. The luck, good and bad, evens out. The hot streaks even out. The cold streaks even out. Yet teams will refuse to see this. It seems the teams that usually lose or haven't won in a long time have the most excuses as to why they didn't win. Whether it's, "Well, the weather wasn't good at home," or, "We got off to a such a slow start in April and May that we just couldn't catch up," or, "A few of our hitters hit so poorly at the beginning of the season that by the time they started to hit, it was too late"—all of these are just excuses.

The reality is that over the course of a season, you'll have guys with career years. You hope to have a few of those guys. If you do, and a number of players have average years, you will be in very good shape. You also will count on a couple of young players who must take that next step and become quality major leaguers. But then we hear from some teams that have some problems, and they just can't seem to get it done.

But it's the good baseball teams that take over late in the season. The bad teams give way. It's just like in a single game, where the good teams take the game away in the seventh, eighth, and ninth and the bad teams give the game away in those innings. You can talk to teams that will make a lot of excuses about what happened, but in the end, the good teams can weather these setbacks, come back, and win.

• • •

I once had a very enlightening exchange with a great hitter who gave me an interesting insight into hitting. Besides the obvious, such as hand-eye coordination and all of the other things he worked on, I asked him, "What is the key that took you from a good hitter to a great hitter?"

He said very simply, "Never wasted an at-bat."

I've talked to many great hitters about that, and they feel the same way. If they're 4-for-4 and they go up for their next at-bat, they want to go 5-for-5. If the score is 12–0 when they come up for their next at-bat, they're not going to make an easy out. They're going to try to grind out every at-bat, and over the course of a season, it turns into much higher numbers.

Although it seems kind of simple, it really isn't. Whether you're ahead or behind by a big number late in the game, the truly great hitters are still trying to get that hit. They're trying to get on base any way they can. I've seen a lot of guys with wasted at-bats. I've seen a lot of guys in blowouts, one way or another, swing at the first pitch—which is a pitcher's pitch—because they believe the game is over and they want to get it over with.

But not the great hitters.

That's the meaning of the credo "Never waste an at-bat." That philosophy can turn an average hitter into a good hitter, and a good hitter into a great hitter.

Acknowledgments

First of all, I'd like to thank Mark Gonzales, whose research, writing, and assembling of facts where my memory failed me was invaluable to the completion of this book. I also could not have explained how front offices work nearly as well without the help of the White Sox assistant general manager Rick Hahn, as well as White Sox general manager Kenny Williams. I had the opportunity to speak with the owner of the White Sox, Jerry Reinsdorf. Jerry gave me an overview of where baseball has been, where it is now, and where he feels it's going. Without that perspective, I wouldn't have been nearly as insightful about our great game.

My thanks also go out to a longtime friend who just happens to be the commissioner of baseball, Bud Selig. From the time that I was a player through the many incarnations of my broadcast career, Bud has always been very generous with his time and been patient with my questions. He's given me the ability to understand what's going on just by sharing his reasons for the decisions he has to make on a daily basis.

I never pretended to be one of the great authors, so I went to a friend of mine who actually is a great author. His political knowledge and breadth of work is amazing, and he just happens to have an abiding love of baseball. So my thanks go out to national, political, and baseball author par excellence, George Will.

I'd also like to thank all of the players I played with and against, as well as all of the managers, coaches, GMs, and assistant GMs who have graciously given me their time and insights, imparting some of their baseball wisdom to me for over a quarter of a century during my broadcast career.

I know that I am probably leaving out many people I've encountered heading into this, my fifth decade in professional baseball, but suffice to say this wonderful game has many wonderful people in it and I have been fortunate to interact with most of them. Without the cooperation, the help, and the knowledge of all these people that I have mentioned, this book would not have been possible.

Catching

I was a free agent in the first free-agent class after the 1976 season. I had a rotator cuff injury—came back from it with no surgery, just a lot of rehabilitation. The Cubs decided that they didn't want to sign me, so they let me go for nothing. And so I became the Cubs' first free agent.

Then I signed with the Chicago White Sox, with Bill Veeck guaranteeing me one year and telling me (although I knew that I gave away my rights to free agency for five years), that he didn't have that kind of money. My 3–6 record the previous season didn't warrant a multiyear contract. But he was willing to take a gamble by guaranteeing me one year, and in an effort to make it equitable, he would give me my free agency at the end of that first year.

So I told him that I was indeed healthy, that things just didn't work out on the north side of town, and wound up leading the White Sox's staff with 15 wins in 1977.

I went to Bill's office toward the end of the season, and he asked me if I was going to exercise my free-agent rights. I told him no, I was not, because I had seen all of his young pitchers, and they weren't ready.

I told him my father always said to balance the scales in life. If someone does something for you, and you have an opportunity to do something for them, then you pay them back for thoughtfulness or anything that enables you to make yourself a little bit better. In this case, Bill Veeck had given me an opportunity to reestablish myself in the major leagues.

"I'm going to give you one year back, and at the end of this year," I told Bill, "I'd also like my free agency."

Bill had no problem with that, virtually doubling my·salary and eventually telling me that he would bring me back, even after that second year. The 1978 season saw me with a 12–12 record. We weren't very good, but I did lead his staff in victories for the second consecutive season. He suggested that I go into free agency and that he would guarantee me a one-year, $200,000 contract if nobody picked me in free agency, so I could go into that year with a clear mind, knowing that I had a job if nobody else wanted me.

Baltimore drafted me and eventually signed me to a four-year contract. But after the Orioles made their lucrative offer, I went in to see Bill Veeck again, and he suggested to me that I had to take the Baltimore offer because it would give me security that he couldn't possibly give me.

So we shook hands—we were even—and I was off. It was in Baltimore at that point where I had enough experience in the major leagues where I finally found out how a winning baseball team was put together and how to be a part of a winning baseball team.

In my first year with the San Francisco Giants in 1971, we won our division. But I was so young and immature as a baseball player at the age of 23 that I really didn't understand how things worked. I just knew that we had four Hall of Famers. We had Juan Marichal as our ace and Gaylord Perry as the No. 2 starter. We had Willie Mays in center field and Willie McCovey at first base. We had Bobby Bonds in right field, a five-time member of the 30-30 club with three different teams. We had a very solid baseball team. So it was kind of lost on me how exactly we did win it, and what we had to do to play winning baseball.

Fast-forward to the winter of 1978–79, when I decided, with a lot of counseling from Bill Veeck, to take the Orioles' offer. I already had been to Baltimore once to help negotiate the contract with my agents but elected to return. During my second visit, I read an article in the daily newspaper that included quotes from Jim Palmer, who questioned why Baltimore needed another middle-of-the-road right-handed starter. He was certainly right about that. I was certainly a middle-of-the-road, right-handed starter, being under .500 at the time. He said Baltimore doesn't need that guy, meaning me. Baltimore was in desperate need of a run-producing outfielder. As it turned out, in that 1979 season when we won 102 games and made it to the World Series, we had a combination of Gary Roenicke and John Lowenstein in left field. They wound up hitting 36 home runs combined. One thing jumped out at me a little later in the article.

When I saw essentially all of the quotes were by Palmer, it was my "welcome to Baltimore" moment. Hank Peters, who was my general manager at the time, replied, "Well, we really respect Jim Palmer because he is a wonderful pitcher and destined for the Hall of Fame." Of course, he was all of that.

"But he really doesn't understand what we do here in Baltimore," Peters continued. "And so we suggest that Jim continue his role as one of our star pitchers and let us continue our role of putting together a winning baseball team. Because the philosophy he has missed with the Baltimore Orioles is when we are 100 percent certain that we have enough pitching, we add another pitcher."

That kind of typified the philosophy of the Baltimore Orioles. Catch the baseball, stay out of the big inning, and when you have enough pitching, you add another pitcher. That worked for many, many years; Baltimore won more games from 1960 to 1985 than anyone in baseball. And they did it with a strong minor league system, good player development, and outstanding pitching—by developing pitchers and occasionally going outside the organization to acquire them. That, in itself, told me all I wanted to know about the Orioles philosophy.

That being said, baseball experts have stressed for years that a baseball team has to be strong up the middle to be effective. By being strong up the middle, that means you have a very good defensive catcher; whatever he hits, he hits, but defense is first. You put a good man on the mound on a daily basis. You have a shortstop and a second baseman that can turn a double play and not give anyone four outs in an inning. And you have a center fielder who can go get them, alley to alley. That's what Baltimore usually did.

But Baltimore wasn't the only team that did this. That was a baseball truism, as they say. There were other teams who did it a different way or used that way partially and then made up for it. There's no doubt that first and third base are your power positions, left and right field are your power positions, but the teams that are consistently strong up the middle are the teams that get the job done.

I take a look at the Cincinnati Reds, the Big Red Machine, with Johnny Bench behind the plate, Davey Concepcion and Joe Morgan in the middle, and Cesar Geronimo in center field. That was a very strong team up the middle, as well as at the corners. You're talking about one of the all-time great baseball teams ever assembled.

The 1972–74 Oakland Athletics were a great team, with Bert Campaneris and Dick Green in the middle of the infield, Billy North in center field, and Gene Tenace behind the plate. Ray Fosse came along later as one of their great catchers. But also they put a great man on the mound every day. Everybody thought with Reggie Jackson and Joe Rudi and guys who could hit the ball, Oakland was a team that offensively could get the job done. But in reality, it was pitching and defense that won for Oakland. You do need the runs, but you also have to be able to limit the other teams' runs, and they were able to do it.

There are many more examples throughout the history of baseball of teams built on being strong up the middle. Being a former pitcher, I'd like to tell you pitchers are the most important player on the field and the smartest player on the field. But the reality of it is, it's not necessarily, in my estimation, the pitcher who should be and is the smartest man on the field. Realistically, I have to give the credit to the catchers.

I believe catcher is the toughest position in baseball, and I don't think it's an accident that many of your great major league catchers have become managers. The demands of their position, everything they have to know that makes them great catchers is the same thing they use to succeed as managers. So with my philosophy of how to put together a winning team, that catcher is essential, and the mechanical aspect of catching is very important.

I was fortunate in Baltimore to have one of the great physical catchers in baseball in Rick Dempsey. He would come out to visit me, and he was aware I was a curveball pitcher. He would tell me, "You can't throw it by me in the dirt. The only way you can get the ball by me is to throw it over my head. So throw me your best curveball with a runner at third base and understand that it's not going to get by me for a wild pitch. That run is not going to score."

Mike Scioscia was the same kind of catcher. In fact, I talked with Roger McDowell, now the pitching coach with the Atlanta Braves, and he said Scioscia basically said the same thing to him when they played together for a brief time with the Los Angeles Dodgers. This was especially important because McDowell was a sinkerball pitcher, and his wipeout pitch was usually one that ended up in the dirt after he got ahead of the hitters.

Scioscia told him, "You won't get the ball by me in the dirt." That gives a pitcher a great sense of comfort, and that's something most of the great catchers have in common. They block pitches well, they move side to side, they don't try to catch pitches in the dirt, but they move their elbows in, slant their upper body forward, let the ball hit off the chest protector, and make sure the ball rolls in front of them and the runners can't advance, especially with a man at third base.

But the catching position goes well beyond that. Much of this has to do a lot with a catcher's responsibilities. First and foremost, a catcher must be able to handle his pitchers and understand not necessarily what the pitcher's best pitch is—everyone knows when a guy has an overwhelming fastball or sinker or slider—it's the sequences of pitches and how you deal with situations like that.

It's understanding how you work a pitcher that comes into play: How to keep a pitcher in rhythm. How to get him in rhythm if he can't seem to get himself there. How to frame pitches. How to set up on the outside corner. My belief has always been if you have a right-handed pitcher who wants a fastball on the outside corner to a left-handed hitter, you put the thumb of your catcher's glove or the part of the glove closest to you on the outside corner. That means the catcher's glove is probably sitting two inches outside.

Do the same thing if you want the ball away if it's a right-handed pitcher to a right-handed hitter. You put the left part of your glove right on the outside corner. This takes a 17-inch plate and actually gives you two inches on each side of the plate, because more times than not, if you do that, you'll get that call from the ump.

Catching the ball and framing the pitch are of critical importance, as is the idea of understanding pitching sequence. Hand in hand with that is knowing the scouting report. Say a pitcher faces some particular hitter with two out and nobody on, and he pitches low and in and gets him out. Then the second time he faces him—maybe this time with two out and a man at first base—he goes low and in again, and gets the guy out.

Well, if he has to face him for a third or fourth time with the game on the line, the hitter is going to realize that the pitcher's hold card is low and in. If the pitcher tries to go back there again, it's going to wind up being a double down the line. A pitcher cannot go to his strength all the time, nor can he go to his hitter's weakness all the time. You may start with the pitcher's strength, and then if the batter can hit a pitcher's strength, then you go to a hitter's weakness. Sounds like a simple idea, but it doesn't happen very often. For instance, my strength was inside fastballs or sliders and breaking balls away. Every pitcher has a strength, and the catcher has to understand that and use it to the team's advantage.

But first and foremost for any catcher is the defensive aspect of the position. There are catchers who understand their main goal is to work that pitching staff, catch it, call it, block it, and throw it. That, to me, is the prerequisite of a catcher. A good arm and good footwork are essential. A good arm can be overcome by a quick release, but good footwork is a prerequisite for getting the ball away quickly. Good fast feet for a catcher are irreplaceable. Some guys have it, some guys don't, so that becomes one of the things you look for in your catcher.

Some catchers are basically offensive guys. They have a good bat, but they also add to the offense by way of a lower ERA. For instance, if a catcher has an ERA one run lower for his pitching staff than his backup, that's like driving in a run a game because you're saving your team one run a game. It's the equivalent of having a catcher who could drive in 162 runs. .

A catcher also has to be able to hit, so he has to know every opposing pitcher in the league and what he's going to do with him. He has to know every pitcher on his team and how to get the best out of him. It would help if he knew tendencies of the opposing manager, because then he would have a pretty good idea about when a guy might be bunting, although pitchouts are called from the dugout more times than not. Occasionally a catcher will be given the latitude to call his own pitchouts. Sometimes he'll be given the latitude to call his own pickoff plays, although that has become a rarity in this day and age.

A catcher has to think defense first. Then he must be able to hit the ball, as well as absorbing a tremendous beating because he's going to take foul tips off his shoulders and legs. On occasion, he's going to be run into by an opposing runner trying to score. In many instances he'll have to block the plate (although that's another skill that's becoming a dying art in baseball). But he's going to have to keep his concentration on a throw coming in from the outfield, especially from right field, where he can't see the runner charging from third. Then he has to put the tag on after catching the baseball cleanly. And you have guys who will make a throw on the fly. You'll have guys who make a throw on a bounce. You have to know which guys throw the ball with a tail, which guys throw the ball straight over the top, and it's going to come to you straight.

It's just an all-consuming position. If you happen to have a good catcher, then you've got yourself a little bit of gold within the framework of your lineup.

• • •

I played professionally for 14 seasons, and I've had quite a number of catchers. Some catchers helped me greatly behind the plate, and some were a little shakier than others. I remember having Jim Essian behind the plate, and Jim was a terrific guy. Jim didn't have the strongest arm, but he had a quick release, was very enthusiastic behind the plate, and later went on to become a major league manager.

I remember in Oakland that Essian and I had a fairly unusual situation come up. There were runners at first and third and only one out, and Jim had a pretty good idea that the man at first was going to run. So he came out to me and said, "Look, if that guy on first base breaks to second, don't react."

I wasn't really sure what he was telling me because there's not much a pitcher can do when a man tries to steal second base, except get out of the way to make sure you don't get hit by the catcher's throw if it is low. You're certainly not going to cut it off. You're going to let it go through. When he said to me, "Don't react," I just said, "Okay, I won't react." And sure enough, on the first pitch, the man from first base did break toward second, and Essian came up throwing.

Then all of a sudden, with the same arm motion he had on all of his throws to second base, I see this throw coming, but then it started to pinwheel up in the air. Just about everyone in the infield, except the base runner, who had a single-minded purpose—to try to steal second base— just watched it as it climbed higher and higher in the middle of the infield and came to rest somewhere behind the mound.

Unfortunately for Jim, the base runner at third also was mesmerized by this pinwheeling object that he had decided to throw. Of course I went to pick it up, and it turned out Jim still had the baseball in his glove. He was waiting for the guy at third to break a step or two toward home plate, and then he was going to throw the ball to third and pick him off. The problem was that the guy at third, after taking one step, was obsessed with what Jim had thrown in the infield because he had never seen a baseball go straight up in the air.

That's because it wasn't a baseball.

As Jim came out and looked at me with this sheepish grin, I said to him, "You tried to get him with the old sponge trick, didn't you?" He just shook his head and said, "Yes." He had thrown the catcher's sponge that he wore inside his glove, and, thinking that the man would take the bait and break toward the plate, he was trying to get a cheap out. As it turned out, I had runners at second and third with no play made by anyone. I handed him back his sponge and tried to pitch my way out of it.

But that story brings up a good point.

A good catcher is going to try to figure out a way to get an out without his pitcher actually making a pitch, and some teams are better at it than others. I go back to the Baltimore Orioles, and of course this was masterminded by the Hall of Fame manager Earl Weaver, who always was looking for ways to get outs without his pitchers throwing a pitch.

One example is something called a "daylight pickoff." That's when a shortstop, with a man at second base, will get fairly close to the man at second base on his lead, and then extend his left glove hand. If a pitcher can see his hand between the bag and the base runner, then the pitcher whirls and throws to second. That requires the pitcher to look back, which means you have to have a quick shortstop, your pitcher has to make a very good throw, and hopefully you can catch a base runner and get an out without making a pitch.

You also have to depend on your catcher at times. We had one of the signals where the pitcher never even looked at second base, and the catcher would give the pitcher whatever sign it might be. For example, say a pitcher doesn't have five pitches. The catcher signals 2-1-3-5 to the pitcher, and now the pitcher knows there is going to be a pickoff at second base. The pitcher looks into his catcher, and as soon as the catcher takes his hand and moves it straight down, the pitcher turns and throws to second.

In this case the base runner, knowing the pitcher hasn't looked at him yet, is probably inching away on his lead. The shortstop, who also looks into the catcher and knows that 5 is the pickoff sign, will be ready to make the play.

A lot of managers don't want to do this because they don't trust their catcher to make this play. But it's a terrific play, and some catchers do it better than others.

My catcher at Kent State was the late Thurman Munson, who I believe was destined to go to the Hall of Fame with the New York Yankees. In our sophomore year—our first year in the Mid-American Conference, where we played together on the varsity—we tried a pickoff play at third.

We were so certain that we could pick the runner off third that we'd use two pitches and throw them in a manner so our third baseman knew what was coming.

With any luck, we'd have an aggressive base runner at third. He didn't have to be overly aggressive; just a guy who would take a pretty good secondary lead when the pitch was on the way to the plate. Thurman would give a sign and I would go into the stretch on the first pitch, keeping my eyes on the man at third base.

My first pitch was always up and in. I didn't want to hit the batter, just push him off the plate. Now I was 1–0, and I would then wave the third baseman away because I went into a windup, not a stretch, at 1–0. If it was a right-handed hitter, I would throw a high, tight fastball and knock him off the plate. If it was a left-handed hitter, I would throw one over the right-handed batter's box so he couldn't touch it.

Thurman would catch it and would either throw it over the batter's head or throw it behind him, depending on where he caught the ball. Munson was a master at throwing the ball exactly where he caught it and getting rid of it exceptionally quickly. He carried that over to the major leagues, where probably 75 percent of the catchers had stronger arms than he did, but very few were more accurate than he was, and none were quicker than he was.

In eight consecutive games during our sophomore year, Thurman picked a man off third base on this play. If you think about it, you're taking a potential run off, but eight straight games of using this play with success convinced the rest of the Mid-American Conference. Thanks to scouts and observers, word got around, and there were no secondary leads against us.

• • •

It's extremely important for a catcher to instill confidence in his pitcher and be realistic in telling him on a daily basis what kind of stuff he has because, honestly, the pitcher usually is the last one to know. It's up to the catcher to remind a pitcher that his fastball might have lost its hop, so they're going to try something else—either use a slider and use it as an off-speed pitch; change speeds on a curve; or change grips on the fastball—and use this when his stuff isn't particularly sharp.

Sandy Koufax, one of the greatest pitchers of all time, once said that he had his best stuff 25 percent of the time. That meant he had to learn to pitch without his best for the other 75 percent of the time.

Ironically, Koufax developed into the pitcher he was because of a catcher with the Dodgers named Norm Sherry, who helped him while catching him in the bullpen.

There was a rule at the time that if you received a signing bonus of $4,000 or higher, you had to stay with the major league team for a couple of seasons rather than going down to the minors. That retarded the progress of some of the young players who otherwise could have been in the minor leagues working on becoming polished players. In the case of Koufax, he was in the major leagues and couldn't get his fastball over the plate. Sherry told him he didn't have to throw every pitch as hard as he could, that it was best to take something off and hit the glove. Koufax worked on throwing to the glove and taking something off his overwhelming fastball and astonishing curveball to throw to various spots. The more he worked on it, the easier it got for him.

Eventually Koufax was able to throw his fastball and his other pitches to various spots. He became one of the great pitchers of all time, as evidenced by his dominance in the short amount of time he played.

That was due to a catcher who was a little observant but never became a star. Sherry took a young pitcher, gave him one thing that he had never heard before, and trained him on a daily basis to turn him into a guy who is still held in reverence when they talk about pitchers. That's one of the things that catchers have to do.

I found that the best catchers are the guys who know where every hitter sets up, look for any adjustment he might make during the course of the game for whatever his pitcher is trying to do to him, and then either tell the pitcher between innings or go to him and say, "This guy has started to look away, so we're going to begin to bust him inside."

Most hitters will line up in the same spot and keep their hands the same way against a pitcher. A catcher must take note of this. Many times if his pitcher isn't all that aware of where a hitter set up the first or second time up, the catcher has to be the one to find out if the hitter is making an adjustment.

Perceptive pitchers like Greg Maddux will know any variation that a hitter is going to make. He's going to watch everything a hitter does, because just like a good catcher, he should have a photographic memory as far as the hitter is concerned. Then he can use that information to get the hitter out.

Major league catchers have to learn the 12 or 13 pitchers on their staff and find a way to get the best out of each one. Catchers have to realize that there are guys that I call "tender psyche" guys. Those are the guys who generally have confidence problems. Sometimes in the course of the game, their confidence will wane and come back, wane and come back. It's up to a catcher—sometimes between innings or during an inning—to communicate to the pitcher that he has good enough stuff to get the job done and to give him what he needs at various times.

A catcher can take a look in a pitcher's eyes and notice when a pitcher is losing his focus or his confidence to get out of a jam in any inning. The good catchers are able to give the pitcher what he needs at any given time. Sometimes it's a kick in the butt; other times it's a confidence-building conversation. Sometimes it's giving him a fist pump, putting down a signal and telling him, "You can make this pitch. And if you make this pitch, you can get this guy out." That's what catchers have to be able to do. It's what separates the ones who simply catch from the really good or great catchers who are the greatest assets to their pitchers.

• • •

One of the things I truly believe is that the game of baseball is won 90 feet at a time. It's either taking 90 feet from the other team or giving it away. A good catcher can save 90 feet on pitches in the dirt or a pickoff at second or a block at home. He can remind a pitcher when he's not varying his looks or varying his time as far as holding the baseball with a good base runner on.

A pitching coach can do that, but he's limited to only one trip to the mound per inning. We've seen catchers make multiple trips to the mound. But more than that, a catcher can remind a pitcher about certain base runners or that he has to perform a particular thing to make himself very effective on a given day. It doesn't always have to be a trip to the mound.

The idea of a solid target is something that several catchers don't understand, and sometimes it comes down to pitcher preference. There are some pitchers who have a fastball that moves so much they like their catcher in the middle of the plate. Other pitchers will want the catcher moving to the spot to give the pitcher a very low target if he wants it down or shifting up if he wants a high fastball. Hitting that target sometimes will determine if that pitcher makes a good pitch or bad pitch. The only thing a catcher has to be very aware of is if he shifts too early with a smart base runner at second or a very aware first-base coach. Some catchers are aware of this, but some aren't, and they might be showing their cards to the opposing team.

We had a very good first-base coach with the San Francisco Giants in Wes Westrum, who was a former catcher who excelled with the New York Giants. Within three innings, Wes knew every pitch the pitcher was throwing, based on a tip-off from either the pitcher or the catcher. Unfortunately, a lot of catchers don't know they are tipping someone off.

When we faced St. Louis, we didn't hit Hall of Famers like Bob Gibson or Steve Carlton, when Carlton was there. But by watching what catcher Ted Simmons was doing, Wes was able to pick up every time a breaking ball was coming. Just by an infinitesimal move of Simmons' right foot.

When Simmons called a slider or breaking ball with a right-handed pitcher on the mound to a right-handed hitter, it wasn't that he set up away; it was that his right foot was actually set up about two or three inches behind his left foot. When he called for a fastball, his feet were in line with each other. Wes, being a former catcher, was able to pick that up and consequently had all of the pitches. We had them from the catcher—not the pitcher. It shows that catchers have habits, just like pitchers do.

Similarly, the Chicago Cubs, at one point, had a tell on Sandy Koufax. When Koufax went into the stretch, he kept his elbows one way for a fastball and another way for a curveball. It didn't matter that he happened to throw a perfect game against the Cubs. But many times catchers will have several distinctive mannerisms too, depending on what pitches are coming. Because of that, they have to be very careful that they're not tipping any pitches.

I always liken baseball to chess: once you learn the movement of the pieces, it's very easy. However, it's played on so many layers that the average player can't conceive of what the grand master is able to see, which is four to seven moves down the road as he sets up his traps and various other things to defeat you.

Now, smart catchers always talk to the defense. They'll look at the defense before every pitch because they've got a very good idea about how they're going to work a given hitter. And if the defense is out of line from a catcher's standpoint, he's going to stand up and motion for a guy to move over, and most of the catchers will do that.

Some catchers will do this subtly. They might walk to the mound and call in the shortstop and second baseman and say, "We're going to work this guy a different way this time. I know what we've set up in the past, but let's play him to pull because it looks like he wants the ball away. Let's go inside. For the second baseman, you play him up the middle. For the shortstop, play him a step to pull." So those guys will go back to their positions and subtly make a move that hopefully the other team can't pick up; you don't want to give anything away to the hitter as far as defensive changes are concerned.

Being able to make these kinds of adjustments is one of the reasons catchers make the best managers. They have to know so much about the offensive and defensive aspects, how to work the starters, long men, setup relievers and closers, as well as how to play every hitter and all the other things that really go into being the captain on the field, whether he's a designated captain or not.

• • •

Rick Dempsey was very sound from a technical standpoint. You could assume he would block any pitch in the dirt. He had a very quick release, a very strong arm, and he was probably my favorite catcher to throw to. He was one of the great characters of the game, as illustrated by the fact that he played for at least parts of 24 major league seasons with six teams, helping two to World Series titles.

He was also involved in his share of funny instances, some with not such great endings.

I was pitching a game against the Cleveland Indians in 1980. I had a 4–0 lead in the second inning with a runner on base and facing the American League Rookie of the Year—Super Joe Charboneau.

Charboneau was a pretty good hitter, but his career quickly faded. His legend included being able to open bottles with his teeth and occasionally chewing on some of the pieces of glass.

But he could hit. With a four-run lead after the first inning, I felt pretty good, had pretty good stuff that day, and had every intention of winning the game. Then I saw Dempsey calling time and walking to the mound. I was wondering what he was going to say to me. It was early, and I was hitting my spots and doing what I needed to do.

Dempsey came out and said, "Hey, whatever you do, don't hang a curveball to this guy because he's the only guy in their lineup who can hit a home run."

It kind of struck me as odd, because I had no thought of hanging a curveball to him. Out of all the things that had entered my mind, hanging a curveball and watching him hit the ball out of the park was never anything I entertained. So he went back behind the plate, called a curveball—which I proceeded to hang—and Charboneau proceeded to hit it out of the park.

That gives you an example of the power of suggestion. A catcher can go out and change the rhythm of a pitcher. He can put a thought into the pitcher's head that he might not have been thinking about otherwise. In the case of Dempsey, it was usually a good thought. But that particular time, it appears the phraseology wasn't particularly good. The end result was a no-decision in a game I probably would have won.

Balance that with all the games that Dempsey did help me win, and it certainly weighs heavily on his side, as he helped me win 25 games and the American League Cy Young Award that season. But I did approach him after the game and said, "Look, when you do come out to the mound, if that's the best you got for me, don't come out and say anything, because I had never even thought about hanging a curveball until that very moment."

I took full responsibility because I threw the pitch, I hung the curveball, but that bit of advice from him was not a positive affirmation. The thought process was short-circuited, and I believe that's not a benefit for any pitcher. So, for all you catchers and parents of prospective catchers, just tell your kids that if they do go out to talk to the pitcher, phrase their advice in positive terms. That way things usually work out a lot better.

Another incident with Rick Dempsey was something he disputes to this day. He remembers it one way, and I remember it another. But since this is my book, I will tell you the story from my standpoint.

It was 1979, and we went to Milwaukee to play the Brewers for our second series of the year. In the first series, they scored 24 runs against us in three games. This, despite the fact that we had a wonderful starting rotation. In fact, Mike Flanagan won a Cy Young Award that year. Our other left-hander, Scotty McGregor, was one of the best left-handers in the American League, and won 20 games that year. Jim Palmer won three Cy Young Awards, was a six-time All-Star, and was elected to the Hall of Fame. The fourth pitcher on the team was Dennis Martinez, who went on to win 245 games, throw a perfect game, and have a magnificent career. I was the fifth starter on that team.

In that first series against Milwaukee, they had a young Hall of Famer in Paul Molitor as their leadoff batter. Cecil Cooper, a perennial .300 hitter with power, was batting third. They had solid hitters in the middle of the order in Ben Oglivie and Gorman Thomas, a prolific home run hitter. Robin Yount, who went on to become a Hall of Famer, batted lower in the order with Jim Gantner, a pesky hitter. They also had older hitters who could still cause damage, like Don Money, Larry Hisle, and Sal Bando.

Well, at Miller Park today, and at old County Stadium if you remember that far back, the Brewers' mascot, Bernie Brewer, sits atop his perch waiting to slide down this ramp whenever the Brewers hit a home run. During that series in County Stadium, I was convinced, right or wrong—and probably wrong—that a combination of Bernie and someone in the scoreboard or in the center-field seats was somehow giving some signals on pitches to the Brewers' hitters.

Now this is not a precedent. It's happened at many places under many circumstances, because baseball is a game where you try to get away with as much as you can until you get caught. There's an old saying that if you're not cheating, you're not trying. I don't exactly adhere to that, but it shows that everyone is looking for an edge.

So with that in mind, we came in to play them for a second series. I called out Dempsey after my warm-ups while the ball was being tossed around the infield. I told him my theory on Bernie Brewer or somebody else in the seats. I said, "I'll tell you what I'll do: you give me the signal 3 and sit away to Paul Molitor on the first pitch. So give me 3, which is a slider, and sit on the outside corner. I'll throw a fastball up under his chin. So be ready for a fastball. If he's leaning out over the plate to get that called slider, we're going to know that they're indeed getting signals from center field or from Bernie."

After the chat, I get the ball in front of the mound and I realize Rick seems to have forgotten my message. How do I know this? Because he sets up, sits down, gets into a crouch, and gives me the signal 1, the fastball, and sits inside.

I quickly called timeout, summoned him to the mound, and said, "That defeats the purpose of what we're trying to accomplish here."

"Oh, okay. That's right."

By that time, we kind of lost the element of surprise and had to call off the experiment. As I said, Rick disputes it to this day. I believe it happened just like that, and because I'm writing this book, he can have a rebuttal in the next one. Rick and I remain good friends, and he is still one of the real characters that I've seen.

One more Rick Dempsey story!

There was a day and age when catchers used to routinely block the plate. You still hear the legendary stories of Mike Scioscia and the fact that if you were running home, you'd better be prepared for a collision, the likes of which you hadn't experienced before because it was like running into a brick wall.

17

For many years, that was the style. I remember many years ago the White Sox had a catcher named Ed Herrmann, who also blocked the plate exceptionally well. One of the things Ed would do was a trick that has been kind of lost, as a lot of things are now. This isn't to say things were better back then. It's to say that things were different.

Ed would put his left leg across the plate, hopefully holding the ball at least a step ahead of the runner. He would angle his body slightly to the right. As the runner came in for the collision Ed would allow the runner to run toward his left hip, since his body was angled. If Ed had you in that position, he would just smack you with his glove and trip you up with his left hip and leg. You would tumble, and many times you would land very close to the on-deck circle. If he didn't have time to do that, he would just stand there and knock you silly because he was a very big, strong man and felt that the plate belonged to him and this run shouldn't score.

Mike Scioscia had the same philosophy with the Los Angeles Dodgers. If there was a close play, you'd better brace yourself because you probably were going to take a beating from him. I think Mike came away the winner on many of those plays.

But these days things have changed somewhat. Catchers will give a whole lot of the plate to the base runner, many times by going out in front of the plate. That's why many times you see catchers either using a swipe tag or actually diving at the runner, who slides headfirst around the plate and tries to tag the back of the plate.

My feeling always was, if a guy came in headfirst, and you're wearing shin guards, plant that shin guard in front of home plate if that throw is close to or on target and try to bury that guy at home plate. Some catchers still do this by anchoring the left leg and tilting it on the outside so the shin guard will take the brunt of the collision with a runner coming in. But more times than not, you see guys dive to the back of the plate, use the swipe tag, and give the player the plate. That way he avoids contact, he doesn't get hurt, and he lives to fight another day.

But in this particular instance, Rick Dempsey was expecting a throw from right field, and he had given the back of the plate to a very strong and very fast young base runner who came to prominence not only in baseball but also in football. His name was Bo Jackson.

I don't know if Bo could slide very well, but I do know that he was proficient at running over people because that's what he did for a living as an NFL running back. So with Dempsey waiting for the ball at the plate, and it not quite arriving yet, instead of sliding to the back part of the plate, Bo Jackson just absolutely knocked him head over heels, rolling him like a ball over home plate. Jackson scored the run, and Dempsey wound up with a broken thumb, which put him out for quite some time.

• • •

One of the jobs a catcher has to perform is protecting his pitcher if a batter charges the mound, depending on the size, strength, and hostility of his pitcher. You see catchers who tackle the hitter from behind before the batter can get to the pitcher, such as after the batter has been thrown at. Or the catcher will get in front of the hitter, thus preventing a batter from charging the mound, chasing or tackling the pitcher, or starting a bench-clearing brawl in the middle of the diamond.

I always felt that was one of the best attributes a catcher could have, especially when his pitcher was 5'9¾" and 180 pounds, and some of the batters were very big men. In many instances, they were hostile men, too. They were very unhappy with being thrown at or being hit.

There are several things a pitcher can do to get his point across that he owns the inside part of the plate, or that he feels the need to retaliate because he believes the opposing pitcher is throwing at his batters. In the American League, some pitchers believe they have to send a message because the pitchers don't bat.

When I played, however, the umpires weren't as sensitive to the inside pitching that we see today. It was before the era of hitters padding their lead arm and standing on top of home plate and not giving any ground. So that high and tight fastball, that pitch that sailed behind the hitter's head, that well-placed fastball in the hitter's ribs or one that hit a base runner in the knee—those things were part of the game, much more so than today.

It's not better. It's not worse. It's just the way the game was played then. It was a much more aggressive and much more violent game a few generations ago. The slides to second base were continually tougher, the collisions were continually harder, and there were more high and tight fastballs thrown and a few more guys hit with intention.

In one case, we were in Oakland where they had a hitter named Glenn Burke. A pitch sailed up and in to Burke, and he didn't particularly care for it. It was after several pitchers from Oakland's staff had thrown at a number of our hitters. Dempsey was behind the plate, and Burke said to Dempsey, "Go out and tell that guy that if that happens again, I'm going to come out and beat the crap out of him."

Dempsey, one of the all-time heroes, took off his mask and said, "You don't have to wait for the next pitch, pal. Let's take care of it here, right now." He took off his mask, stood there, put his glove to his side, and said, "Let's go get 'em."

Burke looked at him like, "Whoa, no, I don't think I want to do that." That was one of the ways Dempsey protected his pitcher, which is something that all pitchers appreciate from their catchers. And Rick was a terrific fighter, one of those guys you want to have in that foxhole when you go to war. He had that one attribute where he felt that his duty was to protect the pitcher, and I certainly have always appreciated that attribute in a catcher.

Especially when throwing to Rick Dempsey.

• • •

It wouldn't be right to leave the catching section without sharing this next story, which involves catcher Ed Herrmann and Chuck Tanner, our manager with the 1973 Chicago White Sox.

I figure Herrmann checked in at about 260 pounds, give or take five pounds on a bad day, and he had these gigantic muttonchop sideburns.

Tanner wasn't the kind of manager who would tell you, "You know what, just shave them off. They look ridiculous." That wasn't his style. Tanner was a manager with several wonderful attributes, and he had a long and illustrious career. He's a terrific guy and was a very good manager. But he had ways of getting his feelings across to his various players, and he had a unique way of communicating his displeasure with Herrmann's muttonchops.

One day Tanner walked into the clubhouse and saw Herrmann sitting on his little stool in front of his locker. Tanner, you have to understand, was an astonishingly strong man, a former major league player but still a guy that nobody on the team—not one player—wanted to mess with. If Tanner called you into his office, many times he would stand in front of the door and have a conversation with you. The only way you were getting out of the room was to agree with whatever he had to say. And he didn't mind fighting you if it came down to that. Usually it didn't come to that because most of the guys were much too smart to fight with Chuck Tanner, because he was probably as strong as any two guys in that locker room.

So Herrmann was on his stool when Chuck approached him, grabbed him by each muttonchop, and pulled him off the stool. Next thing you know, Chuck is lifting this 260-pound catcher off the stool, and he's now suspended in air. He grabs Chuck's forearms because he's noticing that his cheeks are being unceremoniously lifted parallel with the top of his head, and Chuck Tanner just holds him there.

Now, if you can, imagine how strong you have to be to hold a 260-pound man in the air, basically sitting down without the aid of a stool. Chuck looks Ed right in the eye and says, "Have I ever told you how much I like those muttonchops? I got to tell you something: A lot of guys can't get away with those. But that look for you is really working. I really appreciate them."

In the meantime, Ed is grabbing Chuck's forearms and trying to pull down to get his face back in the normal shape because his muttonchops, along with his cheeks, are literally being rearranged by a manager who is facetiously complimenting him on the look.

To Ed Herrmann, it seemed like 10 minutes. But it was probably only 10 seconds when Chuck put him back on his stool and said, "I just want to let you know how good that look is, how much I appreciate it."

Well, as you can imagine, Ed came to the park the next day without his muttonchops. Apparently he felt that he liked his face exactly the way it was and felt the best course of action would be to take the not-so-subtle message of his manager and adhere to it.

CHAPTER **2**

Pitching

You cannot possibly win in the major leagues without pitching.

Just ask the former owner of the Texas Rangers, Tom Hicks, who signed Alex Rodriguez for $252 million—about $70 million above the next highest bidder. Hicks went on to sign just about every hitter he could when he first took over the Rangers. The belief was, in that park, in the American League West, in the AL, the best thing to do was assemble every bit of offense you could. That's how he planned to win games.

When he finished last in 2007, I'm sure somebody finally mentioned to him that it would help to have some pitchers, too.

The wonderful thing about pitching is that everyone has his or her own ideas and theories on what is the most important pitch. Knowledgeable baseball people will each tell you different things.

Some people will tell you the well-located fastball is the best pitch in the game because you can move it up and down and in and out. Plus, if you can locate it, it sets up your other pitches. There's certainly a great case to be made for that.

Some people will tell you if you have a curveball that you can throw for strikes at different speeds, that is the best pitch in the game because, in the end, nobody hits a good curve. As an example of that, I give you Bert Blyleven and his 60 career shutouts. (I will take Sandy Koufax's curveball over any curveball in the history of the game, although there have been some great ones.)

In the 1990s the split-finger fastball was the pitch du jour, and everyone threw that. I'm sure some pitching coaches taught that pitch a lot better than others. I think that a good split-finger fastball or a forkball is a very good pitch. However, I think it also helps to destroy elbows. Because of that, I certainly wouldn't advise it, but the guys who throw it do a pretty good job.

Some pitchers have lived and died with the slider. Larry Andersen pitched for at least parts of 17 seasons, and he threw 98 percent sliders. Everyone went into the at-bat knowing what he was going to throw: a slider low and in to the left-handers; for the right-handers, it was a slider low and away.

In addition to Andersen, Hall of Fame pitcher Bob Gibson had a great slider as well as a hard fastball. Fergie Jenkins—another Hall of Famer—also had a sharp slider.

Another popular pitch nowadays is the backdoor cutter. A right-handed pitcher will try to hit the outside corner to a left-handed batter, while a left-handed pitcher will try to hit the outside corner to a right-handed batter. But those aren't used as often as normal cutters are. I would say the cutter is probably *the* pitch of this particular decade. The circle change was around last decade, and they're using it more this decade. There's also a three-fingered change and a number of other change-ups as well.

But let's go back to the original question: which is the most important pitch in the game?

Greg Maddux was most likely the smartest pitcher of his generation, but there's one aspect of pitching that I disagree with him on. Maddux will tell you the most important pitch in any sequence is the 1–1 pitch because it sets up the rest of the at-bat. If it's 1–2, it's very much a defensive at-bat. If it's 2–1, it becomes very much an offensive at-bat.

But I disagree. Keep in mind that disagreeing with a guy who has that much ability, is that intelligent, and understands the game and has broken it down as well as he has is something I take pause before doing.

But I will do so, nonetheless.

I think the first-pitch strike—whatever type of pitch it is—is the best pitch in the game.

If you throw a first-pitch strike, you then have the opportunity to go 0–2. If you take a look at statistics and computer models, you'll find that the batting averages are ridiculously low on 0–2 counts. So if you're throwing a first-pitch strike, it automatically sets up a defensive at-bat.

Once most professional pitchers get to an 0–2 count, that's pretty much the wipeout pitch at the wipeout time. Even a decent hitter, more times than not, can pretty much forget about it if he goes down 0–2. He's not going to be able to do too much with that next pitch. Even Sandy Koufax said it in one of the many books and articles written about him. He always felt the best pitch in the game was strike one, and so whatever pitch you believe you can throw for strike one becomes the best pitch.

For me, in my career, throwing strike one with a breaking ball made a great deal of sense. One of the things I always heard was, "Remember that you can't strike anyone out on strike one." That meant don't throw your best curveball or your best slider, don't try to hit the outside corner, just barely nipping it with the fastball. Cut the plate into thirds, forget about the middle third, and use the inside third and the outside third to locate your pitch.

I didn't throw hard enough to throw on the inside third for the first pitch, so I preferred the curveball.

When I watch pitchers today, I pay particular attention to pitchers who consistently throw strike one, and it makes all the difference in the world.

• • •

Pitchers are unusual people, so it's not surprising that many unusual things happen to them.

I remember one of my early spring trainings with the San Francisco Giants. The team had invested money in a Korean pitcher named Won Kuk Lee, in order to take advantage of the huge Asian population in San Francisco.

Lee and I were teammates at Class A Fresno, where he had an odd habit that annoyed the Giants. During games, he would order food from some of his favorite restaurants and have his friends deliver the meals to the bullpen. When he would enter the game, there would be a noodle or two from whatever he ate on his uniform. It drove people crazy.

There's one story about Lee that I'll never forget. Charlie Fox, my manager at the time (with whom I was later reunited for a short time with the Chicago Cubs), was constantly being pestered by a longtime friend to permit this guy's nephew to try out for the team. At the time, this was not unusual because most of the tryouts occurred during major league camps. Many players fell through the cracks around the draft, and these tryouts enabled scouts to see undrafted free agents. It was very rare, however, for the major league manager to give a player a so-called private audition during the course of spring training.

So this young kid started taking batting practice in front of Charlie, who was stationed behind the screen. Lee was pitching, and after a few swings, Charlie told him to take it easy on the kid, who struggled to hit. It was quickly apparent this kid wasn't ready to play in the majors or probably even the minors.

But to placate the kid's father and convince him that he had plenty of time for his audition, Charlie told the kid, "Hey, the next time you hit the ball, run to second base. I want to see if you have any speed."

The kid looked at Charlie and said, "Okay, Mr. Fox." Finally, on the fourth or fifth pitch, the kid actually hit a ground ball, and he ran directly the mound. Lee, not knowing what Charlie had said, believed he had embarrassed the kid and thought the kid was charging the mound for an old-fashioned brawl in the middle of the field. So Lee gets into his karate stance and is ready to chop this kid to pieces, only to see the kid sprint past him and run to second base as fast as he could.

Needless to say, the entire infield went into hysterics. Lee turned around and couldn't understand what had happened. This guy was at second base, beaming and thinking he got out of the batter's box quicker than Ty Cobb. The fact that he completely missed that elementary stage of running to first base before you go to second was not something he was concerned about. But Charlie just yelled, "Drag this kid off the field. End of tryout."

That was one of the stranger things I've seen on a baseball diamond.

We had an international-type team in the San Francisco Giants organization. Along with Pittsburgh, the Giants took advantage of the Latin American population. Certainly the occasional Cuban player found his way—even back then—into the major leagues. But it was Pittsburgh and the Giants that got the majority of those players. On my first team in Fresno in 1969, we had an Native American pitcher named Brent Foshie, a teammate of the aforementioned Won Kuk Lee.

During batting practice, they would play a game in which whoever caught the most fly balls would get some clubhouse service from the other guy, such as buying him a Coke or shining his shoes.

Foshie was relentless in playing practical jokes on Lee. He thought that was the funniest thing to come out of that particular season. Lee would show up late, and Foshie was always the guy who would bring it to the attention of Denny Sommers, our manager. Sommers was 28, and fresh off the playing field. He was a diligent worker, a very good baseball man who stayed around for many years, and we were members of his first team.

So Lee would arrive late, and Foshie always would yell, "Hey, Lee, nice to see you." Sommers, recognizing Lee was late for that evening's workout, would proceed to make him run from foul pole to foul pole endlessly.

Everybody got a kick out of it but an aggravated Lee, who had trouble finding ways to get back at Foshie.

One day the two of them were catching baseballs for services, and Lee ran across as Foshie was lined up to catch the ball. Lee ran over and put his glove up to shield Foshie's face in the direction of the ball. At the last instant, Lee pulled the glove away. Of course Foshie had already lowered his hands, and the ball hit him squarely on the mouth. Foshie was sitting there with a lip the size of a golf ball, and Won Kuk Lee was literally rolling on the ground laughing, thinking it was one of the funniest things he had ever seen.

I went on to play with a number of characters, but none were stranger than a relief pitcher for the Baltimore Orioles named Don Stanhouse. Earl Weaver called him "Full Pack" because that's how much Earl smoked during the course of a game when Stanhouse was on the mound. It seemed Stanhouse threw strikes only when he had to. The hitter would help him out by swinging at pitches out of the strike zone, and he would never see a strike.

In one game, we had a one-run lead in the ninth inning in Texas, and Stanhouse was called in to earn the save. In those days, closers didn't get 40 or 50 saves. If you earned 25 or 30 saves in a year, that was a lot, because starting pitchers were used to going the distance more than they are today. Complete games were expected often. Hall of Famers like Bob Gibson, Juan Marichal, Jim Palmer, and Fergie Jenkins often had 25 to 30 complete games in a season.

If Stanhouse didn't inherit a problem, he created a problem for himself. Of course, he would get himself out of it, too. At Texas, Weaver was smoking a few heaters in the little stairway, and Stanhouse quickly retired the first two batters. That part was easy because the hitters obliged him by swinging at pitches out of the strike zone, resulting in easy ground balls.

Stanhouse went on to walk the next three hitters. Weaver, meanwhile, was pacing and smoking at a furious pace. Stanhouse proceeded to throw two balls to the next hitter, and Weaver was getting deep into that pack of cigarettes. Finally, when Stanhouse threw ball three to that hitter, Weaver yelled at pitching coach Ray Miller, "Get out there. Talk to him."

So Miller got up, called time, and walked to the mound. Stanhouse slowly walks off the mound, reaching the grass before Miller reaches the mound to meet him. Before Ray can say a word, Stanhouse, obviously a little hot under the collar, says, "Did the little guy send you out here?"

Miller just nodded his head, and Stanhouse said, "Wait a second. He told you to come out and talk to me because he thinks that I don't know that if I throw another ball and walk this guy, the game is going to be tied and we might lose?"

Miller again nodded his head and didn't say anything. So Stanhouse said, "Doesn't he think I know that? Doesn't he believe I've been here enough to realize that if I throw one more ball that I'm actually going to walk in the tying run? I'll tell you what: turn around, go back in the dugout, and tell the little [expletive] fellow to sit down, shut up, and I'll get this guy out."

So Miller, without saying a word, turned around and returned to the dugout. Weaver asked, "What did he say?"

Ray replied, "You don't want to know."

Don Stanhouse threw strike one, strike two, and got the batter to ground harmlessly to second to end the game.

That was life with the man that Earl Weaver called "Full Pack."

• • •

Mechanics are important in both preventing injury and in being effective. To try to get an advantage, many times pitchers will move a bit on the rubber. Guys will throw from the extreme first-base side or the extreme third-base side, depending on their pitch of choice, what angle they want to have, and what particular part of the plate they want to concentrate on.

I threw mostly from the middle of the rubber, and I would dig out a little bit of the clay. Then I would go about trying to get the mound to the specifications I really liked. Since I was only 5'9¾", I didn't have a long stride. But it was longer than most pitchers my size, so I didn't have a great deal of trouble with the opposing pitcher's stride.

Sometimes you'll find that for pitchers of vastly different heights, such as one pitcher who's 6'1" and another who's 6'7", the landing areas won't be that wide. For a sinkerball pitcher, many times that spot will be across his body. For a fireballer, that area will be even with the plate or slightly open.

If the left foot of a right-handed sinkerball pitcher falls more toward the third-base line, then he's throwing across his body. If he's throwing directly at the plate or open slightly, he can clear his hips and pick up more velocity.

This was a big issue with many fireballers who threw across their body. Most noticeably in Chicago Cubs history, Kerry Wood threw across his body. Now, there's a long list of great sinkerball pitchers who threw across their bodies but were effective. The Cubs had Rick Reuschel, who wasn't a fireballer but threw an effective, hard sinker. We had a left-hander in Baltimore named Scott McGregor who threw across his body and was effective for several years. John Tudor, who came into prominence with St. Louis, threw the same way. The trouble is, throwing that way can lead to injury.

Kerry Wood, year after year, was one of the toughest to hit as far as league batting average against. Unfortunately, he didn't have near the success he should have had with the stuff he had. That was evident in his fifth start—his 20-strikeout game in 1998 against Houston, which I had the pleasure of calling. It looked like the sky was the limit at the time. I made a lot of people on the North Side angry at me when I mentioned his mechanics and eventually what would happen to him, as far as injuries go. Kerry wasn't particularly happy with that prediction.

However, when they wanted to pin the overuse of him on managers like Jim Riggleman or Dusty Baker, Kerry admitted it was his mechanics that wound up doing him in—something I had said from the very beginning.

One of the things I really hate to see, and it's the unfortunate part of the game, whether it's a pitcher or a player, is unrealized potential. There are guys who come up to the majors with the ability to truly be stars of the game. I'm talking about their place in baseball history, what it could have become and what it does become, and often it's because their body betrays them.

Sometimes these players don't fulfill their potential because of happenstance. Bodies just don't hold up or arms don't hold up, and there's nothing you can do about it. Other times they become their own worst enemies because of various habits they develop but can't break. One of them is throwing across their body.

• • •

The job of every pitcher is to get guys out, either through location or by consistently changing velocities. With that in mind, you have to know something about the way bats are made. Most bats either have a label or a signature where the label would go. For instance, the old Louisville Sluggers had that label in the middle of the bat and the name of the individual toward the end of the bat. A hitter usually tries to square every pitch and hit the ball on what they call the "sweet spot," between the label and the name, because that's the biggest part of the bat with the most wood.

My goal was to get the batter to hit the ball between his hands and the label, which is the thinner part of the bat, or between the label and the end of the bat, where you can't get near as much distance as you can when you hit it in the middle of the bat. Doing that required my full repertoire of pitches.

If I could remember where each batter hit the ball on the bat, I'd know if I had fooled him with my pitch. If I threw a batter a certain pitch at a certain speed and he hit it on the good part of the bat but lined out, hit a hard groundout, a deep fly, or a line drive out to the outfield, I would remember he hit the ball on the "sweet spot" and that I had gotten lucky. I recognized that he was seeing me well and that I would need to make an adjustment in his next at-bat. I needed to use every advantage I could possibly use later in my career, because I didn't have nearly the stuff I had in the middle stages, when I became a fairly decent pitcher.

Different hitters had more success against me, and it had more to do with what they did against me rather than the quality of the batter. I had a very difficult time retiring certain batters because they were able to square up on just about every pitch I threw. I would go to my strength first, which was the inside corner to a right-handed batter and the outside corner to a left-handed batter—which was the arm side.

The majority of pitchers have that tendency, although some are gifted enough to be able to "control all four quadrants"—up and away, up and in, low and away, low and in. If you can control all four quadrants with basically your fastball or perhaps your cutter, you're going to be very effective because it allows you to do what most pitchers want to do with a given hitter—change the eye level.

For instance, you'll see pitchers pound the ball low and away for a strike. They'll then pound the ball low and away again. Now it's 0–2. They throw a slider just off the plate—again low and away. Next thing you know, they're throwing a fastball in a spot called "higher than high," which is out of the strike zone, usually face or helmet high, and it changes a hitter's eye level. So instead of looking at one spot, the batter sees that all of a sudden the pitch is going up and out of the zone. Because it looks so tantalizing, the batter might believe he can get a good part of the bat on it. But realistically, that higher-than-high fastball with anything on it often results in a batter hitting the ball straight in the air, fouling it straight back, or missing it entirely.

Today you'll see many pitchers who have a curveball or a little spinning slider that they use for strike one. I can't tell you the exact numbers because I'm not as computer literate as I'd like, but the reality is that hitters don't particularly like to hit a breaking ball—especially the first pitch. They will try to hit a breaking ball if you hang it, usually later in the count.

I remember talking to Hall of Famer Eddie Murray, one of the most powerful switch hitters of all time, who ended his career with 504 home runs. Murray was just an outstanding teammate and a wonderful first baseman. He had a tremendous conception of how to hit from both sides of the plate, which is very difficult to do.

I remember telling him that I noticed one series against the White Sox where every pitcher started him out with a slow curveball. I asked him before his next series in Chicago, "Why don't you just give up the fastball on the first pitch and look for a slow curveball? They're throwing it to you every at-bat, every first pitch."

Murray replied, "No, there's no reason for me to look for that because I don't want to hit it. A lot of pitchers can't throw their first curveball for a strike. Even those who do, I give it to them. I want to hit a fastball. I want to get him into a count where he has to throw me a fastball and probably use too much of the plate. That's the pitch I want to hit."

He parlayed that strategy into a Hall of Fame career. He's one of the guys I truly enjoyed playing with and is one of the true professionals in the game of baseball. Now, I'm not certain that he became a great hitting coach, because it's very rare for the great players to be very good as hitting and pitching coaches when it comes to teaching guys with less talent how to succeed, but he was a heck of a teammate.

What's really strange is if you go back over time, you see that some of the most highly acclaimed pitching coaches were mediocre pitchers, if they were pitchers at all. For instance, Dave Duncan of St. Louis is regarded as the game's top pitching coach, and he was a catcher. Duncan has served under Tony La Russa with the White Sox, the Oakland Athletics (where they won three consecutive American League titles and a World Series), and with the Cardinals when they won the World Series.

Duncan wasn't a pitcher, but he certainly knows a whole lot about pitching.

Another good pitching coach that didn't have much of a career, per se, is the White Sox' Don Cooper. One of Cooper's greatest success stories is setup man Matt Thornton, who throws 97 miles per hour with a sharp slider, cut fastball, and terrific control.

But Seattle gave up on him and traded him to the White Sox for Joe Borchard, a failed first-round draft choice who received a $5.3 million bonus out of Stanford. There's no way in the world you give up a left-hander who throws 97 miles per hour unless he doesn't have control. Thornton, after several years with Seattle with different pitching coaches and instructors, finally was sent to the White Sox because he had no control.

Cooper watched him pitch one inning and took him into the bullpen for one session. I don't know exactly what he told him, but I do know ever since that particular pitching session in the bullpen, Thornton has had control, and it very rarely deserts him.

Pitching coaches need to be a couple different guys all wrapped into one.

First, a pitching coach needs to be a psychologist. He has to know exactly what his pitcher needs on a daily basis.

Second, a pitching coach has to be real mechanic. We're aided today because we have so much videotape on pitchers and can review what they did on a pitch-by-pitch basis—sometimes over the course of years. But from an immediacy standpoint, a coach can see what a pitcher has done the past five games and see if he's diverted from what makes him successful.

It used to be that as long as a pitcher was pitching well, the pitching coach probably would say very little to him. But when he deviated from something, a pitching coach could pick it up right away and mention one thing, such as staying closed. By that I mean keeping your weight over your back foot and your front shoulder closed off so that you can time the front foot hitting the ground. There are a lot of guys who have trouble staying closed.

33

When a guy opens up too quickly, he's not keeping his weight centered over his back foot, failing to pitch off the mound or use his lower body. In my opinion, using your lower body is very important because it carries most of your weight. My saying always was, "If your legs will take you six, your arm will take you the next three," meaning, if you use your legs for six innings to push off the mound, you will have enough arm strength to complete the baseball game.

If your legs aren't strong enough, you must allow your arm to take over, and you find guys leaving games in the sixth and seventh inning. When a right-hander opens too quickly, that front foot is going to come around, his arm is not going to be able to catch up, and he'll open too quickly. The result is the curveball will hang or the fastball will stay high and away to every left-handed hitter.

One of the things I had to learn as a pitcher was breaking a difficult task down to its simplest parts. The revelation came to me one day in Yankee Stadium. I had never beaten the Yankees in Yankee Stadium, and they were a proficient left-handed pull-hitting team, taking advantage of that very short porch. It was very difficult to pitch there because the Yankees usually had six or seven left-handed pull hitters in that lineup to take advantage of that short porch.

I remember warming up in the bullpen, and as I was warming up, I stepped off and took a look at the monuments at old Monument Park. For whatever reason, I was drifting away and thinking about the monumental task of facing guys like Reggie Jackson, Graig Nettles, and at the time, Oscar Gamble. They would occasionally play Jim Spencer, who initially was a defensive whiz before becoming a dead-pull left-handed hitter. They had Chris Chambliss in those lineups, and it was left-handed slugger after left-handed slugger, pull hitter after pull hitter.

Out of the blue, it dawned on me that I really didn't have to beat the Yankees in Yankee Stadium. That was a phenomenally large goal. What I needed was to break it down into its simplest parts.

I figured all I actually had to do was make one good pitch to Willie Randolph. Randolph was their leadoff hitter, but he was a right-handed leadoff hitter. I said to myself, "Well, can you make one good pitch to

Willie Randolph? Of course you can. You've made hundreds of thousands of pitches in your life. It's very easy to make one good pitch to Willie Randolph."

Having succeeded in that, the next thing I'd have to do was throw the next good pitch to Willie Randolph, assuming I didn't retire him on the first pitch. So I started to develop a philosophy of breaking down this particular tremendous accomplishment into its simplest parts.

I began to learn how to concentrate on each pitch as if it were the only thing in the world that existed. I wouldn't worry who was coming up next or what bad pitch I had made before, because that had no bearing on what I was going to do now. That created for me what I call the "green and brown theory."

The theory went something like this: When I was on the grass, I would allow myself any emotion that I wanted to have. If I wanted to be mad, I would sometimes yell into my glove. If I wanted to bemoan my fate because someone made an error behind me, I would feel that way. If I wanted to feel a sense of satisfaction, then I would do that.

Because we have five senses, and we're constantly bombarded by all of them, it's very easy to lose that concentration once you've originally gotten it. I imagine concentration as being a very narrow beam of light, similar to what you see in a movie where a guy is centered up with a red laser, usually in the middle of his chest or middle of his forehead and—boom!—the bullet comes, and the guy is dead. Well, concentration is that narrow beam of light.

So as long as I was on the green grass, I could permit myself any emotion I wanted to because pitching is an emotional roller coaster. It's first and foremost an intellectual pursuit, because you have to think about what you're going to do against every batter. You have to get him out with the best stuff you possibly can but not necessarily with two out and nobody on the first time you face him. Sometimes you have to go away from what you know works so that later in the game, in a tough situation, you can go back to that spot. You're on a roller coaster.

But as long as I was on the grass, I would allow myself the luxury—and it is a luxury—to indulge my various moods at any given time. When I got to the brown part of the mound, however—the dirt part—I would stand

35

atop it and allow all the emotions to absolutely drain away to the point where nothing existed at all except the next pitch. Make one good pitch and don't worry about how that pitch might affect something else. Every pitch should be well thought out. For me, that doesn't mean throwing a fastball for a strike. That is a positive affirmation, but it's not a well-thought-out pitch. A well-thought-out pitch is this—determining to throw a cut fastball on the outside third of the plate at the knees, and then throwing it.

In other words, you've told yourself what pitch you're going to throw, you've told yourself what location you're going to throw it at, and you do it. You might also tell yourself that if it's the first pitch, you want to throw it at 75 percent of your ability and velocity. Because going with the philosophy that you just as soon throw one pitch and get one out, if you throw your best cut fastball low and away on the first pitch, there's a very good chance the guy is not going to make any good contact or he's not going to swing. He'll just take it for strike one because that's a pitcher's pitch.

The better the hitter, the less he will get himself out on a pitcher's pitch. If you use a third of the plate and give him something to look at, maybe he'll hit a hard ground ball to second if he's a right-handed hitter. If he's a left-handed hitter, maybe he'll hit you a one-hopper to first base or he'll fly out harmlessly to right. But if you don't think out that pitch, then you open up the door to defeat.

When this all came to me in the middle of 1979, the guy who caught the majority of my games was Rick Dempsey. I would see the ball lodge into the glove, if Dempsey happened to be giving a signal out there and he happened to be sitting out there. But there were times when I aimed not necessarily at the glove but at parts of his body, such as his right shoulder, because I wanted to throw the pitch a tad higher. There were many times when Rick would be sitting inside, giving me a low target inside, but I didn't want to throw it there. I determined where I wanted to throw it, and I threw it there.

There's a saying that the game of baseball is more mental than it is physical. You have a whole bunch of guys who are physically all in the same class, so what sets them apart? It's the mental toughness. When I was playing, I would often wonder why it was that every team I'd been with had between three and five physical trainers for that 25 percent of the game and no mental trainers for the remaining 75 percent of the game.

That's one of things we've seen in recent vintage—the sports psychologists. And there are some great ones out there. Harvey Dorfman, who has helped many guys, is one of the great ones. Bob Rotella is also very good.

I'm all in favor of these guys, but there are things that a sports psychologist can't tell you. In the case of a pitcher, it's telling you what it is like to stand 60'6" away from a guy who you absolutely know has better talent than you. I know this from my career, standing on the mound and pitching to the likes of Johnny Bench, Billy Williams, Roberto Clemente, Willie Stargell, Joe Morgan, Pete Rose, and Hank Aaron. I could go down a list from both leagues that includes Reggie Jackson, Andre Dawson, and Jim Rice (who killed me, by the way). I knew I had to retire batters who were destined for the Hall of Fame or guys I suspected were headed there. I knew what it felt like to be 60'6" away from them.

For sports psychologists, it would be very difficult to explain to a performer how to get the job done against these guys if they hadn't done it themselves. Again, sports psychologists have done a pretty good job of trying to help players. I've worked with tennis players, golfers, and baseball players on the psychological aspects of the game, such as how to concentrate, how to use various sets of mental gymnastics, and a number of other factors. I go back to self-hypnosis, imagery, creative visualization, positive affirmations, and a number of other things that I used. Of course, you tailor it to the personality of the individuals, and then you talk to them about making themselves better, winning with less than their best. There are days when you just don't feel well, and on those days, you have to learn to win with less than your best.

All in all, it's very important to train for the mental part of the game, that 75 percent. Because oftentimes, that makes the difference between winning and losing.

• • •

You may have heard the saying, "Never throw the same pitch at the same speed in the same location to the same hitter in the same at-bat." If you adhere to that and display that ability, you'll be unpredictable and very difficult to hit. Every pitcher is looking for an edge when it comes to developing a new pitch or a variation of a new pitch.

During a couple of my better seasons, I decided I would try to incorporate a split-finger fastball into my arsenal. But that came around only because I was trying to find a change-up. Everyone has a different way to grip a change-up. The most fashionable way is the circle change, where you have your index finger and your thumb together. You actually hold the ball against that index finger and deliver it almost like a screwball.

What makes a change-up so effective is when you throw it from the same release point with the same arm velocity that you would a fastball. The difference is the change-up doesn't travel as fast and usually sinks low and away from a left-handed pitcher to a right-handed hitter, and the same movement occurs for a right-handed pitcher to a left-handed pitcher. But very few left-handers will throw their straight change to left-handed hitters for whatever reason.

In my search for a change-up I was using all kinds of different grips. I was using the three-fingered change-up and the drag-the-back-foot change-up, where you release the baseball but don't come around, in my case, with my right foot. Fergie Jenkins used to throw the latter pitch, and he went into the Hall of Fame and won 20 games six consecutive years for the Chicago Cubs. Fergie was masterful with his control.

I talked to him about it, and he emphasized dragging his back foot. He would throw the pitch with the same arm velocity and release point, but the velocity wouldn't be the same because he wouldn't come around with his back foot and follow through.

I tried that. It just scuffed up my shoes.

I was trying to discover a change-up, and I figured the farther you split your fingers apart, the slower the ball has to go. I eventually discovered that if I split my fingers far enough apart, I could keep the baseball in there and throw a very good split-finger fastball. That became the change-up that I used at various points in my career.

I elected to use it during a part of the 1970s when I was with the White Sox. To do it successfully, you aim for the middle of the plate. If you have one finger placed higher than the other, the ball will move another way. Finger pressure is another consideration. But most of the time if you throw it straight down the middle, the ball will come in without a whole lot of spin and drop straight down. It put Bruce Sutter into the Hall of Fame. It was a great pitch for me, for a brief time.

Occasionally, though, you have pretty good low-ball hitters. When that's the case, the ball comes right back at you—sometimes more quickly.

I remember pitching to Al Cowens of the Kansas City Royals, and he hit me in the thigh after I threw a splitter in the 1977 season. The pitch was down the middle and had very good sink, disappearing at the last second. But Cowens drilled it off my right thigh so hard that I thought it went right through me.

Obviously, that bruise stayed with me for a while. Had Cowens hit the ball on my glove side—the left side—I probably would have been able to field it. But he hit it on my right side, where I would have to move my glove across my body to reach it, very difficult especially since I tended to flip my glove slightly behind me when I delivered the baseball. That makes it tough to get the glove in position to field, especially when there's a rocket hit back to your throwing-hand side.

Cowens' drive off my thigh discouraged me from throwing many splitters after that. I was a curveball pitcher, and I went on to lead the White Sox with a 12–12 record in 1978 after a 15–12 season in 1977.

I elected to break the splitter out again during the 1979 season with Baltimore because I was 6–7 at the All-Star break, and my team was headed for 102 wins and the World Series. I was not a winning pitcher at the break, so I decided to add the splitter and refine it.

And it came back. I remember manager Earl Weaver promised me only two starts after the All-Star break. Those were against Oakland and Seattle, and I beat them.

In the game against Oakland, I struck out 10 and allowed no walks, and the splitter was absolutely magnificent. Then I threw a complete-game win over Seattle.

I was on my way, although I later discovered the splitter wasn't very good for me. That was before I faced the California Angels, who were on track to winning the AL West that year. We beat them in the American League Championship Series to advance to the World Series.

But the Angels had a strong team, and two of their three exceptional hitters were developed in the Baltimore organization. One was Bobby Grich, and the other was Don Baylor. Along with Rod Carew, they were the stars of that team.

In the fifth inning of that game, I was facing Grich and threw him a pretty good splitter for a strike. So I came back with another splitter that I thought was better, but Grich hit it off the same spot on my right thigh. I felt like I had been shot. I went down and crawled to the baseball because if a guy is going to hit you, then you certainly don't want him to get a base hit. When I reached the ball I fired it to first base from my knees.

The problem was that first base was not anchored to the coach's box. This one went well wide of the bag, over the coach's box, and into right field. Not only did Grich get a base hit, but he wound up at second. That added insult to the injury, and I concluded two things: first, I didn't think my thigh could take any more abuse, and second, being a curveball pitcher and throwing that splitter, the strain in my right elbow was too much.

But the splitter helped me through the second half of that season, and I went undefeated from July 6 on. I won only five games in my 14 starts but didn't lose any, and the splitter was a big part of that. Then I decided that my elbow probably would fall off if I continued to throw it, and I would need football thigh pads or risk having a wooden leg somewhere later in my life.

So the splitter went bye-bye, and the curveball became even more prevalent. The 1980 season came along, and it was an enchanted season. But it was sans split-finger.

Two batters killed me. One was Jim Rice, who was 21-for-37 with four home runs and 11 RBIs against me. The other was Cecil Cooper. Of Cooper's 12 hits (in 39 at-bats) against me, five were home runs. Although I had great luck against the Milwaukee Brewers, I couldn't get out Cooper.

He couldn't have hit me more if the catcher had told him what pitch was coming. Cooper beat me like the proverbial rented donkey.

I was getting at least four starts against Milwaukee each year. That didn't help me much because that was about 20 at-bats a year against Cooper. It was just a slaughter.

Mostly, if I threw at guys, I did it to defend my hitters. I didn't throw at too many hitters over the course of my career just because they hit well against me. But one of those throws was at Cooper.

In this particular game, the first time Cooper came up there was nobody on base. I figured that rather than have him hit the ball out of the ballpark or hit one of the many doubles or hard-hit balls that he hit against me, I was going to hit him before he could hit me.

But I didn't try to hit him where he wound up getting hit. I threw the first pitch inside, aiming for his lead arm or his back. But the ball sailed up and in and hit him right in the neck.

Cooper was a very big, fast man, and I had the thought of this enraged first baseman chasing me around the infield, trying to kill me. That was not my game plan that year because I was playing for a very good team, throwing the ball very well, and didn't really need to have that happen. So I walked directly toward Cooper. He was grabbing his neck and glaring at me with this fierceness in his eyes. He said (and I'll leave the expletive out), "What the hell are you doing?"

I said, very rationally, "Cecil, I face you 25 to 30 times a year. The last couple of years you've just been killing me. Have I ever knocked you down before?"

Cooper said, "No."

I said, "Right. No. I wasn't trying to knock you down this time. That ball just got away."

So he just put the bat down and went to first base.

The newspaper stories reported the next day that it was a good show of sportsmanship to see if Cecil was okay. In reality, it was self-preservation, believing I could probably talk him out of his rage and prevent him from charging the mound, which would have been embarrassing for me and likely led to a suspension for him.

• • •

I remember one story that will explain why a pitcher should be honest with his manager, and sometimes you have to take your ego out of the equation. This also involved Cecil Cooper.

This occurred in 1979, during a Monday night game that Howard Cosell was broadcasting. The last batter I was going to face with two out in the bottom of the ninth inning was Don Money—with Cooper in the on-deck circle. Believe me, I knew Cooper was in the on-deck circle, and Tippy Martinez was warming up in the bullpen. Earl Weaver, at that point, had come to trust me as far as pitching deep into ballgames. He didn't do this when I first arrived in Baltimore, despite my experience, but he had come to depend on me.

So I quickly got an 0–2 count on Money. I knew that if I threw one more curveball over the plate, I was going to strike him out, retire 21 straight batters, and win the game 2–1.

I missed with the first curveball. It was not a setup pitch; it was a wipeout pitch. Then I missed with a second curveball to even the count at 2–2, knowing if I could just get one more curve over the plate, I could strike him out. I missed with the third curveball and, realizing that I had one more pitch before Cooper came to bat as the winning run with a man at first base, I put all my concentration, everything that I had learned, into that last pitch.

As fate would have it, I missed with it. Money didn't swing at any of them. They were all out of the strike zone, all wipeout curveballs, and I just wanted to make sure I didn't hang them. So if he didn't swing, he wound up at first, which is exactly what happened.

Cooper walked to the plate, and Weaver came out of the dugout. But for the first time in a long time, he did not motion to the bullpen. He had a standing rule that if he came out, he was going to take you out of the game. He would always motion to the bullpen before he got to the foul line because there were times in his career where he would let the pitcher talk him out of taking him out of the game, only to get burned. In some instances, Weaver got scorched before he was back in the dugout.

I remember one night Weaver came out after I had given up a long fly ball with an 0–2 count. The ball was 100 feet foul as I hung a curve to a hitter I can't recall, but I do remember that I was leading. It was late and this guy just happened to hit a long foul ball. And I looked over, and here comes Earl. He came walking to the mound and put his hand out, asking for the ball.

I said, "What are you doing? That was a foul ball."

Then in that raspy voice of his, he said, "Yeah, that was foul. The next one is not going to be foul, so that's why I'm going to the bullpen and bringing that guy in."

Well, he was probably right, but he didn't leave me a choice.

In this instance in Milwaukee, he did leave me a choice. He came out but did not motion to the bullpen, where Tippy was warming up. Tippy was a great left-handed reliever with an outstanding curveball that most left-handers and right-handers just didn't hit. Earl knew I pitched a tremendous game and he was going to give me the opportunity to complete the game and keep my destiny in my own hands.

Weaver looked at me square in the eye, as Cecil Cooper was ready to get in the batter's box. Weaver said, "You think you can get that guy out?"

Well, a younger pitcher or a guy with a lot of machismo—or as some would say, a stupid pitcher—would have replied, "Absolutely, Skip," and Weaver would have walked back to the dugout.

When posed with that query at that point of my career—my ninth year in the major leagues—I looked at Cecil Cooper. I looked at Earl. I remembered Cooper hit five home runs off me in two years, and I said to Earl, "Hell no. Bring in Tippy."

Sure enough, Weaver pointed to his left hand and brought in Tippy Martinez. One pitch, a fly ball to left-center field, and we won the game. Tippy got the save, the Orioles won, I won, and I think I always had the trust of Earl Weaver after that. But I had to concede to Cecil Cooper that he was better than I was, and there was no way that I was going to allow him to beat my team with me on the mound, knowing this guy had been that tough on me.

So, congratulations, Tippy, wherever you are, for getting me out of that situation.

Here's something else I remember about that game. I called my father afterward, and he said, "Hey, Howard Cosell had wonderful things to say about you. Did he talk to you?"

I said, "Howard Cosell wouldn't know me if I was on fire."

Jerry Klein, his researcher, had talked to me, and that's why Howard was able to tell all those pithy stories in the sixth inning when he realized that pitcher Jim Slaton of Milwaukee wasn't the story. I was winning 2–1, rallying to take the lead after Charlie Moore hit a home run in the third inning. After the homer, I retired 20 consecutive batters.

So Howard, being no dummy, realized that the storyline had shifted somewhat and began to break out all of the stories that Klein had written on three-by-five cards three or four days in advance. These were for Howard, who knew very little, if anything, about baseball—but he delivered it very well.

Howard was a wonderful wordsmith. He was one of the first guys I worked with in the TV booth, and he wasn't any more likeable when I worked with him than he was at other times in his life. But he did give me some good broadcasting experiences.

• • •

These days, middle relievers and closers are very important. Just about everyone I talk to wants to know why it's so difficult to find excellent middle relievers. As baseball has developed, we know that the setup man, the eighth-inning guy, is a valuable man. That's the case with the White Sox and left-hander Matt Thornton.

Just about every team has a pretty decent setup man. That would mean there are 30 of them. Some teams have a setup man for the right and left side. That would mean there are 60 of them.

So the setup man is a very important player.

But in the world of Major League Baseball—which encompasses a huge majority of the greatest players—there are only 10 lockdown closers at any given time. When I say lockdown closer, for me that's an 85-percent-and-above success rate. I consider only 10 in this category. If it were an easy job, there would be more. Sometimes there are fewer than 10 lockdown closers. That's because it takes a certain character as well as quality stuff and a special attitude to be that closer—to be the man who wants the ball at the end of the game, getting those key outs day after day after day.

A closer must have a short memory, because even if a team beats him today, he must return the next day and put the finishing touches on the ninth inning. We now put a lot of stock in the setup man. The seventh-inning reliever is valuable, but he can be interchangeable. Understand that it's tough for the middle relievers—pitchers you might use in the fourth inning if your starter gets knocked out or the sixth inning if your starter runs out of gas—to be converted into quality pitchers.

That's because many of these pitchers failed at something else, or they wouldn't be there. Your failed starters usually are long relievers. Your failed closers and setup men usually are your seventh- or sixth-inning guys. So out of every position on your team—whether it be a starting pitcher, a starting first baseman, setup man, or closer—they all have to be earned. Middle relief is the only position on the baseball team that you actually get by default. In the heart of a long reliever is some starting pitcher waiting to get out.

In this vein, one thing that is of utmost importance is acceptance of the role before you. That is the only way you can excel. And it doesn't matter what that role is, because I have been the eleventh pitcher on the 11-man staff. I've been the sixth starter on the five-man rotation. I've been the fourth starter in a three-man rotation for the 1973 White Sox with Johnny Sain as their pitching coach and Chuck Tanner as the manager. You have to accept that role. I never did very well because I never really accepted being in the bullpen. I always viewed myself as a starting pitcher. That was probably one of the reasons why I had very little, if any, success out of the bullpen.

But I did have one save—one save in my entire career—and that was in Oakland. We were in the twelfth inning, and Chuck Tanner used Terry Forster for three innings and Cy Acosta pitched two and two-thirds innings.

Chuck summoned me to protect a one-run lead in the twelfth. I was a starter for most of that year, so being in the bullpen wasn't a great thing for me. Also, because I never had success in the bullpen before, it was very difficult. But as the bullpen phone rang, as Oakland was putting together a rally in the bottom of the twelfth, I was the only guy there. They told me to get up and start throwing.

As I started to throw, Oakland got another man on base, and now they had two men on. Then Oakland got a third man on to load the bases with two of their better hitters coming up—Joe Rudi and Gene Tenace. They made up the heart and soul of those three consecutive world championship teams (1972–74).

I see Chuck Tanner going to the mound, and sure enough, he calls me into the game. With the bases loaded, I have to retire Rudi and Tenace.

So I did what I thought was best. I threw six straight curveballs, struck them out, and wound up getting the only save of my entire career. They never asked me to save another game.

In 1974, the Cubs gave me an opportunity to try to preserve a 5–5 tie in the twelfth. It was early in April, and I was in the bullpen, where I was doing a terrible job. It was freezing, just a horrible April day. Anyone who knows Wrigley Field will realize how bad it can get. And there I was, asked to warm up again. As it turned out, Pittsburgh had runners at first and second and two out, with a middle infielder named Frank Taveras coming up.

I remember coming into the game. I was freezing. I had been in the bullpen all day. I was freezing when I took my jacket off, I was freezing when I started to warm up, and I was freezing when I came into the game.

Billy Williams walked up, met me at the mound after Whitey Lockman handed me the baseball, and he looked at me and said, "You cold?"

I said, "Yeah, I'm a little cold."

Williams said, "I was wondering because your lips are blue."

Well, there was not much I could do. So I hung the first curveball to Taveras for a single, Manny Sanguillen hit a two-run double to left field, and we lost the game.

I don't know how many more late-inning opportunities I was going to get. But they didn't put me in save situations too often because I didn't have a powerful fastball or a bona fide strikeout pitch. Plus, the fact that I felt I was a starter didn't make me suitable to get called upon to close too many games—certainly not in April, certainly not at Wrigley Field, and certainly not feeling like the ice man coming into the game.

But I do remember Billy commenting on my blue lips, which probably went very well with my pinstriped Cubbie-blue uniform.

• • •

I have a philosophy about pitchers, and it goes back to a story of a pitcher I played with who never made it to the major leagues. You won't recognize his name, so I'll leave it out.

The story is this: One day someone asked this pitcher if he played professional baseball, and he said, "No, I'm a pitcher." That wasn't meant to demean the art of pitching or to mean that he wasn't an athlete. He was a terrific athlete. But that player's mindset prompted this next idea: I truly believe that every team, if they want to develop more pitchers, more successful pitchers, and more consistent pitchers, should have a pitching school attached to each spring training.

As it is now, teams will work on parts of what a pitcher has to be, but very rarely will they work on all of what a pitcher has to be. So let's figure out how we can make pitchers much better, because pitchers have a tremendous amount of responsibility in the game.

For example, let's say pitchers must cover home plate three or four times a year. This occurs after a short passed ball or a wild pitch with a runner at third base. First, you have to run in and concentrate on catching the ball from the catcher. Second, you must give the base runner part of the plate to slide to. Finally, you must be able to make a tag with your concentration someplace else. That's because if you don't concentrate on catching the baseball, or if you don't give the guy some part of home plate to slide to (which means that he can and will, on occasion, run you over), or if you can't then apply the tag and get him before he gets there, you're going to give up a run or two or three during the course of a year. That could possibly cost you a game or two.

In talking to many officials involved in running organizations as well as pitchers from various organizations, I have found that few, if any, actually work on that play. They also don't work on pitchouts or intentional walks. It may sound strange, but you'll see a highlight when a guy is attempting an intentional walk, and one of his pitches will sail over the catcher's head.

47

Everyone takes for granted that the pitcher can actually throw four pitches wide of the plate, have velocity on those pitches, and hit the catcher. But it could cost you a ballgame. In this case, remembering the idea that baseball is won and lost 90 feet at a time, you would be giving up 90 feet. So that's another thing a pitcher has to work on.

You must remember if you're going to pitch, once you release the baseball, you become the fifth infielder. Those pitchers who can field plug up the biggest hole on the diamond, that hole up the middle. That's one of the things that enables pitchers, especially sinkerball pitchers, to turn 1-6-3 or 1-4-3 double plays. They're able to knock down baseballs that would ordinarily be in center field for a hit.

But to do that, you must work with pitchers on their follow-through and how they come off the mound after completing their deliveries. The hard throwers usually have more problems squaring off on their follow-through than the other types of pitchers. The main reason is that the more effort you put into a pitch, the more apt you are if you are right-handed to fall off the mound on the first-base side and the third-base side if you're left-handed.

This is something to work on, as is the fielding aspect of it. Fielding, for a pitcher, is all-encompassing. It's not only knocking down and catching the baseball and making a throw to second base to start a double play. It also includes charging a bunt to the third-base line, charging a bunt straight in, charging a bunt to the first-base line, knowing when to flip it underhand, when to throw it overhand.

Of course, pitchers must also learn to cover first base correctly. In that respect, you want to tag the inside part of the bag with the right foot. Over the course of a year you'll see a pitcher forgetting to run to the right side on a ground ball. He won't be able to pick up a bunt. What I dislike the most is seeing pitchers who try to barehand every play, because many times they won't be able to get a good grip on the ball, and many times they will not be able to make the play they otherwise would if they used their glove.

That's repetition, and that's something for the pitching school because you can't take for granted that these young men can do anything. You just have to work it over and over until it becomes part of their muscle memory.

The thing that most pitchers try to avoid at all costs when fielding the ball is crossing over the base line, endangering them from getting run into or stepped on by players on the base paths. Occasionally we have seen guys who tore up an Achilles tendon in a collision at first base or got knocked down after a play. That's something you constantly have to remind the pitcher to be aware of.

Here's another situation you would review in the pitching school: there's a runner at second base with fewer than two outs, there's a play to the right side to either the first or second baseman, and the pitcher is going to take the throw at first base. In this situation, the pitcher has to remember to catch the ball, tag the bag, and wheel around and look at that man at third, because that's the guy who can really hurt you.

Certain guys will lose track of the outs, and that can really burn them. That's why I suggest to most catchers and infielders that if you have a forgetful pitcher, always show him how many outs there are because—again in the land of never taking anything for granted—that's a mistake that you see a couple of times a year.

Now, your very smart baseball teams will limit those mistakes, and your very smart pitchers will never let that happen. But we have to assume that not everyone is brilliant, so they have to be consistently reminded.

In spring training, teams conduct pitchers' fielding practice, known as PFP, when balls are hit to the right side. Everyone will yell, "Get over there" on anything hit to the right side. In spring training, you're constantly conducting that drill. But it has to be constantly reinforced. That's why I suggest a pitching school that takes guys away from the regular ballclub and teaches them the nuances of what they have to do.

To continue exploring this idea of the pitching school, there are so many tasks that pitchers really need to learn. For example, pickoffs are completely different for a right-handed pitcher than for a left-handed pitcher. The left-handed pitcher uses deception, such as with a raised right leg where he doesn't go back over the mound and suspends his knee and leg and then moves home. If a left-hander takes his right foot back over the pitching rubber, he must deliver the pitch to the plate. That's a tipoff to a base runner that he can take off for second base.

If a left-hander brings his knee or leg back over the pitching rubber then goes to first base, just about every good umpire will call a balk. So it's the guys who suspend the front leg who are the most difficult to run on.

The observant pitcher is going to watch a guy as he takes his lead. Most base runners are taught to never take crossover steps as they take their lead because it's very difficult to get back. That's a tip for all you good pitchers to take a good look at. How does the base runner take his lead? Does he shuffle to take his lead? Does he get to his lead and then wait for you to go into your stretch? Is he continuing to move off as you continue to go into your stretch? If he's doing that, then he has to be leaning toward second base, and that's a great opportunity to pick him off. But unless a pitcher has worked on that, for one thing he's not going to be able to notice that quite as quickly, and for another, he's not going to be able to take advantage of that.

The right-handed pickoff move is completely different at first base because it depends almost primarily on speed. It also depends on varying the moves. Some pitchers will make a move to first base from a set position, meaning the pitcher will bring his hands up, bring his hands down. Now he's in a set position. Then he throws to first base, depending on quick feet.

Others will throw on the way up. Some will throw on the way down where their hands aren't set. None of these moves are balks. It's not deceiving the runner. For a right-hander, it will be quickness, as opposed to that deception, that gets results.

Coordinating with the catcher is also essential. You have to get your signs right. How do you signal a pickoff? Sometimes if a pitcher doesn't have a fifth pitch, the catcher will put down five fingers. Now the pitcher knows a pickoff play is on. Other times, a catcher taps his shin guard, prompting the pitcher to turn around and throw to second base. The middle infielder must be aware because he must watch the catcher and recognize that a pickoff play is on when the catcher signals for it.

Others work on a count system. For instance, a catcher might put down five fingers or a fist for the middle infielders to see. And then you work on a count system in which the pitcher and the infielder assigned to cover the bag start to count. On the second count, the infielder breaks for the bag. On the third count, the pitcher turns and throws, and that's how you get some pickoffs without even looking at second base. Consequently, when the pitcher doesn't look at second base before he gets into his stretch position, many times the base runner hasn't really paid much attention to the infielders because he's never seen that move before from that particular pitcher.

It's usually the element of surprise for one time. It should be used in critical situations, not just in the first or second inning when you have nothing better to do.

Handling bunts is yet another duty this pitching school would teach. Charging straight in, to your right, or to your left in a bunt situation when you have a slow base runner at first; you must know how to turn and throw to second base. You must understand that the catcher is the captain of that play. The reason is, you have the play behind you. You trust your catcher to come out when a ball is bunted, understanding how hard the ball is bunted, and you and the catcher should know the speed of the runner on first, but you trust your catcher to call the play.

When you pick up the ball, you don't have to look at second because you're trained to hear your catcher's voice. He's going to yell "First," "Second," or "Third," depending on the situation, and then you're going to wheel and make the throw. If you don't work on this repeatedly, then it's going to be very difficult when you're asked to perform this play in a game.

It just takes one bad throw to second base to cost you a game. That's why pitchers must understand how to field their position. That includes knowing exactly where to go, depending on where the ball is hit.

On certain plays, a pitcher must be ready and understand how to be involved in a rundown. For instance, a normal infielder understands that when he delivers the baseball, he has to move away from the base runner. If an infielder stands in the base paths after throwing the ball, a smart base runner will try to run into the infielder. Pitchers who haven't had the experience in rundowns may find themselves getting caught up and eventually hit by a base runner, resulting in interference. Instead of an out, the runner is awarded a base and the pitcher winds up in a situation that might cost him a game.

When you think about all of these things, it's fairly complicated. That's why it takes quite a while to learn it. But you do as much as you possibly can during spring training. You start with your youngsters. You also do it with your major leaguers, not leaving anything to chance, because you're going to deal with a lot of guys in the major leagues who haven't come through your organization. If they've come through your organization, they should know everything they have to do when they get to the major leagues. But it doesn't always happen that way. That's why a pitching school is something I believe will make every pitcher that much better.

◆ ◆ ◆

The importance of knowing the count and the situation is imperative to a pitcher. A concentration lapse can be costly, as was the case on one of baseball's biggest stages.

The 1989 Chicago Cubs had the momentum of a 4–3 lead in the bottom of the seventh inning with their best-of-seven National League Championship Series against San Francisco tied at 1–1.

The Cubs exchanged leads with the Giants before moving ahead on a sacrifice fly by Ryan Sandberg that scored pinch runner Greg Maddux— yes, the same Greg Maddux who went on to win five National League Cy Young Awards.

Manager Don Zimmer had a knack for pulling off the unexpected and playing hunches en route to a 93-win season that gave the Cubs their second NL East title in six seasons.

Every out became more precious to the Cubs. After Brett Butler hit a single with one out in the seventh, Zimmer elected to change pitchers after left-hander Paul Assenmacher threw a first-pitch ball to right-handed hitter Robby Thompson.

This wasn't the first time in 1989 that Zimmer changed pitchers in the middle of an at-bat, but electing for a right-handed reliever made sense against Thompson even with hot-hitting Will Clark on deck.

Les Lancaster entered the game and threw a ball to Thompson to change the count to 2–0. But Lancaster, who thought the count already was 2–0 when he was summoned, threw his next pitch for a fastball that

Thompson whacked for a two-run home run that gave San Francisco a 5–4 lead.

The Giants went on to win that game and the next two contests to win their first NL title in 27 years, while the Cubs extended their World Series drought.

"If I knew it was 2–0," Lancaster told reporters after the game, "I would've thrown another slider instead of a fastball."

• • •

I wasn't much of a hitter in the early stages of my career, nor did I develop into one later. But I do remember my first year going 0-for-34. It's hard to believe you could go a full season in the major leagues without getting a hit, but I was able to do that.

By spring training of 1972, my second year with the Giants, everyone on the team knew I couldn't hit at all. I remember one day Willie McCovey, our Hall of Fame first baseman, was sitting on one of the tables in the training room working on one of his bats with some tape.

Hitters are very sensitive to the fixing of their bats. Some guys used to have what they call "a boned bat," which is a bat that has been rubbed with one of those soup bone gadgets. It was thought this soup bone would help the grain and make the bat a little bit harder. You don't see it as much as you used to, but in those days it was a popular thing to do.

Other batters would sometimes shave down the handle because the handle came in a little too thick. They liked the barrel of that particular model, so they would shave the handle down, and they would tape the knob of the bat so that it kind of eased its way into the actual handle of the bat instead of just being there at the bottom. Some guys would have a bat without the knob at the bottom.

But Willie McCovey would like his bats taped a certain way, and he was sitting there, winding the tape around and around, retaping it a different way, crisscrossing it. Whatever the case, I didn't pay attention because I couldn't hit.

But I took this opportunity to say to Willie, "Stretch, that's probably my problem."

He said, "What's that?"

I said, "I'm just not taping my bats the right way."

McCovey said to me, "Son, I could give you this tape, and my suggestion to you would be the only way this is going to help you is if you tape the pitcher's arm to his leg."

Obviously that wasn't the response I wanted, but it was a very accurate comment. That prompted Willie Mays, who was sitting in the locker room with us, to bet McCovey that I would get four hits that year. McCovey said, "Four hits? You think he, who didn't get a hit all of last year, is going to get four hits?"

Mays said yes.

So they bet $100.

But then Mays wanted to change the bet. He said, "You got to count walks."

Of course, McCovey said no. "Four hits is going to be four hits."

But Mays would not take that bet. The irony of it is that I got exactly four hits my second year.

I didn't even have to tape the pitcher's arm to his leg. It wouldn't have been a bad idea, however, because I was just awful and readily admitted it.

I ended my career with an even .100 batting average. So at least I could say I was in triple digits, and here I had two Hall of Famers—Mays and McCovey—wanting to place a bet on the excellence of my batting stroke. In the end, the bet never came off, even though Mays would have won yet another $100.

• • •

There was an era when baseball was a completely different game and pitchers were much meaner. They would throw at you for several reasons. Some did it because they had to protect their teammates. Some did it because you had the audacity to get a hit or two off them. Or sometimes that was just what they liked to do.

One of my first pitching coaches was a man I truly like and is a scout with the Washington Nationals. He was the original "Big Hurt."

I know with most fans, when they think of the Big Hurt they think of Frank Thomas. My partner in the broadcast booth, Hawk Harrelson, nicknamed him the Big Hurt a number of years back. But the first time I heard the name the Big Hurt, it was associated with Stan Williams. Williams had gigantic hands and was astonishingly strong, and he had the habit of sometimes doing things that his teammates didn't care for.

For example, when he was a teammate of Luis Tiant in Cleveland, he would get behind Luis, place his huge hand over the top of Luis' head, and just squeeze. He would squeeze until Luis dropped to his knees and was ready to pass out. Stan thought that was the most amazing thing he'd ever seen. He got a big chuckle out of it, as Luis slowly came back to consciousness.

This was the same man who, when you shook his hand, would get you in a death grip, and if you emerged without any of the small bones in your hand being absolutely liquefied, you were a very happy man. You learned quite quickly not to shake hands with Stan Williams.

But Stan kept a book, and in that book was a list of all the players he planned to hit, for whatever reason, whether it was perceived slights, protecting teammates, or something else. Understand that Stan had been part of a very mean staff with the Los Angeles Dodgers. Don Drysdale gets well-deserved credit for being one of the meaner guys around. They also had Larry Sherry, who was especially mean.

But Williams wouldn't back down from anyone, even the most formidable sluggers in baseball. In one game, Stan grazed the bill of Hank Aaron's hat with a high and tight fastball with two out and first base open. Aaron went to first base, and Williams retired the next batter to end the inning.

As they crossed paths after the inning ended, Williams said he told Aaron, "I'm sorry I hit your hat. I was trying to hit you in the neck."

That's how baseball was played.

Williams had a pretty good memory. He recalled an exhibition game in 1959 in which he unintentionally hit Bubba Phillips of the Chicago White Sox. Barry Latman, who was Phillips' teammate at the time, proceeded to nail Williams in his next at-bat. There was supposed to be a rematch four days later in which Williams would be able to retaliate for Latman's purpose pitch. But Williams recalled that Latman was scratched.

That wasn't forgotten by Williams, who had to wait six years for his shot at Latman.

It occurred in an exhibition game at Sicks Stadium, where the Seattle Pilots played in their only season, in 1969, before moving to Milwaukee. Williams was trying to resurrect his career with Cleveland after suffering arm injuries.

Sure enough, Latman—now with the Angels—came to the plate with Williams on the mound. Williams, with a fertile memory, nailed Latman with a fastball on the first pitch.

That prompted Williams to say, "I got the last guy left in my book," and he suggested to Latman that they could either fight or call it even.

The drilling was enough to get Latman's attention and for Williams to close his book.

This is a tough game, and you have to be fairly tough to play it. However, I did have to draw the line in one case involving a player/pitching coach named Don McMahon. Don was an active pitcher with the San Francisco Giants at the time, and he taught me how to throw a cut fastball in to left-handed hitters. This was Don's signature pitch, and I couldn't get my fastball in to left-handers consistently. So he said if you learn to cut it and have the same velocity on it, you can break it inside on a left-handed hitter's hand.

In the spring of 1972, we were facing the Milwaukee Brewers, who were in the American League at that time. They had a gigantic first baseman named George Scott who had been recently traded from Boston. His nickname was Boomer, and he was very big and strong. I suspected he was much faster than I was.

So I was warming in the bullpen, preparing to enter the game in the fourth or fifth inning, when McMahon approached me and said, "I want you to hit the first hitter next inning." Well, being an observant type of pitcher, I knew that when I came in to pitch my first inning, the first hitter I was going to face was George Scott.

I said, "Don, the first hitter I'm going to face is George Scott."

McMahon replied, "I know. I want you to hit him."

"Why?"

"Don't ask me why. Just hit him. If I tell you to hit a guy, you hit him."

All I had in the back of my mind was this vision of George Scott, this gigantic hitter, from another league that had done nothing to any of my hitters or anything to me that I knew of, chasing me around the infield after hitting him. That wouldn't have been a manly sight but might have been my fate had I hit Scott.

I told Don, "I'll tell you what, big boy. You're still active, and if you have a problem with George Scott, you hit him. But I'm not going to hit him because I don't have a problem with him, and they haven't thrown at any of our hitters."

A little bit later they traded me to the Chicago White Sox, and one of the things that Giants owner Horace Stoneham said later was, "One of the reasons we traded Steve to the White Sox was that we didn't believe he was tough enough."

So I always remembered the George Scott situation and my refusal to hit him, and maybe, in some small way, it contributed to my actually discovering the great city of Chicago. It gave me an opportunity, along with outfielder Ken Henderson, to wind up with the Chicago White Sox, which eventually led me to the Chicago Cubs.

You see how strange the turns of life are.

• • •

Chuck Tanner was my manager with the 1973 Chicago White Sox, and he later gained a measure of fame by winning the 1979 World Series with the Pittsburgh Pirates. He was a baseball lifer and a good man who had this wonderful way of getting a message across to you.

Chuck was very good at communicating that he was the boss when you first came to the ballclub. He was a very strong man, and he was one of those guys who always wanted to show you just how strong he was. He also would leave you an unforgettable message that he wanted you to adhere to.

I was in my third year in the major leagues, and we had two of the youngest and best relievers to come up together that I had ever seen. They may have been the two best bookend relievers to come up at the same time in the history of baseball. It was a young Goose Gossage and young Terry Forster.

Forster was a left-hander, and Gossage was a right-hander. Gossage is now a member of the Hall of Fame, but he didn't have stuff as strong as Forster. Forster had three absolutely unhittable pitches. He threw a hard, sinking fastball that most hitters describe as a "heavy" ball. Forster would pitch three innings one night against the New York Yankees and then pitch three and two-thirds innings the following night against those same Yankees. He would literally throw the ball through some of the bats. That was before the maple bats that seem to explode whenever guys swing.

One game, I was leading and thought I was pitching very well, but Chuck came to pull me in favor of Goose. Goose routinely would get seven, eight, sometimes even nine-out saves. He would enter in the seventh many times, finish the game, and get the save. It wasn't any big deal for him because he was a starting pitcher in the minor leagues. But that's how closers were used. That one-inning closer that became popular with manager Tony La Russa using Dennis Eckersley in Oakland wasn't around yet.

I wasn't overly happy with Goose's relieving me, so I kind of flipped the ball to Tanner. Goose saved the game, we won it, and I got credit for the victory.

I was sitting by my locker after the game and Tanner came over with a big smile. He said to me, "I want to talk to you about something." I said, "What's that?" Tanner replied, "Hey, look. I know you're new to the ballclub. I just want to tell you about the way we do things around here. I let you pitch as long as I think you should pitch. Then, when I don't think you should pitch anymore, I turn it over to one of those two big guys in the bullpen—Gossage or Forster. They will pitch as long as I want them to pitch, and they usually save the ballgame.

"That's what happens around here, and that's what I do. So I just want you to understand that's for the best. You pitch until I don't want you to pitch anymore. And if I don't want you to pitch anymore, I'll get someone else. But more times than not, either of those guys will close out whatever game I put them in. I just want to know if you understand that?"

I wasn't all that convinced, but I nodded my head. There was a big smile on Chuck's face at this point.

"So I really want to know, do you understand that or not?" Chuck asked.

I said, "Yeah, I guess I do."

Chuck smiled and said, "I'm glad we got that cleared up."

Then he took his finger, which was like a piece of rebar, and he poked me in the chest so hard that I do believe that it just healed up a couple of days ago. This was back in 1973. So we're talking about an indelible impression 37 years ago. When Chuck wanted to get something through to me, all I could think of was, *Agree with him very quickly and make sure he doesn't stick that finger in my chest anymore.* It felt like he literally put it through my chest to my back.

Chuck had that way of communicating what he wanted to with a big smile on his face. He didn't get angry; he just explained to you in a way that you would understand, that this is the way it was going to be on his baseball team. So that was another thing learned on my path through professional baseball, and I learned it very early.

CHAPTER 3

First Base

There are different philosophies about first basemen, whether taller is better or shorter is better. Now, there have been some great small first basemen. I think of Steve Garvey and Jeff Bagwell, just to name a couple guys who were smaller than most first basemen. Then you look at midsized first basemen like Mark Grace and Keith Hernandez, who excelled in the 6'1", 6'2" range. Yet, some of the best defenders in this era of baseball are guys who are a little bit taller. Derrek Lee of Baltimore stands about 6'5". Paul Konerko of the White Sox is a terrific first baseman; he doesn't have great range but he has very smooth hands and makes the 3-6-3 double play and the 3-6-1 double play as well as anyone around because of the accuracy of his throwing arm.

An accurate arm is essential for this position. First, you have to be very careful about the angle you get on your throw. That's why you see some first basemen will move in a little on the grass to make that throw after they catch a ground ball. Or they move back in an effort to throw the ball preferably around the base runner as opposed to over the top. If you throw the ball over the top of the base runner, it becomes a very difficult proposition. If the throw is too low, obviously you hit the runner. You might skip it off his helmet, or you might throw it over the head of an infielder, usually the shortstop, who is covering on a ball hit to you.

Another facet of first base comes into play when you get a very crafty veteran base runner. That runner can make a determination on how to take his lead based on which arm the first baseman throws with. Let's say a base runner breaks from first on a ground ball hit to the first baseman, who is right-handed and was playing even with the runner or a step behind him. That base runner is going to move a little away from the grass and attempt to take away that angle from the first baseman throwing with his right arm.

If a first baseman throws with his left arm, then that base runner is trying to get close to the grass, sometimes even on the grass—again, to try to take that angle away from the first baseman. That's why those first basemen who really have four strong assets—a good idea, a strong arm, an accurate arm, and an understanding of what the base runner is going to do when he makes that throw—those first basemen usually get the job done and help their pitcher out with a double play.

Also, you have guys who scoop the ball out of the dirt better than most of the other guys. I know Konerko has told me he prefers to scoop the ball on a low throw with his backhand. He feels, for whatever reason, that's where he's most comfortable. If you watch over the course of the year, almost without exception, the balls that he scoops are to his backhand, and he will go with the forehand only when there's nothing else he can do.

Other first basemen have other preferences. Many first basemen don't set up on the bag early. The reason for that is to keep their options open, depending on from where the throw is coming. Most guys will set up with their feet in front of the bag and then, depending on where the throw is, will stretch. Many first basemen who make the stretch maybe get that extra 12 inches that can sometimes turn the play into an out. Of course, they have to be very flexible to do it.

But you want to be careful with this. If the ball is going to be in the dirt, and you've already started to stretch out to get the throw, then you might have a problem because if that ball is to your left or right, you won't be able to get to it quickly enough. That sounds rudimentary, but some folks don't understand the intricacies of that position.

It used to be that baseball teams would take that slugging giant who didn't have enough speed and put him at first base. You could count on him for perhaps 35 home runs and 120 RBIs and believe that first base was the place where he could do the least harm. Your first choice would be left field, assuming the guy can run a little bit and can sometimes catch what he runs under. But some guys are not capable of playing left field, so they wind up at first base.

I think we've steered away from that. You want a first baseman who's going to help sometimes off-balance infielders make that throw by scooping it out of the dirt and getting that out. What you don't want is a first baseman who is not as talented and who is going to let that ball go by him. Then the batter is either going to be safe at first base or make it to second if the ball winds up in the dugout or in the seats.

There are a whole lot of people around baseball who consistently look at ground ball–to–fly ball ratios from pitchers. They would like 2:1, two ground balls to every fly ball issued. One of the best pitchers around in that regard was a right-hander named Kevin Brown, who historically in his career was about 3.5:1, ground balls to fly balls, sometimes 4:1.

With this preference for ground ball pitchers comes the importance of a first baseman who can help the infielders, for the simple reason that there will be more plays in the infield. When you look around these days and see first base, many times managers want to tell you how good that first baseman is, or how much he's improved, and they work quite a bit with the first basemen now. They don't take for granted that he's going to be at first because he can't play anywhere else, thinking, *He's going to hit me a lot of home runs and drive in a lot of runs. We're going to put him at first base knowing he's going to be a liability but we can live with that.*

We're now dealing in the post-steroid era with HGH testing very close to being implemented and amphetamines banned from the game. This means that slugball isn't going to be quite as present as it once was. Because of that, you're going to be playing tighter, low-scoring games. As a result, you want a first baseman who is going to save you runs, not give them up.

The Baltimore organization was the best organization I played with as far as player development goes. When you arrived at the big-league level and addressed execution, the Orioles' philosophy was very simple: "Stay out of the big inning." Also, "Stay close enough to the other ballclub because they will make a mistake before we will." Consequently, that was the whole philosophy of the Orioles for many years. It was called the "Oriole Way," and you learned it in the minor leagues through their system. They had wonderful instructors. They told you from the beginning to the major leagues, and it was consistent.

Because of that, when you came to Baltimore from another team, you were always given a crash course in the Oriole Way. One of your teammates would come over, and Earl Weaver would mention it, but maybe not as gently as a teammate would, to stay out of the big inning. Keep it close.

This was told to me a number of times. "Keep us close in the game because later in the game, that other team will make a mistake. And if we're close enough, we're going to capitalize on that mistake and we will beat them." And that mistake, a lot of times, came around first base because of the philosophy of putting a guy over there because he could hit, as opposed to thinking you'd love for him to hit, but it's essential that he also fields.

I see no real advantage between the right-handed first baseman and the left-handed first baseman; each one has different challenges. For instance, on just the pickoff play: the routine pickoff play to a left-handed first baseman is when he can put his glove straight down, catch the ball very easily, and put the tag on as the runner comes sliding back headfirst. Meanwhile, the right-handed first baseman has to cross over his body, catch the throw backhanded, and maybe go an extra inch or two to put that tag on.

We've seen some great first basemen in the past few years who didn't let anything get by them, had good range, and could really adjust on the bunt plays. I always point to Jeff Bagwell, whom Houston acquired when they sent reliever Larry Andersen to Boston. Bagwell was a small but slugging third baseman at the time. He was so good on the wheel play, in which he charged toward home plate in an obvious bunting situation with runners at first and second.

This play often occurs when there are no outs. The first baseman charges from first, the third baseman stays back, and the pitcher charges straight ahead. Bagwell would charge straight in from first base before heading to the third-base line. He would field the ball on the third-base side of the pitching rubber and fire to third to get the lead runner. Sometimes he would do it so quickly that he would actually get the man at second on the relay throw.

By cutting down the lead runner for the first out, you have a man at second instead of third, so he can't score on a wild pitch, passed ball, or fly ball. That is a big play. I know that Keith Hernandez, from the left side, was one of the best I'd ever seen at doing the same thing—charging that bunt hard, getting the ball, and making that throw to third base.

There are many incarnations of the wheel play, and all of the infielders have a role to play. The first baseman will either charge straight in, in case the hitter bunts to first; or in the case of a quicker and more agile first baseman, he might come in and then over toward the third-base line.

In case the batter tries to make that bunt toward the third-base line, the third baseman has to stay anchored at the bag. This presupposes the bunt isn't going to be hard enough to get it toward the third baseman. In this case, the pitcher will go over that way as well. Because if a batter sees both the first baseman and the pitcher, he's not going to bunt it to the right side or up the middle. He going to try everything he can to bunt it to the third-base side.

In either event, if the first baseman gets to the ball quickly enough and is schooled properly, he will get the lead runner. It's an enormous advantage to keep that man off third base with less than two out, because major league hitters take a great deal of pride in driving in that runner from third with less than two out, whether that's by hitting a fly ball or a soft grounder with the infield back. Scoring the run is important because the opponent wants to stay out of the big inning. You eliminate all of that by cutting down the lead runner.

First basemen also have responsibilities on popups, and one is protecting their catcher. Anything on the right side that's hit in the air, especially if it drifts five to 10 feet away from home plate, up the first-base line, especially in foul territory, that catcher will really appreciate a first baseman who comes over, gets to it quickly, calls him off, and makes the play.

It's always the man coming in, as opposed to the man drifting back, who has the easiest shot at it. Even for the best of catchers, that becomes a difficult play. For a first baseman, though, that's a relatively easy play. But you have to get there quickly enough.

The first baseman, just like the third baseman or some outfielders, must know where he is when he drifts back. Many first basemen will take a peek to locate where the ball is, then check to see where they are. Unlike outfielders, who have the warning track, infielders have a very difficult time knowing just how many steps they have on that gravel part from that grass in front of the dugout or the grass down the right-field line before they get to the seats or the dugout. If the ball is hit high enough, first basemen will feel for the rail near the dugout. If they have time, they will set up and lean as far as they can into the dugout to try to make the play.

• • •

How far does a first baseman have to range to the right of the base to be able to get ground balls? We've seen this question come up often. Miguel Cabrera of the Detroit Tigers is one of those first basemen who loves to range far to his right—and many times to the detriment of the play.

By now nearly everyone has heard about Armando Galarraga's perfect game that wasn't. Galarraga had a perfect game with two outs in the ninth, when the final batter, Jason Donald, reached first safely to spoil it. It started with Cabrera ranging far to his right and then throwing to Galarraga, who was covering at first. Replays show Galarraga actually did get to the bag before the base runner and did hold on to the baseball—which was unfortunate for umpire Jim Joyce, who made a bad call. However, it would have been completely unnecessary had Cabrera understood where the second baseman had set up.

When the second baseman is playing up the middle, the first baseman must range far to his right. The farther away the first baseman is from the first-base bag determines the type of throw he'll make to the pitcher covering first. If the first baseman ranges wide of the bag, then he must make an overhand or sidearm throw to the pitcher—whatever is his preference. But he must make that throw and try to hit him a couple of steps from the bag to allow him to right his footwork.

Now, if the first baseman is closer to the bag or playing back in preparation for a dead-pulling left-handed hitter, then he'll want to make that underhand throw. He'll show the pitcher the ball all the way and make an underhand flip to him with enough on the toss ahead of time so the pitcher can get his footwork right. Sometimes you don't have the luxury of doing that, so you have to make the overhand throw. Pitchers prefer that throw above the waist, preferably chest high, either in the middle of the body or to their right, taking them toward the bag so that they can right themselves.

If a pitcher has to turn to his left to make the catch, whether he's a left-handed or right-handed pitcher, then his footwork is skewed. Odds are he's either going to be beaten by the runner or he's going to turn an ankle, dropping the baseball—doing all of those things that are not particularly good when you're trying to get an out.

First basemen are taught to hit that pitcher in the middle of his body, preferably keeping the ball above the waist. Or if they have to lead them a little bit, much like a quarterback leads a wide receiver, then lead him by a step, lead him with the throw so he can catch the ball with enough time to right his footwork and touch the inside of the bag with his right foot.

Pitchers and first basemen work together on that drill continually in spring training. But if the first baseman has a tendency to range way wide of the bag, then he's always out of the play. The pitcher always has to get there, often in a bang-bang play at first base. Or sometimes if he gets there before the runner, he must set up like a first baseman and wait for the throw from the second baseman, who might be off-balance because he has a long way to go to try to get it. You never know exactly where that throw is going to be unless the second baseman makes a good throw.

Many times when you see that happen, it's the first baseman who doesn't take a look to see where the second baseman is setting up. He takes himself out of the play instead of understanding if he just goes back to the bag, the second baseman will make that play. In the Galarraga situation, with the second baseman setting up between first and second, Cabrera should have set up closer to the bag, and the second baseman would have fielded the ball. Again, the guy coming in has a better chance fielding than the guy fading back. Unfortunately for Galarraga, that's not what happened.

So it's not only the base runners that have to check where the defenders are set up. The first baseman must also have an understanding on every pitch where the second baseman is, and that will determine how wide of the bag he has to range.

When you look for a good first baseman, you see the Mark Teixeiras, the Derrek Lees, and Paul Konerkos of this world. There are other current players who are very good as well, such as Adrian Gonzalez of Boston and Carlos Pena of the Cubs. Those guys save their team run after run just by digging out low throws and making stops on balls that could easily have been into right field.

When you see these guys and appreciate their play, you realize that many of them are more than just sluggers. It's not just his batting average. It's also how many runs he saves. Every run you save is just like driving in a run. The good first baseman will save you maybe as much as a run a game. Sometimes if your defense is having a particularly tough time throwing the baseball, he'll save you more than that. So putting that guy at first base because he can hit but doesn't have good hands, doesn't have good feet, doesn't have a sense of how to throw that ball to the pitcher coming over, that's becoming rarer. Because the importance of first base on closer games and more low-scoring games is becoming increasingly more apparent.

• • •

Dick Allen was the first baseman when I joined the White Sox in 1973, and he was a unique character, to say the least. In fact, Dick was one of the most talented guys that I have ever been with, and I have played with and against several Hall of Famers. That includes Juan Marichal, Gaylord Perry, Willie Mays, Willie McCovey, and Billy Williams, as well as Eddie Murray and Jim Palmer later in my career. I also played with some great players who, for whatever reason, might not have applied themselves, liked a few things they should not have liked, or didn't have their priorities quite squared away.

Two players come to mind who, talent-wise, really should have been Hall of Famers but never got there: Bobby Bonds—father of noted slugger Barry Bonds—and Dick Allen.

I always thought Allen could do just about anything he wanted to do as far as first base was concerned, especially hitting. When I got to the White Sox, he was the star of the team. He helped them make a very good run in 1972, and they thought that they could make a strong push in 1973. Our ace pitcher was Wilbur Wood, and our best hitter, far and away, was Dick Allen.

Dick's reputation had preceded him. Everyone knew how good he was when he came over from the Los Angeles Dodgers. He played for the Philadelphia Phillies, where he had some problems in his career. Shortly after he joined the White Sox, the city fell in love with him. Chuck Tanner, our manager, had a set of rules for 24 guys, which everybody adhered to. There was a completely different set of rules for Dick Allen, who could do whatever he wanted to do. Tanner was quick to set the record straight with every player who talked to him about the set of rules he laid down.

"As soon as you can play as well as Dick Allen, then you can do exactly what you want to do," Tanner said. "And until that day, then you have to do what I tell you to do. And Dick can do what he wants to do."

I think in those times the game would start at 8:00 PM. There were many more times than probably anyone realized that Allen wouldn't be there for batting practice. In those days, we took infield practice, and Allen wouldn't be there for infield practice either. About 7:45 PM, Allen would come rolling in. He wouldn't have swung a bat; he wouldn't have taken a throw. He didn't loosen up. He didn't take any sprints. He just put on his uniform, and when we took the field at 8:00, he took his position at first base with no preparation.

Usually he played the game better than anyone else. If you look back to his 1972 season, he hit 37 home runs, drove in 113 runs, and batted .308. So when you look at those numbers and realize how tough it was to hit at Comiskey Park in those days, you realize how good Dick Allen was.

Dick played one of the most amazing tricks on me in spring training after I joined the White Sox. One day he asked me if I wanted to go to

69

dinner with him. I thought it was a remarkable gesture by the star of the team. I was a guy who only might be a starting pitcher, and here was their star asking me to go to dinner. So I said, "Of course, I'd love to do that."

He said okay and told me to meet him in the lobby at 8:00 PM; Dick liked to eat a little bit later.

I arrived at the lobby about 15 minutes before 8:00, but Dick wasn't around. Then it was 8:00, and Dick still wasn't there. When 8:15 arrived, all of a sudden I got a telephone call from Dick.

He said, "Hey, are you in the lobby?"

"Yeah, I'm answering the phone. The switchboard lady told me you were on the phone."

"You know, we're going to have to put off dinner."

I said, "That's disappointing."

He said, "Well, we actually just traded you."

"What?"

"We actually just traded you," Dick said.

"I just got here," I replied. "I haven't really thrown any pitches in spring training yet."

Allen said, "I know. But we really needed some infield help, and, look, I know it's tough on you. I know you were just traded from the Giants. But look, you've got to take this the way it is. Everyone gets traded and, in your case, so you've been traded a couple times. But I think you'll like where you are going."

"Where am I going?" I asked.

"You're going to the Cleveland Indians."

"I was just traded to the Cleveland Indians?" I replied.

"Yes."

"Well, that's where I'm from."

Allen said, "Yeah, that's why I thought you'd like it. You'll be okay."

"Great. That part of it is good. I thought I was playing in Chicago. I got a place to stay after I was being traded and that was probably being taken care of."

"Yeah," Allen said. "That's where you are going."

"So who was I traded for?" I asked.

70

"Well, we traded you even up for Jack Brohamer."

I said, "Wait a second. I'm a starting pitcher. You traded me even up for Jack Brohamer?"

He said, "I didn't trade you. Roland Hemond traded you. But yes, even up for Jack Brohamer."

I said, "Wow. That doesn't sound right to me. That's all you got, Jack Brohamer?"

"We needed a second baseman. He hits left-handed. That was something we were looking for. We got him."

"Okay, well even up for Jack Brohamer. Okay."

Allen said, "You know what? Stay in the lobby. Roland Hemond is going to explain everything to you. You might want to call your folks. Sorry, maybe somewhere down the road we can be teammates again and we can have that dinner."

I said, "Well, thanks, Dick. That's really good."

So I called my parents and said, "You'll never guess what happened."

They said, "What?"

"I just got traded."

"Yeah? Where did you get traded?"

"I'm coming to Cleveland. I got traded to the Indians."

My parents were ecstatic. Absolutely ecstatic. Here I was, a local guy, being traded to my hometown team, a team that I had rooted for continuously while growing up.

My dad said, "Who did you get traded for?"

"Even up for Jack Brohamer."

My dad, like me beforehand, said, "Even up for Jack Brohamer?"

"Yeah."

My dad replied, "He's okay, but he's not all that good."

I said, "Well, the Sox needed a second baseman. I was supposed to have dinner with Dick Allen. He told me that I was traded even up for Jack Brohamer and was going to Cleveland and that part of it would make me happy, and I thought you guys would be absolutely ecstatic."

So they said, "Oh my God. This is great. You get to play here, and we get to see you all the time. Just terrific."

I said, "Look, I'll give you the details and everything else later on. I have to wait. I'm in the hotel lobby in Sarasota and I have to wait for Roland Hemond, who is going to come down and he's going to tell me the whats, whos, whens, and whys, where I go, who do I talk to—all of those things. So wait around a bit, and I'll call you back."

We said our good-byes and hung up.

So I'm in the lobby, waiting, and now it's 8:30. Soon enough it's a quarter to nine and I'm looking at my watch, wondering where Roland was.

About 9:15 PM I said to the switchboard girl, "Can you call Roland Hemond's office? He's supposed to meet me down here and tell me about a trade that happened, and there's nobody down here."

The woman at the switchboard apparently was in on all of this, because she said, "Hey, look. Dick wanted me to keep you hanging around this lobby for a while. I got to tell you, you weren't traded. Roland is not around anyplace. He's probably at dinner. Dick is certainly at dinner, and this was kind of a 'welcome to the White Sox' for you. Nice having you here, and I think you should probably get something to eat, because none of what Dick told you was true. You also might want to tell your parents that you're unfortunately not coming to Cleveland."

I just sat there. I was stunned. I guess that was part of the ritual for being indoctrinated into the '73 Chicago White Sox. But there I was in the lobby, for the better part of 90 minutes, thinking that my world was just turned upside down, going to Cleveland from Chicago, where I hadn't been in the first place because I was traded from San Francisco, which was shock enough. I had to call my parents again and tell them it was a little practical joke played on me by the best player on the Chicago White Sox, and that Roland Hemond had no part of it.

Later, when I explained it to Hemond, he got a laugh out of it. My folks were a bit disappointed, but knowing that I was in a good city in Chicago took the sting out of it. Sure enough, I went out to dinner much later than I had anticipated without Dick Allen. We never did go out for dinner that year we were teammates, but I never have forgotten that day.

• • •

These next two stories will give you some kind of idea of just how good Dick Allen was, and I can attest to these stories because they all involved me.

I was with the White Sox, and we were playing one night against the Baltimore Orioles. You might remember that the 1971 Orioles had four 20-game winners on the same staff—Jim Palmer (who went on to do it eight times), Dave McNally, Mike Cuellar, and Pat Dobson. Four men, four 20-game winners. A most unbelievable accomplishment that I don't ever think we'll see again. But because of the four-man rotation in those days, you saw it with the Orioles.

This particular evening, Cuellar was starting against us in the old Comiskey Park, and Dick Allen was talking to me before the game. He said, "Every time I face Cuellar, he starts me off with a slow hook. I usually don't like to hit breaking balls on the first pitch, but he starts me off with a slow hook."

Dick continued, "If he starts me off with a slow hook tonight, I'm going to give up the fastball or the change-up, or anything else. I'm just going to look for that slow hook. If he throws me a slow hook on the first pitch, I'm going to hit it over the roof."

At that time, there had been only 10 balls in the history of Comiskey that hit on or sailed over that roof. That was a pretty big statement. Obviously, I was riveted to Dick's first at-bat in the bottom of the first inning.

Cuellar was on the mound, taking his warm-ups. He had a terrific curveball. It was fairly slow, but he got such a tremendous rotation on it that it broke very sharply. I know it sounds like a contradiction, and I know everyone believes that a sharp-breaking curveball is usually thrown hard. It isn't the case.

A curveball breaks because of the rotation on the baseball, and the quicker you can get the rotation on the baseball—that is, the faster you can make it spin—the sharper it breaks. If you hold the ball in the back of your hand, you can get it to spin very quickly, especially if you pull down with your middle finger on a seam and you push up with your thumb, usually on a seam, and you usually can get it to really break sharply even though you're throwing it a little slower.

73

Cuellar had that kind of curveball. It was called a biting curveball, and he threw it fairly slow. So I was watching Dick as he got into the batter's box, and sure enough, Cuellar threw him that first-ball biting curveball.

Dick promptly hit it over the roof.

The 11th guy in the history of that ballpark to hit it over the roof.

At that time, I began to think that Dick was really something special, and later on in that season, he was to reinforce it one more time.

Dick and I, along with Goose Gossage, had an extensive conversation one night in Dick's room. He was explaining to me how he hurt his hand, and the explanation was that he was pushing a car for a friend, trying to get this car out of a rut in the snow, when his right hand went through the headlight.

Whatever the truth of that story is, what he did was sever some nerves at the bottom of his hand and it really rendered the ring finger and the little finger on his right hand numb most of the time. That meant he had to completely change his batting style, a remarkable thing for a hitter to do.

Once a guy has a place where he puts the bat in his hands, a blister forms on the bottom hand—the left hand for a right-handed hitter, the right hand for a left-handed hitter—and eventually there will be a distinct callous. Well, Dick showed us his hand, and he had two of these calluses: one from before the accident and one from after the accident, when he had to completely change his batting style. His ability to make that adjustment attested to just how good he was.

Anyway, the White Sox went with a three-man rotation in 1973, which was not a particularly smart idea, but Chuck Tanner and Johnny Sain wanted to give Wilbur Wood as many starts as possible. So it started out Wilbur Wood, Stan Bahnsen, and Eddie Fisher in the three-man rotation. It morphed into Wilbur Wood, Stan Bahnsen, and me because Fisher couldn't pitch much anymore. He was a bit older, but that knuckleball just didn't knuckle. So I got my first start on June 2.

We were in Milwaukee, and it was one of those very cold days in old County Stadium. In that stadium, the wind blew straight in from right field, and it blew in a gale. To hit the ball out in right field was a monumental task, even for a left-handed hitter, let alone a right-handed hitter. I was pitching a very strong game. It was one of my early starts, and I was to only go seven innings in that game. (I say "only" because seven wasn't a whole lot in those days. Now seven innings is what everyone strives for.)

It was a scoreless game, and there was one out and a man at second base, and a ground ball was hit to shortstop Eddie Leon, who rifled the ball to Dick Allen at first base, retiring the batter for the second out. At that point the base runner at second, who was moving up on the throw, decided he was going to head for third base. It was a play that Dick could have made easily, but being a cold day in Milwaukee and the fact that he had lost the feeling in those fingers on his right hand, he went to transfer the ball from his glove to his hand, and the ball just dropped out.

When the ball dropped, the runner was safe, and it didn't end the inning. The Brewers wound up scoring two runs that inning, and I trailed 2–0. Dick knew he should have made that play, which would have saved me those two runs. Instead, Tanner told me I was out of the game, and we entered the top of the eighth trailing 2–0. We did get a man on with two outs, and Dick got a bat. But before he got a bat, he came by me and looked at me and said, "I'll get them back for you." I said, "Okay, go get them."

I was not sitting on the home plate side of the dugout by that point. My day was done, and I was wearing a jacket while sitting toward the other side. But Dick went up there and got the count to where it was favorable, and he made contact. He hit a line-drive rocket into the teeth of the wind, which I didn't think was humanly possible, and that ball went about halfway up the bleachers in right field. And at old County Stadium, it was exposed. The bleachers weren't that high, so the wind could come over the bleachers a lot like at Wrigley Field. Yet he was able to take it out of the park and tie it at 2.

He came back and put his helmet away, put his bat away, and walked down a couple steps in the middle of the dugout, took a look over at me, just winked, and walked back and we made the third out, and he went out to first base.

It was about at that point that I believed that this guy could literally do anything that he wanted to do on the baseball field. He was our best base runner. Not our fastest, but our best. He was a very good first baseman. Not one of the greatest, but a very good one. But with the bat, he was infinitely talented, astonishingly strong, and to his teammates, a pretty good guy. We really liked him. That was an interesting part of what Dick Allen brought to the table.

I won't say that he didn't take it seriously, because between the lines he did. But he had a few demons that he had to exorcise, and sometimes they got the best of him.

Rich Gossage and I spent a night with Dick Allen in Minnesota—just Rich, Dick, and me. That's when Goose and I were still young players. Dick, of course, was a veteran and a guy we all looked up to. All of us had our favorite relaxation libations at that time, and we wound up spending five hours talking with him. It was one of the most interesting, most educational, and most unique experiences I ever had in the game. Because here was a superstar talking with two kids. Goose, of course, went on to become a Hall of Famer. Dick, as you know, had a good career, although he never really accomplished all that he needed to. But he started telling us some of the situations in his life. He told us about a batting race in the Eastern League, when he was in Double A, between him and a rising superstar from the San Francisco Giants' organization named Jim Ray Hart.

Hart was the star of Springfield, Massachusetts, and Dick Allen was the star of Williamsport, Pennsylvania, for the Phillies. On the second-to-last day of the 1962 season the two teams were playing at Williamsport. They ended that night game in a dead tie for first place for the batting title.

Now, Dick told us he was friends with Jimmy Ray, and he said that Jimmy Ray hit the baseball harder than anyone he knew. He said you could close your eyes and just hear the difference. Keep in mind that the Giants had Willie McCovey, Orlando Cepeda, all the Alou brothers, Willie Mays, and two guys named Willie Kirkland and Leon Wagner. They brought up slugger after slugger through their system. And they said if you stood around home plate during batting practice and closed your eyes at the batting cage, you could tell when Jim Ray Hart came to bat because he hit the ball perceptively harder than the rest of those guys, which is quite an accomplishment.

So here they are, dead even, on the second-to-last day of the season. Dick told us he knew that he could outdrink Jimmy Ray. He knew that

Jimmy Ray's drink of choice was Old Crow. Dick drank Johnnie Walker Red. So he told Jimmy Ray that they would go out that night after the game and have a good time. Jimmy Ray, like Dick, was always up for a party.

Dick said his plan was to keep Jimmy Ray out for as long as he could and try to drink him under the table. If he could do that, and he knew he could, he would win the batting title the next day. So they went to an after-hours club that Dick was very familiar with, and, as he told it to us, "I bought a bottle of Old Crow and put it in front of Jimmy, and I bought a bottle of Johnnie Walker Red and put it in front of me."

They told stories and some lies, had some laughs, talked about baseball, life, growing up, what they were going to do—all those things that guys talk about late at night while trying to drink themselves into a stupor. Or in the case of Dick Allen, trying to outdrink Jimmy Ray so that Jimmy Ray wouldn't be able to do much the next night.

So that bottle of Old Crow disappeared fairly quickly, as did the bottle of Johnnie Walker Red. Dick ordered another bottle. They drank about a third or so of that bottle, and by that time, it was nearing sunup. He told us, "I let Jimmy keep his bottle; I kept my bottle. I drove him back to his hotel. The sun was up, it was morning, and I was pretty convinced I was going to win the batting title.

"So we go to the park the next day. He couldn't have gotten much sleep, because I know I didn't get much sleep."

Of course we wanted to know if his plan worked. Well, Dick went 4-for-5, but Jimmy Ray Hart went 5-for-5 and won the batting title.

It was a great story, and Dick Allen continued to captivate Goose Gossage and me throughout that evening with various anecdotes of his baseball life and times. It was one of the most unusual evenings I ever had in baseball.

• • •

You might remember the 1977 Chicago White Sox were called the South Side Hitmen. On that team, we had two first basemen whose duties were split. One was Jim Spencer, an exceptional left-handed fielder who went on

77

to play with the Yankees. When we needed a right-handed hitter, we'd go to Lamar Johnson, a very nice, big, strong guy.

Lamar wasn't as good defensively as Jim, but he could really smash the baseball, and that's what the South Side Hitmen were really known for. We had nine guys in our lineup who hit at least 10 home runs. We had two guys who hit at least 30, which in those days was an exceptional accomplishment. Oscar Gamble hit 31, Richie Zisk hit 30, and Eric Soderholm hit 25.

During one evening in Anaheim, I was on the mound facing a right-handed hitter who loved to push bunt to the right side. His name escapes me, but I do remember Lamar Johnson had just committed a misplay at first base. It was either a low throw that he didn't scoop or some other play he didn't make. But you knew with Lamar there, he would most likely get it back with the bat. It was one of those things. The pitchers on that South Side Hitmen team took for granted that we weren't going to field it very well, but we were probably going to score six, seven, or eight runs a game, so the ERA didn't matter too much. But after the mistake, Lamar was a little sensitive.

I remember looking over to him because this right-handed batter had push-bunted on me before to the right side. His job was to get it by me and hope the first baseman would range wide off the bag and make the play, and he felt that he could either beat me to the bag or that there wasn't enough coordination between—in this case—second baseman Jorge Orta and Lamar Johnson.

It takes a rare second baseman to be able to get to first base in time on a push bunt that skips past the pitcher with the first baseman fielding it to actually make that play at first. The best I saw was the coordination that Mark Grace had with Ryne Sandberg. Sandberg was exceptional with that particular play because as soon as that push bunt got by the pitcher, Grace went to get it, and Sandberg would always be there covering first base. It would take a lot of pressure off the pitcher because he really couldn't get there. The first thing the pitcher would try to do was catch the ball. But on a perfectly placed bunt, he couldn't get to it, forcing the first baseman to catch it.

In this instance, I was looking at Lamar and motioning to him to watch the push bunt.

Well, he thought, for some reason, that I was trying to show him up in front of the fans about the misplay that he had made before, which would really make no sense for the simple reason that I wouldn't signal the bunt sign on a play that had happened just before, and there's no reason to show up a guy in front of all the fans in Anaheim, especially a guy who was much bigger, much stronger, and probably a lot more hostile than I was in the first place.

But Lamar was steaming. We finally got out of the inning with no runs scored. I put my glove down and started to walk up the ramp to the locker room to change shirts. Then here comes an enraged Lamar Johnson. His eyes were bulging out of his mind, angry as hell. He came running up to me and said, "You're trying to show me up?"

I said, "No. What are you talking about?"

"You were out there, making those gestures. You were trying to show me up on that play that I didn't make?"

I replied, "Lamar, first of all, a lot of guys don't make plays. Second, I was trying to tell you that that right-handed hitter had a tendency to bunt to the right side. I was trying to alert you to that fact."

All of a sudden he went from axe-murderer angry to where it finally dawned on him that I really wasn't trying to show him up, and he completely relaxed.

He said, "Oh, oh. That's what you were trying to tell me?"

I said, "Yeah. What good would it have been to me to tell you about a push bunt on a play that happened before that had nothing to do with that?"

He said, "Okay. All right."

He was a very good-natured guy most of the time. Fortunately, he believed that story, which actually happened to be true. So I was saved another beating from a very large, very hostile man at that point. So I just went to change my shirt and thought, *Phew, that was close.*

Occasionally you'll have disagreements on the ballfield. Occasionally they're settled with some fisticuffs either in the locker room or in the runway up to the locker room. Fortunately, this incident with Lamar ended well for me, because I figured he was checking in at about 6'2", and I'll graciously say he was about 275 pounds. So being outweighed by 100 pounds and a few inches in height, I didn't think it was in my best interests to settle this by fisticuffs.

• • •

Ron Blomberg was a designated hitter who started with the New York Yankees and later played with the Chicago White Sox. Before he arrived with the Sox, two of the many things we had heard about Blomberg were (1) he had tremendous skills with the Yankees; he could run and was as quick as anyone despite being a big, strong guy, and (2) the position of designated hitter was actually made for him because he couldn't field very well. But when he did field, he played first base.

One other thing we heard about Blomberg was that he was one of the most prodigious eaters in baseball. It was really strange because he was a nice-sized guy, but he wasn't that Frank Howard type of build. He wasn't 6'7". He wasn't 300 pounds. He was a normal-sized guy at 6'1", 195 pounds. But you could tell he could hit the ball out of the park because he was very strong, and his reputation preceded him.

As the story went, when he was with the Yankees, there was an all-you-can-eat place in Fort Lauderdale that served average-sized lobster tails. Ron ate there one night. The guys who were with him started counting. Ron had a few other dishes, but he ended up eating 47 lobster tails. Forty-seven! He was known as an eater, but he was apparently able to burn it off because he wasn't a fat guy.

Eventually, the owner of the place came over, after watching this magnificent display of gluttony, and told him, "Look. I'm going to buy your dinner tonight. You won't have to pay for it. But I want you to be assured that I will remember you, and I never want to see you in here again."

So Ron was banned from the all-you-can-eat place because I guess it was all-you-can-eat except if you were Ron Blomberg, and then you couldn't eat there because you could eat them out of business.

I remember the first time I went to dinner with Blomberg after he joined the White Sox. It was at a Chinese restaurant, and it was Ron, me, a few teammates, and I believe it was Bobby Molinaro, who at the time was best friends with Ron. The waiter came over to take our orders. Ron started first, and I remember he ordered three appetizers. Then he ordered five entrees, a plate of fried rice, and a couple of side dishes.

We were looking at the menus and thought, *Okay, he's ordering for the table. What the hell. It's going to be good, anyway. It's a good restaurant.*

Ron put down the menu, looked at us, and said, "What are you guys going to have?"

We honestly thought he was kidding. He replied, "No, I'm serious. What are you guys going to have? That's what I have. Just don't worry. I'll pick up the check, but you guys order what you want."

Ron put on a display that was absolutely awesome. He not only ate everything he ordered, but he ate it easily. It wasn't one of those forced things; it wasn't like Takeru Kobayashi or Joey Chestnut in the Nathan's hot dog eating contest where they force themselves in 10 minutes to eat in the neighborhood of 50 or 60 hot dogs with the buns. It was just his normal eating pattern. It's a moment indelibly etched in my memory— Ron Blomberg plowing through that ridiculously large meal at that Chinese restaurant. I didn't go on to have many more dinners with him, because it took way too long. By the way, he also helped clean up some of the other plates where guys ordered too much and couldn't finish the rest of their dinners.

So everything I heard about him was absolutely true, and that particular evening he showed us that there are some human beings on this planet who can eat everyone else, literally, under the table. That was so memorable, I couldn't feel fulfilled in a book without mentioning Ron Blomberg.

• • •

The Cubs had a first baseman who became a dear friend and a partner of mine in an ill-fated restaurant in Scottsdale, Arizona. His name was Pete LaCock, and Pete was a very nice guy who probably got as much out of his ability as he possibly could.

LaCock was not known for his power, but he was a decent hitter, and one night he was facing Bob Gibson, during the later stages of Bob's career.

If Bob were in his heyday, Pete wouldn't get too many hits off him, let alone a home run. Indeed, in 1974, LaCock hit a double off Gibson, only to get drilled in the shin with one of Gibson's best fastballs in his next at-bat. But in September 1975, this was one of the last times that Bob, who was 38 years old, was going to throw professionally because he was about ready to retire. In fact, Bob was facing Pete and the Cubs in relief.

This time, Pete hit a pinch-hit grand slam off Gibson that gave the Cubs an 11–6 lead in the seventh. Those were the days where if you hit a home run off a pitcher like Bob Gibson, and you weren't a home run hitter or he didn't particularly feel like you should have hit that home run, then he would make sure you felt it the next time.

Gibson didn't get another shot at LaCock, but Bob made sure LaCock knew he wasn't happy as he followed him around the bases rendering a litany of unpleasant words directed at him. Bob was saying things that really don't belong in a book to be consumed by some of our younger generation.

It was one of those things where you just looked at him and said, "This guy is going to the Hall of Fame, yet he's still intense enough and still competitive enough to really take exception to the fact that this light-hitting first baseman from the Chicago Cubs just got a grand slam off him."

That was our first baseman and friend Pete LaCock, and one of the most competitive and one of the greatest pitchers who ever played the game, Bob Gibson.

CHAPTER 4

Second Base

One of the best descriptions I ever heard about a second baseman was by Frank Cashen, a longtime and successful general manager who understood the Oriole Way through the Baltimore system.

Cashen once told me he wanted his second baseman to be a "dirtball." I asked him, "Please explain what you mean by a dirtball."

He said, "There are going to be a lot of plays, 5-4-3, 6-4-3, a lot of ground balls hit to the left side, and I want my second baseman to be able to turn that double play. I want him to stand in there and make sure he gets a throw off, regardless of where the relay throw is to him, or regardless of how long it takes to get there. He's got to sometimes take the hit but get the throw off." The dirtballs are going to do that.

That's why you see several guys who were not particularly great players that qualify in that dirtball role, such as Wally Backman of the New York Mets in the late 1980s and Richie Dauer, a teammate of mine in Baltimore. There are others who fit that role; they will stand in, take the hit, and make sure they get the throw off because they don't want to give another team four outs, especially a team with a little thunder in the lineup.

That's of critical importance for a second baseman.

Teams have a tendency to shift players from third or shortstop to second because either they've lost a step in range or their arm isn't as strong as it should be. For instance, the White Sox's Gordon Beckham was moved from third to second shortly after the 2009 season. But maybe one of the all-time great examples of the move to second is Ryne Sandberg.

Sandberg was a shortstop in the Philadelphia organization. The scouting report on him was that he didn't have the arm for a shortstop. Despite what you've heard from some people who want to indulge their revisionist history, Sandberg was a throw-in in the Larry Bowa deal. Dallas Green originally wanted Luis Aguayo. Because the reports on Sandberg as a shortstop weren't particularly good, Philadelphia was willing to part with him.

Green took him and shortstop Larry Bowa. Ryno played his first season with the Cubs at third, where he was solid defensively. But later they shifted him to second base, where he played well enough to go into the Hall of Fame. His longest errorless streak was 123 games at second base, which is remarkable when you consider that you are the cutoff man on several throws from the outfield, either down the right-field line or into right-center field.

Many times a second baseman must serve as the cutoff man. He's in charge of making that accurate throw to try to nail a runner trying to take an extra base, as well as fielding all the ground balls like every other infielder does, and execute the double plays. That can become problematic, especially for guys who shift over from shortstop. The reason is that shortstops are used to having the play in front of them. That means they can see the base runner all the way. They can take a throw either from first or second on a double play. Consequently, as they come across the bag, they know exactly where that runner is going to be. They know where he's running. They can see where he attempts to slide. Or they can tell if the base runner is trying to roll them, and prepare themselves for that.

The second baseman, on the other hand, has the double play with the runner coming in behind him. If you are a converted shortstop who is used to seeing the runner all the way, this is a difficult transition. You're trusting that the throw to you from third base or shortstop is going to be to the glove side, preferably letter-high, and hopefully a couple steps ahead of that runner.

In some instances, the second baseman has to act like a first baseman. He has to recognize a slowly developing play with the guy running with enough speed where he's probably not going to be able to turn two. Therefore, he will set up at second base like a first baseman would set up and try just to get the force play. He has to give up the idea of the double play.

But more often he'll have a chance to get that throw off. Then he has to do various things to try to protect himself. There are many second basemen who will stand behind the bag, get the throw and use the bag as a piece of protection against the sliding base runner.

There are several second basemen who are new to the position who end up making a flat-footed throw. Those are the guys who are going to take some contact and they're going to take quite a lot of it. You want to make sure that you don't have both feet on the ground when you're making the throw and absorbing the contact. If you have both feet on the ground and a guy comes barreling into you, there's a good chance you're going to get hurt. I've seen a lot of knee injuries with both feet planted.

The object is to throw from whatever foot you're going to throw off. That is, if you're throwing off your right foot, you want your left foot in the air. That way when you take contact, you can absorb the contact and usually fall on top of the base runner. Many second basemen who don't particularly care for the way a guy slides will go up in the air and land right on the sliding base runner. Now, there are a lot of people who would say that's not ethical; that's not the way the game is played. It's actually the way the game has been played for a long time. Of course, depending on how much you've aggravated the pivot man, especially the second baseman, there's a chance he can go right up in the air and come down on you. Consequently, the runner takes the brunt of the collision.

A second baseman must be concerned with the knowledge of who is coming down and trying to break it up, because some players slide harder than others. The second baseman must be aware of the base runner who makes a clean slide but intends to get a piece of you and tries to break up the double play. Every good second baseman knows which guys on the opposing team slide as hard as they possibly can.

85

Then you must know which guys will slide and roll. There are several base runners who will take that slide and then roll with their shoulder, trying to hit you around the midsection and knock you up in the air. Usually they're rolling after the bag. Some umpires will call that, but most won't. But for a second baseman's health and welfare, he's got to know the slide-and-roll guys.

When throwing from second to first on a double play, the second baseman must make that runner get down and out of the way of the play. If he's throwing over the top, aim toward the bill of the runner's helmet. He'll get down. Many second basemen will grab the ball and throw it a little more to the side and try to keep as low a throw as possible, but make sure it goes right over the runner's head. If you get a reputation as a second baseman who will come across and don't mind hitting a runner right between the eyes or right off the helmet, those runners are going to start their slide a little bit sooner, or they're going to slide right to the bag and let you get your throw off.

But with cutoff plays, second basemen have other responsibilities as well. There are a lot of second basemen who don't have quality arms, and that's why they're at second and not short or third. But even at second, you need some amount of accuracy and strength. That was one of the things that helped Sandberg, as good a player as he was; he had a plus arm at second base. He didn't have what you need at short, but at second base, he had it. A modern-day example of that would be the White Sox's Gordon Beckham. Beckham might not have had a plus arm at short, but he certainly has a plus arm at second base. He goes straight over the top and gets as much velocity as possible on his throw. He has a pretty strong arm, so when he doesn't complete a double play, it's not for lack of arm strength.

In looking at Sandberg's career, very rarely did he ever get knocked around at second base, because he was very quick and very smart. He knew how to avoid contact and still get the throw off. Because he had a plus arm for a second baseman, he could move maybe an extra step to get away from contact and still have enough left to throw the guy out at first. That's just something second basemen have to do.

Another important play that involves the second baseman is when a right fielder must retrieve a ball hit into the corner. When that happens, the second baseman is the primary cutoff man and should run down the line to get into position. Then he must rely on one of his teammates to tell him where the play is. If he must turn around and look before throwing, he's lost a critical second or 1.5 seconds. That first baseman should be telling him exactly where the play is going to be.

Pop-ups can also trick some second basemen if they don't know how to field them. Some guys do it much better than others. When Alexei Ramirez of the White Sox took over at second base in the 2008 season, he wanted to go everywhere for pop-ups. And because that pop-up down the first-base line is a little easier for a second baseman than it is for a first baseman, it would help if that guy could get to it. Unfortunately, we've seen mishaps between the first baseman and second baseman when they don't communicate. We saw it in the 2010 season with a collision between Minnesota's Denard Span and Orlando Hudson that put Hudson on the shelf for a while.

A second baseman is very vulnerable when he runs with his back to the infield and tries to catch the ball. That's why it's imperative for either the center fielder, if the ball is in right center, or the right fielder, if it's in right, to yell as early as he can, "I've got it." The rule is that the second baseman is going to try to get everything he can until he hears the voice of somebody calling him off—whether it is the center fielder, the right fielder, or the third baseman. That means communication out there is key.

The best guy I've seen at fielding like that, as far as any infield position, was Shawon Dunston. Dunston wanted to get fly balls. Any time a ball was hit in the air, he thought it was his. Alexei Ramirez was exceptional at this when he played second, and he's still very good at this at shortstop. About the middle of his career, whenever Sandberg became teamed up with Mark Grace, they were great together and it provided one of the great defensive right sides—maybe in the history of baseball.

Grace was terrific at first base. Sandberg was just outstanding at second base. There are other twosomes who are maybe in the same neighborhood as those guys, but it's very hard for me to conceive of too many tandems on the right side better than those two guys. But the one idiosyncrasy that Ryno had, especially as his career moved on, was that he took fewer and fewer fly balls.

Just about every time a popup went up, you pretty much knew it was, "Go get it, Gracie." And between whoever was playing right field and Mark Grace, they covered most everything on that right side. Again, it's hard to criticize Ryno for anything because he was that good of a player, that good of a hitter, a clutch hitter, a guy who went from an opposite-field hitter to a power hitter, and now is a Hall of Famer. But the one little hole in his game was his ability on popups to go back.

So second basemen have plenty of responsibilities, and the good ones always make the catch they have to make and get that throw off when it has to be thrown. The good ones also save a whole lot of runs, turn a lot of double plays, and get pitchers out of tough innings by making sure they get that throw away every time they have even a glimmer of a shot at that base runner heading up the first-base line.

• • •

I played with an array of second basemen, including Richie Dauer when we were in Baltimore. Richie started his collegiate career at the University of Southern California during its glory years under Rod Dedeaux and is now a coach with Colorado.

When Dauer came to the Orioles and played second base, he was very dependable with the glove, hard to strike out, but he didn't have much power—much to the dismay of Earl Weaver. On a number of occasions, I heard Earl go up to him and say, "Didn't you play baseball at Southern California?"

Dauer would reply, "Yeah, I did."

"If I'm not mistaken, didn't you hit more home runs than Fred Lynn hit?"

"Yeah."

Weaver would say, "Where in the hell did the power go? You hit more home runs than Lynn, and he's still hitting home runs. You're not hitting any home runs. Where did the power go?"

Dauer, of course, took pride in his ability to make contact and move the ball around and do all those things. Sometimes college power doesn't translate into major league power, but Earl loved the three-run homer. In fact, he loved the homer of any kind, and he would periodically get on Dauer about it.

Another second baseman during my Baltimore days was Lenn Sakata, an interesting second baseman of Japanese heritage. He had a steady glove, but for some reason, he could never produce against the Chicago White Sox. I think at one point he might have been 0-for-44 against the White Sox, and he ended with a career .069 average against them.

Sakata was just a youngster when Harry Caray and Jimmy Piersall were announcing games for the Sox, and Piersall was very hard on him. Everything that Sakata did, Piersall would point it out, saying he did it wrong, or he took a bad swing. Harry just went along with it for a while. It was never-ending. It started in one of the first games they ever watched him play, and it continued for a while because of his long slump against only the Chicago White Sox. He wasn't a great hitter, and he couldn't hit the White Sox's pitching.

Finally, between innings in one game, Harry looked over at Piersall and said, "Hey, Jimmy. You know you're being a little hard on that guy. He's just a young player at second base. You've been very tough on him for this series."

Piersall said, "Well, yeah, you'd do the same thing if you had a brother that died at Pearl Harbor."

So Harry thought, *Well, okay. Jimmy is a little off-center anyway. But okay.*

But Harry looked it up. It turns out Jimmy had an older brother who died suddenly, but there was no documentation that he died at Pearl Harbor.

Meanwhile, Sakata didn't start every day, but he was used as a swing man and did a decent enough job.

Another guy who came up in the Baltimore system was Bobby Grich. Grich came through with Don Baylor, but he really came to prominence in that first free-agent class with the California Angels. He and Baylor signed with the Angels, where they had terrific careers.

Grich was one of those guys who, when he was covering on a pickoff play at second base, or when he was covering on a steal, if you slid in headfirst, he would bury his knee right between your neck and your shoulder—right in that soft spot above the clavicle. He would do everything he could to put a big hurting on you to the point where you didn't want to come in headfirst anymore, or you shortened up your lead because you were going to come right into that very pointed knee of his.

I remember him more than a few times leaving some guys in the dirt. That was one of the tricks he used just to let the guy know coming into second base that he was going to be there, and to let the guy know on a pickoff play that he's going to have to come back into Grich.

Jorge Orta was our second baseman on the 1977 Chicago White Sox. Jorge was a terrific hitter, and he fit right in with the South Side Hitmen, who could bat but didn't field very well.

Orta was very robotic at second base. You see some second basemen who have that fluidity about them. Jorge was just the opposite. As I remember the South Side Hitmen, we were still looking for a 6-4-3 or a 4-6-3 double play. The infield turned a few double plays—they just didn't make too many. But Jorge could hit, as everyone else could on that 1977 team. That's the reason he played second base; it was by default because there wasn't anyone else to play it and hit the way he did. He was in there because of his bat. He didn't have much range and the rest of his game was a little suspect. But that was to go on with most of the guys who played on that team.

However, we had a tremendous time. We gave the fans of Chicago a good run for four and a half months until we were chased down by Kansas City, which was a better team than we were. They wound up winning the American League West that year. And they beat us by plenty, as I recall. So once they caught us, there was no looking back.

• • •

From an acquisition standpoint for a general manager, it's almost impossible to get your team 10 percent better by making one move. Certainly the occasion comes up when you make a blockbuster move or a blockbuster signing that makes you 5 percent better. But 10 percent is really not doable.

The object with all of the moves that executives make, is to get your team incrementally better—1 percent at a time. Maybe in a big move, it's 2 percent better. That has to do with baseball acumen, a player's aptitude for the game. If you bring in smarter players, then your team starts to get smarter, and at the end of the day if you buy the philosophy that I have that the game is always won or lost 90 feet at a time, the smarter the players you bring in, the smarter your team is going to be.

Conversely, if you bring in players who don't have strong baseball acumen, who don't have a strong philosophy about the game of baseball or don't understand baseball aptitude, the dumber your team is going to be.

That means if your team is not getting any smarter and is, in fact, as a team, getting dumber, you have to be that much better physically than the opposition to beat them. Because all things being equal, there are many years where the postseason is determined by one game, one way or the other. The wild-card can be determined by one game, whether that's a game you gave away or a game you took away. If you have the smarter team, you're going to win that game. The other team might be thinking, *Boy, that's a very lucky team*, but in reality, it's not luck at all. It's a smarter team beating a team that will beat itself.

• • •

A second baseman I observed in my many years of broadcasting turned out to be a hero with the Arizona Diamondbacks when they won the World Series in 2001. Tony Womack joined the Chicago Cubs in 2003, the same year they were testing baseball in Puerto Rico. There was an 18-game schedule to be played, six three-game series between the Montreal Expos, who at that point were being run by Major League Baseball, against whatever team they happened to be playing.

Because we had Sammy Sosa on the Cubs, they made an exception. They actually extended their schedule from 18 to 21 games, and we went to Puerto Rico to Hiram Bithorn Stadium in San Juan.

I have at least three remembrances about Hiram Bithorn Stadium. First, it was very, very shallow in the outfield. Second, the lights weren't that good. Third, from a broadcast standpoint, we were right in front of the one concession stand that distributed food throughout the stadium. They were cooking for nine innings, and it smelled like they were cooking goats.

It was one of the most difficult broadcasts in history because, first, there was not even the thought of air-conditioning and it was 1 billion degrees down there with the humidity just under 1 billion percent.

Second, the stench from whatever was being cooked—and Lord knows what it was, but if it wasn't goat, it had to be some kind of rodent—was almost intolerable. But we tolerated it, nonetheless, because the folks in Puerto Rico wanted to see Sammy, and Sammy was the star of the Cubs at the time.

So the Cubs took a trip that was supposed to be to Milwaukee, Montreal, and back home for a day game. They changed it to Milwaukee, San Juan, back to Chicago, and they let us play at 3:05 PM. It was still a day game, but not the usual 1:20 start—so that five-plus-hour flight wasn't the greatest thing.

But this story is about Tony Womack.

Three groups of people must understand the strength of a second baseman's arm on relay throws: First, the coaches. Second, the advance scout. Finally, the ballplayers. Tony was nursing a sore elbow. It wasn't his fault. It just happened to be sore. He didn't have the strongest arm in the first place, but he had a very bad elbow, which limited his ability to throw.

I remember Orlando Cabrera, who then was a star of a player and nearly drove in 100 runs for the Expos in 2001. Cabrera remains a good quality player. Montreal still had Vladimir Guerrero then, as well. Montreal had a solid team, but the Expos were nomads and they were just looking for a home, and eventually that home became Washington as the Expos became the Nationals.

Cabrera hit a ball down the right-field line, which normally would have been a double. I can't remember who was playing right field at the time, but I do remember that he got the ball back to Womack, and because they knew that Tony didn't have a strong arm, Cabrera never stopped. He didn't even look to check. He knew Tony was going to be the cutoff man, and he knew there was no way Tony was going to be able to throw him out at third base.

So we wound up losing that game, partly because Cabrera took third, eventually scoring on a fly ball. We lost that one because either the advance scouts or the coaches realized that Womack didn't have much of an arm, and he was going to be the cutoff man.

It's essential to know what kind of arm an infielder has, but for a second baseman, it would help if his arm was strong enough to get it to third. If he does act as the cutoff man, he needs to be able to get that throw in. In that case, he didn't. In that case, it cost us a game.

Third Base

Third base is known as the hot corner because when big, burly, right-handed sluggers pull the ball, they're going to pull it right at the third baseman as hard as they can. You normally don't play even with the bag against those right-handed sluggers. But if you happen to, you're 90 feet away from the ball that's being hit at you at the 110–115 mph range.

However, I always felt calling third the hot corner was a bit of a misnomer in that when a pitcher delivers the ball, the pitcher is about 55 feet away from the hitter. The third baseman has much more time to react than a pitcher. But I guess they don't want to call it the hot middle, so they call it the hot corner for the third baseman.

Third base has different requirements from other positions, and many guys who are a little bigger, perhaps a little stronger, come up as shortstops. Many of them who don't have a whole lot of range usually shift to second base or third base.

Ryne Sandberg, for instance, came up through the system with the Philadelphia Phillies. When the Cubs acquired him, they used him at third base—where he played remarkably well—before shifting to second base, where he went on to have his Hall of Fame career.

Just the opposite, Cal Ripken came to the major leagues as a third baseman. He had played third his entire way through the Orioles organization, and then Earl Weaver, very much to the dismay of many people who inhabited the Orioles organization at the time, really felt that

Ripken had the brains, the anticipation, the ability to set up, certainly a good enough arm to play shortstop. That turned into a Hall of Fame career as well, and he was a very big man.

But at third base, you really don't need a lot of range; what you need is first-step quickness. There is no substitute at third base for first-step quickness to either side. For third basemen, going toward the line to their right or toward the hole to their left, they must have that great first step. Preferably, that quickness is coupled with soft hands. To see what I mean by soft hands, I urge you to take a look at Evan Longoria and watch him play because he's absolutely magnificent.

I talk about it as absorbing the baseball. Longoria's hands are never out front stabbing at the ball. He waits for it to come into his body. The main thing about any infield position, especially at third base where the ball gets a little bit quicker, is that you have to keep the glove down and come up on the hop. That is true everywhere, but no more so than at third. You keep your butt low, you keep your glove low, and you come up with the hop and absorb it into your body. That's what Longoria does exceptionally well.

When you take a look around baseball, there are some pretty good third basemen. Adrian Beltre, for years with various clubs and most recently the Texas Rangers, is one of those guys who has soft hands and seems to absorb the baseball.

Many guys have unusual throwing angles. Consider Graig Nettles, who threw just about everything from the side. Same thing can be said for Beltre and occasionally for Longoria, who does throw three-quarters much of the time. But the absorbing of the baseball is the key, and both Beltre and Longoria have that great first step. Obviously, a third baseman must also have a strong arm because many times when he moves to his left, he doesn't have a great deal of time to position himself to make a good throw with perfect footwork. In fact, we've seen some third basemen throw from their knees. A player must have a very strong arm to do that—especially when going to the right. When a third baseman moves to his right a step or two, it carries him into foul territory and he must make the throw from there. The good third basemen who make those plays throw over the top.

They hope to grab the ball across the seams so the ball stays straight and gets there ahead of the runner.

Probably the best example of a third baseman with a great arm was the late Ken Caminiti, who was with Houston and San Diego. I remember he threw right over the top, with rocketlike velocity. It was very, very difficult to outrun that arm. Over the years, there have been some great arms at third base. But that's not a prerequisite, because some guys get rid of the ball so quickly that they make up for a less than sterling throwing arm.

Also, they used to say in order to play third base, you had to have a strong chest. The reason for that is you get a lot of those overspin one-hoppers that might line right off the dirt, pick up the overspin, and come up, and you can't get your hands up in time. If you stay in front of everything—which you should—then it's going to hit you in the chest.

I remember a conversation I had with Tim Wallach, who played third base for 13 of his 17 years with the Montreal Expos. Tim told me he could read the angle of the bat through the strike zone. He had a pretty good idea what balls were going to come to him and just exactly, depending on the pitch, where they were going to go. There are a lot of third basemen who want to know when a breaking ball is coming.

Routinely, shortstops used to give a signal to the third baseman when a curveball or a slider or a cutter inside to the right-handed hitter was coming. The third baseman might cheat a bit toward the line because many times a ball is going to be hit down there. However, in talking with several players these days, I've learned they don't give signals to a third baseman too often, which doesn't allow the guy at third to take advantage of an extra step in anticipation. But the reading of the angle through the strike zone and angle of the bat is something that third basemen seem to be able to do, especially the very good ones.

Of course, the state of the art was Brooks Robinson. He's someone who immediately comes to mind when thinking about third-base defense. Many people forget his clutch hitting because he didn't have a high career batting average, but he could turn the game around with his glove. He was the prototypical wonderful third baseman who played for more than 20 seasons with the Baltimore Orioles and became a Hall of Famer.

The same can be said for Ron Santo, who was a terrific third baseman in his own right but for a shorter period of time. Nevertheless, he was state of the art in the National League. Ronnie was known as a very gifted third baseman with five Gold Gloves to show for it. Brooks Robinson won 16.

But keep in mind the good third basemen will come in all shapes and sizes. In fact, guys come in all shapes and sizes for all the various positions in baseball, which is one of the reasons it's such a magnificent game. You don't have to be a giant, unlike in many instances with the NBA, and you don't have to be one of those huge offensive and defensive linemen who you see in the NFL. You can be normal-sized guys and play just about anyplace in the major leagues.

It's imperative for the third baseman to do two things: understand the signs from the manager, which isn't all that difficult, and give the signs to the infielders and tell the pitcher which way he's going to charge, which can be more complicated.

Perhaps the toughest duty for a third baseman is being charged with looking over toward the manager or the infield coach to get the set of signs on the wheel play, which happens with runners at first and second. You know it's a bunt situation, and there are either no outs or one out. It's much more imperative to understand the wheel play with no outs because you certainly want to cut down the lead man at third.

So the third baseman looks into the dugout. The way we were taught was that he gets a set of signs from the manager and passes those signs to the catcher, the shortstop, the second baseman, and the first baseman. But he usually takes a couple of steps and will tell the pitcher either to charge in or charge down the third-base line to try to cut off the bunt, spin, and throw to third base.

If the third baseman charges straight in, many times the shortstop is going to break in back of the runner for just an instant and then sprint to third base to get the force-out at third. The third baseman has to make a decision as far as if the shortstop is going to be charged with going back toward second base for the potential pickoff attempt.

If the shortstop is not moving to third base and they want the third baseman to hold his position with the pitcher charging toward the line, then the third baseman—for a short time—is in no-man's-land, because if the ball is bunted very hard, there will be nobody at third base to make that play. They must have the rotation that sends the shortstop over, because he'll be able to beat that runner over to third base. But more times than not, there won't be anybody at third, so that third baseman has to hang back to see how hard the ball is bunted.

Agile pitchers who spring off the mound—depending on how hard the ball is bunted—will be able to field it, and then the third baseman tries to get back to the bag and get that lead runner because cutting that man down at third with less than two outs can be a critical play in the game. This becomes apparent if you can't get him and it puts runners at second and third, and your manager chooses to pitch to the next hitter. If it's not critical in the game or it's early in the game, they're going to play the infield back and concede the run on a sacrifice fly, a ground ball, a wild pitch or passed ball, or even an error in the infield.

The main thing about third—and this holds true for first base also—is that you don't do your own umpiring. You're on the foul line and might be thinking something is foul when it's not, but you have to play the ball no matter what the call is.

You take for granted that you're going to catch pop-ups on the infield. One of the responsibilities for third basemen on shorter pop-ups is, if you can, take it away from the catcher because many times the catcher will be running with his face to the outfield. On a pop-up, the third baseman will be coming in, which is a much easier play.

When a third baseman moves back on pop-ups, he must be able to move like a first baseman, only on the other side. The better angle on pop-ups going into that area is for the shortstop. However, the third baseman has the same responsibility, and what he has to do is get closer to the tarp, closer to the stands, or closer to the dugout. Understand that if your dugout is not on the third-base side, your third baseman is not going to get much help from the inhabitants of that dugout because they don't really care if your third baseman falls or trips over the rail. The third baseman must feel for either the railing of the dugout, the railing of the stands, or the tarp.

The third baseman must understand how far he has to move, and he must realize the ball is going to rotate toward the field of play. When the popup goes up, whether it's up the first-base or third-base side, the ball invariably rotates toward the field of play. It's one of the strange things in baseball. Also, every ball is going to either slice or hook toward the foul line. A right-hander is going to hook the ball toward the third-base line if he pulls it. A left-hander is going to slice the ball toward the third-base line if he hits it that way. That's one of the things that you have to bear in mind when you play those corner positions.

Once he catches that popup, the third baseman must know where to give the strong feed to the pivot man at second base. The quicker he gets the ball to the second baseman as he comes across the bag, the more accurate of a throw the second baseman is going to make to first base. The second baseman is going to be eternally grateful to the man at third.

As the second baseman is coming across the bag, the third baseman tries to target the middle of the body to the glove side, and he wants to get the throw there quickly. He tries to place the throw above the waist to make sure the second baseman has enough time to right himself as he comes across the bag. The second baseman knows the play is going to be behind him, and he wants to have that ball just about as quickly as possible to be sure he gets his runner out.

Normally on a tag play at third base, you're going to straddle the bag and wait for the throw, often coming in from left field. In that case, you are leaning toward the outfield and waiting for that ball to get there. Many times, if it's going to be a bang-bang play, you might even want to reach for the ball a little bit, then bring it back and apply a quick tag as fast as you possibly can. You want to put that glove there, slap it on him, and lift the glove up. You don't want to keep your glove there because it's pretty easy to get the ball knocked out of the glove, and if not that, then you get spiked on the wrist. So that quick tag at third base is essential.

Quickness becomes even more important if a guy is going to steal third base, particularly if the third baseman is playing very deep. The opposition might have a good base stealer at second base with a strong right-handed pull hitter up to bat. After the pitch is thrown, you must race to the bag to get the throw from the catcher and then straddle that bag and try to tag the base runner. Runners will try different things to get into third base. Some will slide early. I've seen third basemen use that sweeping tag, and the guy stops short and jabs his leg under him and gets to the bag.

Finally, we've seen guys going to third base, trying to get very creative. Juan Pierre has begun sliding headfirst. He gives that fielder a look at his left arm, then lifts the left arm up as he's sliding to tag the base with his right arm. He does it more at second than he does at third, but that's a possibility. That's what you have to look for.

You don't have to look for spikes on those guys that slide headfirst. I think, for a third baseman as well as any other position, that would be the ideal thing. The guy comes in headfirst, and you're able to put the tag on him. A lot of third basemen will reach out and try to give that sliding guy a face full of mitt as he tags him, just as a reminder that the next time you come in, you remember that. The runner might not slide quite as hard.

The headfirst guys who come into third base aren't that big of a problem. But it's the concentration you need on a throw, a short hop, and that's one of the toughest plays for a third baseman. Depending on how far away the throw is coming, there are many times when a left fielder figures it's a much better throw if he can heave it the entire distance on the fly. Sometimes it doesn't happen that way.

If the short hop is close to you at third base, it's pretty easy to pick. If it's a little further away, the tendency is for that ball to come up. That makes it more difficult for the third baseman because when that throw hits the dirt and that ball hops up, you have to come up to catch it and then back down to be able to apply the tag. So you're hoping the fielder has a decent arm and keeps the ball low enough so that it doesn't have a high hop, and you can catch that one-hopper basically around the knees so that you can stay down and make the tag.

The same thing will hold true from the center fielder, although you don't find many who will throw on the fly. You can get the throw on the long hop, although you hope that long hop has a tendency to smooth out a bit and you catch it lower. From the right fielder, the same holds true. Normally what a third baseman gets is a ball that hits off the dirt. Usually, he does not get a ball that hits off the grass where you have to worry about the ball skidding. Obviously, from left center or right, you're getting a whole lot of them that come in and hit the dirt ahead of them.

Occasionally if a throw is off-target from right field, it hits the infield grass, and skids. The third baseman's first responsibility is the baseball. If he has to abandon the bag to get the baseball, understand that the dugout and the stands are behind him, depending on how many men are on. A third baseman is going to concede all those runs if he doesn't knock down the ball.

A smart pitcher on a good team will be backing up the play at third or at least drifting to see where the play is going to be. And by drifting, he's going to be between third and home, depending on where that play is and then drift to that proper position using enough distance between himself and, in this case, the third baseman or the catcher to be able to back up properly.

So, just like a first baseman whose first responsibility is the ball instead of the bag, if you have to abandon the bag to catch the ball, the same thing holds true at third. Only the big difference is that if the third baseman misses it and the ball goes into the stands, it can be disastrous. Not only with the man coming to third, but a trail runner if he's a step past second, he's awarded home as well. So that puts a little more pressure on him. Another thing third basemen must understand is line drives. Sometimes you get line drives hit to you so hard that they're sinking. Sometimes you get line drives that are sailing. It really depends on where the batter hits the ball. Sometimes a hitter will catch a seam on the baseball, and that ball will come to you knuckling. Those are the balls that are highly unpredictable.

Here again, the third baseman needs to have quick reactions and soft hands. That really is essential in the making of the third baseman.

Now let's talk about bunts—specifically bunts to third base. You'll see third basemen line up baseballs, sometimes as many as 10 in a row, right in the bunting area where either a right- or left-handed hitter will bunt the ball. The third basemen will practice running in, bending down, barehanding the ball, and throwing in the same motion. They will prefer throwing off their right foot. That's ideal. Sometimes on a bang-bang play they don't have that luxury, but that's what they prefer. They'll charge and repeatedly barehand the ball and throw to first.

This drill is obviously limited in that the ball isn't moving. The third baseman is doing this with somebody at first base or under the tutelage of the infield coach. But he's practicing his footwork, practicing that throw from down under. He wants to see how quickly he can throw it over there. He wants to see how much there is on the throw to first base.

A good first baseman will give you a good target. He's also going to be prepared for that throw up the line because the tendency, more times than not on that play, is to throw the ball into the base runner, as opposed to throwing it wide of the bag to the outfield side.

I see many first basemen getting hurt on just this type of play—either a swinging bunt or a regular bunt. The guy comes in, barehands it, throws off maybe the wrong leg—the left leg—and that throw comes with a little movement. It has the kind of movement that will take that first baseman into the path of the runner. We've seen a lot of broken arms, a lot of broken wrists, and a lot of baseballs get knocked out of gloves because of throws that aren't sharp. That's why your first baseman will be indebted to you if you're accurate on that play.

You also see the swinging bunt. Many times this is a tough play because a third baseman will be playing deep with a powerful hitter, or it's going to be a left-handed hitter who perhaps has a little power and you might play him to pull. All of a sudden this swinging bunt rolls up the third-base side. You charge as hard as you possibly can and then you still have to get that throw off and certainly make it a good one. You must work on this play repeatedly.

There's another play a third baseman has to work on, and it's the high chopper. Omar Vizquel, at shortstop, was one of the best I've ever seen at barehanding that high chopper and throwing in the same motion. The same holds true for third basemen; they also have to come in. Occasionally, they have to field the ball barehanded and throw in the same motion. That's what you're looking for many times in a third baseman—a guy who has an understanding of who's hitting and also an understanding of his pitcher on that given day. That guy will be able to anticipate the high chopper.

For instance, on the White Sox, when Mark Buehrle and John Danks pitch, they use cutters into right-handed hitters and throw a lot of changeups. Many of those balls are pulled to the left side. So the third baseman is going to get a little more work, especially with a changeup. It's easy to pull that ball and hit a little nubber up the third base side, and those are the ones that you have to charge, the ones you have to be able to collect and throw quickly and accurately.

If you look at National League third basemen who make all the plays required and possess strong arms, you'll find guys like Ryan Zimmerman, David Wright, and Scott Rolen. Those guys are consistently good, year in and year out. We won't go through the Gold Glove, because there's that argument that if you don't hit, you won't win a Gold Glove, depending on how good you are defensively. Let's talk instead about a guy's ability to play that position and play it just about as well as you possibly can.

In the American League, I think Evan Longoria and Adrian Beltre are absolutely terrific. They can make all the plays.

When you're scouting a third baseman, you want to see how good he is to the glove side, which is the left side. You want to see how good he is to the arm side, the right side. You want to see how quick he is, how many times he gets to the ball, and how many times he can stay in front of the ball. You're also looking to see how he can do when he gives some ground on the long hop. Although you would like to choose your hop, and sometimes you can come in and smother the short hop, sometimes you just can't do that. So you play it on the long hop, which means you're going to need a little more arm for that play.

The five third basemen I mentioned—Zimmerman, Wright, and Rolen in the National League, and Longoria and Beltre of the American League— each has a strong enough arm to get the ball where it needs to go, can play the ball on the long hop on occasion, and does the other things that go into making a very good third baseman.

• • •

One of the most interesting characters at third base, whom I played against but not with, was Doug Rader, who went on to manage in the majors and coach for a number of teams. His nickname was the Rooster, because of his red hair. He had terrific power, was a solid third baseman, and had a great sense of the lunacy of the game.

One thing I remember about the Houston Astrodome is that two teams I played with had miserable records playing there. The Cubs and Giants went into the Astrodome and got absolutely handled, and it didn't matter which team they put on the field. They just didn't have particularly good runners, and in those days Houston had wonderful pitchers. The combination of the visibility and the fact we weren't made for the artificial surface made for two of the worst teams to ever play in the Astrodome in head-to-head play against the Astros.

In this one game in Houston, there was a popup over the third-base dugout. We had the third-base dugout, and everybody on the bench stood up to see if this popup would stay in play or not, and we were up on the rail to see if the ball would come into the dugout. In those days you could actually go into the dugout and make the catch because there were openings on each side. You saw guys do that in the opposing dugout. You wanted to see if the ball would hit the dugout or go into the seats.

Well, a ball was hit over the dugout, and six or seven of the players got up and watched that ball going into the seats. Rader came over to field it, and he knew the ball was going to be in the seats. It was just like an old Three Stooges segment: Rader just went right down the line through six or seven guys and slapped them right on the side of the face, then ran back laughing to his third-base position.

He thought it was the funniest thing in the world, as the guys were sitting there, not too happy. But Rader was a very big and strong man. Needless to say, no fights broke out, and many people attributed that to just one of the great characters in the game—Mr. Rader.

Another situation came up with Rader, and it involved Joe Pepitone. Pepitone came up with the New York Yankees and thought he was going to become an all-time great, but Joe liked the nightlife a little bit. He had tremendous skills, but he didn't get those skills out of himself the way people might have liked.

In 1970 Pepitone came to Houston, and one of the first things he did shortly after getting traded was to call a team meeting. He told his teammates, "Hey guys, I like to have a lot of fun, just like anyone else on the ballclub. You can do whatever you want with me. If you want to mess around with my clothes, that's fine. You want to mess around with my uniform, that's fine. You want to do anything to my spikes, that's fine. You want to do anything to my street shoes, I don't care. Whatever you want to do, it's fine.

"But please, please, I have very expensive wigs, and just don't do anything to the wigs. Please, it's the one thing I ask of all of you."

So that was like waving the red flag in front of a bull. In that first game, Doug Rader called the entire team into the bathroom, wanting to show us something. I will leave the specifics up to your imagination, this being a family book and all, but I will say this: at the bottom of the toilet was the wig of one Joe Pepitone, looking like some sort of rodent, in with a mixture of a few things. All the guys were beside themselves with laughter. This was one of the funniest things they had seen in quite some time, very typical of Doug Rader and his sense of humor.

But as was the case with Rader, whenever he did something along those lines—and those things will remain in baseball posterity—he also then took out a blank check, signed it, handed it to Joe Pepitone, and told him to get another wig.

Doug was an interesting man, a good baseball man, and one of the true characters of the game. He spent a lot of time in the game and deserved to. He always kept it lively.

• • •

There are a lot of players who don't like to wear the protective cup. They find it to be either impinging on their movement or just uncomfortable. But if you don't wear a protective cup, you have to have magnificent hands. I remember Roy McMillan, who was a very good shortstop in his day, mostly with the Cincinnati Reds. I ran into him when he was the manager of Visalia, California, which was a Class A team of the New York Mets at the time. And Roy spent a long and successful career there.

I was walking into the Visalia ballpark at the same time as a member of the Fresno Giants. As I walked in, I spotted Roy. I never passed up a chance to talk with a former major leaguer, so I said to him, "Roy, did you always wear a cup when you played?"

He had no idea who I was.

He said, "Son, I've been around this game long enough that I wear a cup when I watch a game on TV."

So it comes in handy at times, as Doug DeCinces would soon find out. Doug was my third baseman with the Baltimore Orioles. In this particular game, there were runners on first and second with nobody out, and it was a called wheel play. It was in the old Kingdome, in Seattle, where the visibility wasn't great.

I was in a tremendous jam, and I was facing a batter who could bunt but also pull the bat back and put the bat on the ball. I'm not sure who the batter was, but I do remember that DeCinces looked in the dugout, gave the signs to the infielders, then told me he was going to charge and have the shortstop—Mark Belanger or Kiko Garcia—slide over to third base with the second baseman covering second.

That meant the first baseman couldn't get any backside help from the second baseman, so he would have to not charge quite as hard. As the pitcher, I was supposed to charge straight in, and if I could get to the ball, I knew my shortstop would be at third and we could get the lead runner. The hitter squared early and looked like he was going to bunt, so DeCinces got much closer. I don't believe he was farther than 45 feet away, and at the last instant, the batter pulled back and took a swing.

He hit that ball so hard, on one hop, right in the middle of the lower part of DeCinces' body—right below the belt—and it came, fortunately for him, on one hop. And somehow—I don't know how—he was able to get his glove down and stop this ball. He turned a 5-4-3 double play—one of the most amazing I had ever seen. It was an absolutely unbelievable play.

Although there was a lot of pressure on Doug because he took over for Brooks Robinson at third base, I just remember the look on his face as that ball was hit to him. I wasn't that far from him and, as I recall, that batter hit it with everything he had. But DeCinces made the play, and that shows you good hands are irreplaceable for a third baseman, especially if you're going to play to take away the bunt, and the hitter isn't bunting. Of course, if you miss, you better be wearing that cup.

Many times you'll look over at third basemen, and their eyes are just like those of an owl—wide open, very bright, with a sudden awareness that they're in awfully close for a guy who is swinging away. That's one of the things you have to worry about at third base, but Doug was able to make a spectacular play and turn it into a double play.

• • •

One of the truly great characters among all third basemen was a man who was beloved to all Cubs fans. He was the Cubs radio broadcaster for quite some time, battled through tremendous physical problems due to diabetes at an early age, and worked tirelessly to raise awareness as well as a fortune for juvenile diabetes. That man was Ron Santo.

Most of the things I remember from Ron really didn't come on the field, but off the field. Probably as funny as any story I can remember about Ron Santo happened at Shea Stadium. You have to understand from 1969 to the very end, Ron Santo had this fierce dislike or, you might say, hatred for the Mets and New York, because of what happened in 1969. The Mets flew by the Cubs, who squandered a very large lead while on their way to winning the National League East. That was a wonderfully good Mets team and an exceptional Cubs team that just didn't get the job done.

Now, Ron was in the radio booth, and apparently Fred Wilpon, the owner of the Mets, had decided that he wanted his booth enlarged. So the radio booth moved from the left of the TV booth, where it had been for a long time, to the right of the TV booth. It was in that left booth where line drives came up very quickly, as they did to the right. But at this particular time, a line drive came up very quickly and Ron, known for great hands and his Gold Glove Awards as a player, was not quite as quick in his later years, as happens to all of us.

So when he went up to catch the baseball, he missed it, and it literally exploded the Rolex watch he was wearing and took it right off his wrist. Obviously, Ron, being a very successful businessman as well as a terribly well-paid broadcaster was able to pick up a new one somewhere down the line. He always told the story of how he had a watch literally explode, being ripped off his hand with a foul ball.

But that wasn't the story.

The story came when the radio booth shifted to our right, the right of the television booth. The media booths had these antiquated overhead heaters that had a heating tube placed right over our heads. Ron was in the new radio booth for the first time and was not accustomed to the idiosyncrasies of it just yet.

It was Opening Day, and it was very cold. Before the start of play, we stood for the National Anthem, and Ron didn't realize, for whatever reason, that the heating coil was on in the new booth. It didn't make much sense to have the heating coil above our heads, because as everyone with a third- or fourth-grade education would know, heat rises. So we would have been better served with a heater at our feet. However, this was above our heads.

During the National Anthem, with Ron Santo having some coffee in front of him, he stood up to salute our country and the kickoff of the first game at Shea Stadium, when all of a sudden he smelled something that resembled burnt rodent.

He started sniffing around, and then he started feeling this unusual heat on the top of his head. Now bear in mind that Ron was a very good sport about his toupees, talking about his "gamer" toupee all the time as well as the other few he had. But he somehow had managed to have his toupee catch fire. Of course, with the toupee being synthetic, this was not a good thing.

So the next thing you know, Ron is taking his coffee and pouring it over his toupee—while it is still on his head—to make sure his fairly combustible toupee doesn't go up into a complete conflagration. I look over, he has coffee in one hand and he's rubbing his head with the other, and I'm wondering what he's doing.

All of a sudden we realize what happened: he was standing too close to that overhead coil. Of course, when he got done, he looked a whole lot like Rod Stewart, and it was one of those things that you look at, and say to yourself, "Jeez, I wonder how that happened?" But then you say to yourself, "Oh. It was Ron."

Playing golf with Ron was an adventure, to say the least. We would play frequently, and I would often beat him by one or two strokes. If we had partners, we would mix it up so that Ron and I would play against each other.

There were times when I would be trailing heading into the 16th hole. In those situations, I would suggest to Ron's partner that he tell him what a great baseball player Ron was, lathering him with praise. I would also tell him it would motivate Ron if he asked him what his batting average was in the postseason.

After hearing his partner's laudatory speech, only to be questioned about his postseason performance that never existed, Ron's face would turn crimson. Ron would end up slicing a shot and end up losing. There was one time in Cincinnati that we ended up digging up a sand trap because his shot sailed so errantly.

Another golf escapade occurred in Denver, where Ron pushed the ball off the first tee and shanked his shot as high winds kicked up. Ronnie had the nerve to accuse me of "willing" the ball off the tee!

I told Ronnie that one of the things I couldn't do was will someone's ball to the right.

The name of one of Ron's two daughters was Linda. And at one time, she was single. At one time, I made a point of telling Ron, "Ron, just think. If I married Linda, you'd be my father-in-law. We would be one happy family. Just think of all the father/son-in-law tournaments we'd win!"

Ron was unimpressed. "They would find you wearing cement shoes at the bottom of Lake Michigan," he said.

On a trip to Atlanta, Ron and I actually teamed up to play Don Sutton, who was announcing Braves games at the time, and another person.

We reached the 18th hole dead even. We were playing for big money, and Ron and I hit our first shots down the middle. As Sutton's partner approached the tee for his shot, I mentioned that, "There's a lot of trouble on the right."

So naturally, Sutton's partner hits the ball to the right and is stuck in a rough.

Only one problem for us.

"That's unethical," Santo said, insinuating that I was trying to get into the head of Sutton's partner. "You can't do that."

So Ron tells Sutton's partner to replay his shot, and they end up winning and it cost us some money.

Another time we were golfing under windy conditions at Torrey Pines, just north of San Diego. The hole was a par 3, and Ron sliced his shot as a gust kicked up, prompting him to take his right hand off the club as the ball sailed about 20 yards to the right.

The funny part wasn't his errant shot. It was that the gust caused his toupee and his hat to sail off his head.

Somehow, with the club in his left hand, Ron was able to snag his toupee and cap out of midair with his right hand in one of the greatest displays of dexterity in human history.

Ron would get some help on the road when it came to his hair. In addition to the pre- and postgame shows, Andy Masur would handle an inning on the radio broadcasts and would occupy a room on the road next to Santo to aid him with any duties.

One time Andy received a telephone call in his room. "Andy, you have to come to my room," Ron said. "I have only one wig, and I can't find it."

There was a sense of urgency because it was getaway day, meaning they were checking out of the hotel that day, and there's no way Ron is going to wear a Cubs cap on the team's charter flight.

For 45 minutes, their pursuit is unsuccessful. They flip every couch pillow, look under the bed and mattress, but can't find the toupee.

Finally, Andy notices a FedEx box sitting on a table. Enclosed in the box is a pack of scripts for Ronnie to rehearse for some commercials. Andy proceeded to pick up the box and found the toupee stuck to the box.

It's a pretty firm toupee, as evidenced by the fact that Andy struggled for several moments before successfully yanking it off the box.

Ronnie took great pride in his toupees. He called his No. 1 toupee his "gamer." The toupee looked fine with his tan—except when it failed to cover a part of his head that wasn't tanned.

For several years in the 1990s, Thom Brennaman was part of the Cubs' broadcast crew and he would work most of the time with Ron. One time, Ron calls Thom and asks him to come to his room.

Thom proceeded to knock on the door, only for the door to be opened by Ron—minus a toupee.

The rare sight of seeing Ron without a toupee frightened Thom, who was so scared that he leaped a foot backward after seeing this man sporting a tan face but a white scalp.

After Ron had his second leg removed, I asked him, "Why don't they make the prosthetics long enough so that you could stand 6'5" or 6'6"? Instead of being 6'1" all your life, you could see over a crowd. It would be great. You could be as tall as the players."

Ron wasn't impressed.

"They couldn't make me 6'5" because I wear a size 12 shoe," Ron said.

"Ron," I replied. "You have no feet. You could wear Bozo the Clown's shoes, and it would make no difference!"

Ron had no clue.

Another great story came up in Cincinnati. We had just come from Pittsburgh to announce a game in Cincinnati. By this time he had lost both of his legs to diabetes, and he used what he termed his "shower legs" so he could get in and take a shower on a daily basis. He'd gone through a lot, and the fact he was still announcing baseball in 2010 is a testament to just how tough a guy he was.

On this trip, however, he forgot his shower legs in Pittsburgh. He was known to forget many things, so maybe this wasn't too surprising. But one can only imagine the look on the cleaning woman's face when she found these two legs there still in the hotel room, not knowing just exactly what they were.

Anyway, Ron told Jimmy Bank, our traveling secretary, about it, and they arranged to have these shower legs sent to Cincinnati. It took probably a few days for Ron to get his shower legs back and actually be able to take a shower instead of one of those sponge baths. Needless to say, I didn't get too close to Ron during the first two games of the Cincinnati series.

Back at the hotel in Cincinnati, Chip Caray, who was my broadcasting partner at the time, and I were in the elevator, and I remember Ron coming down. I think he wanted to change his room. So as he was getting off the elevator, I just said to him, "Hey, Ron, what room are you in?"

Ron replied, "504."

I said okay, and he gave me this quizzical look. I got back on the elevator and Chip asks me, "Why did you ask Ron what room he's in?"

I said, "Because I'm going to sign every one of my meals to him."

Then I suggested that Chip do the same. "Just sign 'Ron Santo, room 504.' Eventually he'll figure it out when he looks it over and figures exactly how many meals he ate in a three-game trip and just exactly how many meals are on his bill."

Fast-forward a few days, and the series was over. We were waiting for the bus, and Ron came over and paid his bill. He apparently didn't look at it at all. He just put it in his pocket. He didn't say anything unusual to me or Chip as we were waiting for the bus in the lobby of the hotel.

Finally I said, "Boy, this place is expensive. This is Cincinnati. This seemed to be as expensive as New York."

Ron said, "I don't even look at my bills."

I replied, "My bill had some inaccuracies. They charged me for some things that I didn't do. They got me for the honor bar, which I didn't take anything from. I think it's wise that you check your bill before you leave here."

He got his bill out, looked at it, and had a hard time deciphering what was what. I asked to look at his bill, saying they double-billed me on a couple of things.

Of course, they hadn't, but I said, "For instance, did you have three breakfasts yesterday?"

"No, I had one breakfast. Room service."

I said, "Ron, look. Three breakfasts here. Did you have two lunches the first day in town?"

He replied, "No. I had one lunch." I pointed to the two lunches he was charged.

We went through his bill, item by item, and he started to get up and walk over to the desk. He was turning redder in the face because he was billed an extraordinary amount over what he should have been billed. Finally, before he made it to the desk, I called Ron over.

"Remember me asking you what your room number was?" I said.

"Yeah."

"Well," I said, "I signed a couple of charges to you, and I think maybe Chip did one."

Ron looked at me, and I took out a $100 bill and handed it to him, and he snapped, "You owe me more than that."

I said, "Hold on for a second. You didn't know I owed you anything. How do you know I owe you more than that? That's probably more than enough. Keep it as a tip. Good luck to you."

But one of the best pranks pulled on Ron was perpetrated by Chip Caray. It sounds a bit cold, but we call it "poking the bear." Ron usually took it in a good-natured manner, although sometimes he got a little aggravated with us.

Well, not some of the time.

Most of the time.

This one time, I remember, Ron came in the lunch room at Wrigley Field and he was raving about dietetic candy and how wonderful this sugar-free candy was. It was See's Candies, and somebody got him a couple of pounds of the sugar-free variety. Ron was extolling the virtues of it and telling us how wonderful it was that he could eat a lot of dietetic candy and didn't have to worry about the diabetes. This was one of those times where he could just do exactly what he wanted to do, which included eating candy whenever he wanted to, not only during the game but also at home.

Chip kind of winked at me, so I engaged Ron in a very serious conversation about whatever was going on. Chip snuck into the radio booth. There was the box of See's Candies—three layers of sugar-free candy. Chip had a pen and he started biting into every one of the candies and leaving teeth marks and making pen marks in them and squashing some of them. Then he went into the second layer and did the same thing.

He didn't eat them but chewed them up, squashed them, and put pen marks in them and destroyed all three layers of them. Of course, he placed them neatly back in the box, put the lid on it, and came back in and sat down and winked at me. So I knew the crime had been perpetrated.

So we went to our booth, which was two doors down from where Ron's radio booth was. We waited and waited, because we knew that after having his lunch, Ron was going to sink into the See's Candies. After a while Ron opened up the box and took a look, and there was a look of almost incredulity on his face.

He looked at the first row and saw all of these smashed pieces that looked like a squirrel had broken into the booth. A squirrel with a pen, of course, that had decided he didn't want Ron to eat the sugar-free candy. Then he looked at the second layer, got to the third layer, and with every passing layer, his face got redder and redder and redder until he realized this entire box of See's was absolutely destroyed.

Now keep in mind that Ron had just discovered that there was this sugar-free candy—which had been out for some time, by the way, at that point. But as soon as he got through the third layer, Chip and I were literally crying in the television booth, lying back in our seats and laughing hysterically. Ron looked over and was just infuriated. Had he possessed a bit more mobility at the time, I think we would have had to lock our door or had to deal with an enraged third baseman that just saw his latest novelty—sugar-free candy—destroyed by the folks in the TV booth.

Ron gave us some really interesting moments over the years, and one of them came on the plane. This was Chip Caray who did this. We split our aggravating of Ron and taking advantage of his great sense of humor and his enjoyment of the whimsy of baseball, although sometimes he didn't quite see it that way.

Ron started to get up to go to the bathroom, which was vacant. Chip got up before him. We were actually sitting closer to it than he was, and he knew Ron was headed that way. So Chip, who had a Baby Ruth in his pocket, got up and went to the bathroom just before Ron. He took that candy bar, left half in the bowl and the other half on the rim of the bowl, then came out and waited until Ron got up and went into the bathroom.

Well, although the humor was sophomoric, as you would expect, Ron, after about 10 seconds of trying to arrange himself and taking a look down, the door comes flying open. We were sitting in coach, and he yells from the first-class cabin; a profanity started the tirade, followed by "Don't you ever flush the [blankety-blank] toilet?"

Of course, after he calmed down we explained to him it was a Baby Ruth and not what he thought it was, and if he would kindly knock it into the toilet and flush it down, everything would be fine for him.

Needless to say, he didn't find great humor in that, although we did.

There were times when Ron and I didn't get along that well. I'm sure that surprises you, based on all the stunts that we used to pull on him. But as funny of a thing that ever happened came about in 2001, and it involved John McDonough, now the president of the Chicago Blackhawks. This is one I cooked up, and it was the first year I was sick and away from the booth. I had Valley Fever and actually left the broadcast for a couple of years trying to recover from this. It was pretty difficult.

But to the credit of the Cubs, they invited me back to throw the ceremonial first pitch in the 2001 season. Ron was the radio broadcaster, and along with Pat Hughes, they did a great job on radio and were very funny together. And Pat treated Ron exceptionally well, although Ron was slowing down somewhat near the end. Pat did great with him, and it was very entertaining to listen to.

Anyway, I was asked to throw out the first pitch, and before the game, I went to McDonough's office, which is what I usually did, and started to cook up a plan that I thought was guaranteed to really get Mr. Santo's goat.

We decided we were going to put out a press release stating that my sickness wasn't nearly as bad as everyone thought. But because they had already hired a couple of replacements on television—Dave Otto and Joe Carter—the Cubs were announcing a three-man radio booth: Pat Hughes, Ron Santo, and Steve Stone, with Steve Stone returning to the broadcasts on the radio starting May 15. This press release was sheer genius. It was John's writing, and he was so flowery and laudatory about my efforts: "We think that Steve is the best color man in baseball, and to add him to the radio broadcast, along with Pat Hughes, we believe it's going to be just a wonderful broadcast."

There was no mention of Ron Santo, and it talked about how good and informative I was: "We feel this is the way to go to the future. It's a way to get Steve back into broadcasting and everyone associated with the Chicago Cubs is excited."

The last sentence read: "Oh, by the way, Ron Santo also will be there," as if he was just an afterthought in all of this.

So I went down to prepare to throw the first pitch, and McDonough called Santo into his office. This was about 20 minutes before game time, and

John told Ron, "We just wanted to show you this before we put this out just before Steve throws the first pitch. So take a look at it and see what you think."

Ron starts to read it, and it suddenly starts to sink in to him that, first, they're going to go from a two-man to a three-man radio booth. Second, that the third man is going to be me, after all of the years I had antagonized him and played many, many tricks on him and done a number of things to raise his ire and other things, mostly good natured. Some, well, maybe some over the line of good-natured. But certainly none that would eventually hurt him along those lines.

Well, as he read this, John McDonough told me, Ron got madder and madder. With Ron, and that classic Italian temper he had, he just got bright red and screamed an obscenity at John McDonough. He crumpled the piece of paper, threw it down, and started to walk out of John's office.

He looked at John and said, "[Blank] you," and, referring to the WGN Radio broadcast van parked across from Wrigley, he added, "I'm going across the street, I'm going to punch [whoever was in charge of radio at the time] in the nose, and I'm going home!

"I QUIT! THAT'S IT!"

He was screaming this as he walked away from John's office. John was behind the desk, and he was laughing before he realized that Ron was absolutely serious and he couldn't let him go across the street and punch the station manager at WGN in the nose.

Of course John doesn't want him to quit because I'm not going into the radio booth, and they don't want Pat to do this alone, even for a day. They don't want Ron driving all the way back to his home in Bannockburn. So just before Ron could get to the top of the steps to head straight down and out the door and across the street, McDonough intercepted him, grabbed his arm, and said, "Ron, Ron."

Ron looked at him and said, "Let go of me."

John replied, "Ron, it's a joke! It's a joke! There's no three-man booth. Stone is not coming in."

Ron said, "Goddammit. Why do you always have to do this to me? I got to do a broadcast. Why do you guys do this to me all the time?"

117

All of this happened with me away, although I had planted the seed with McDonough. We came up with some of the wording together, but John wrote it, and it was beautiful.

Unfortunately, as happened so many times with our practical jokes, Ron was the butt of the joke, so that didn't make him particularly happy.

But I couldn't have written this book and had a third baseman section without mentioning one of the most colorful third basemen. I will say, and I don't believe it will happen by the time this book comes out, but I truly do believe—some guys don't—that Ron Santo deserves to be in the Hall of Fame.

Of course, like many of the Cubs of his era, although he played on great teams, he was never able to play in the playoffs. The team retired his number and put it up on the flagpole, one of the great thrills in the life of Ron Santo. But the Hall of Fame would be the crowning glory for what was a pretty good career for a guy who has come to be synonymous with the Cubs, along with Ernie Banks as Mr. Cub and some of the other numbers retired, such as Billy Williams, Greg Maddux, and Ryne Sandberg.

But Ron Santo, having been on radio and being a beloved character around the north side of Chicago, richly deserves that honor, and I think it will come to him.

With that in mind, I will leave you with the last story about Ron Santo. Not too long ago, I told him, "Look, don't worry about not getting into the Hall of Fame as a player. I know it's important, but not all that important. It could very well be that it might not be your lot in life to get there."

But I assured him that I would back his candidacy to the hilt to get into the broadcasting wing of the Hall of Fame. I said, "I'm going to do it, and I'm going to do it posthumously very hard the rest of my life to make that happen."

First, he was incensed that I would take him out of the players' wing and back him as a broadcaster. Then, when he found out what *posthumously* meant, he was not particularly happy about that either. So that was something I used to tell him on a regular basis, along with a number of other things that would get his blood boiling.

I used to call him Mr. Tomato Head because he would, during our many arguments, come away much madder at me than I was at him. But that's the character that was Ron Santo. Through it all, for the most part, he took it in a very good-natured way, and we always had a good time.

CHAPTER

Shortstop

The state of the art—maybe forever—at shortstop has to be Omar Vizquel. I watched him several times in his prime. I remember telling my father about Vizquel many, many years ago. Vizquel came up with the Seattle Mariners, but apparently Seattle couldn't live without Felix Fermin because they traded Vizquel after the 1993 season to the Cleveland Indians (with outfielder Reggie Jefferson) for Fermin, who had a largely forgettable career but at the time could hit a little bit.

I remember telling my father at the time, "You don't know this guy's name. You've never heard of him. But his name is Omar Vizquel. And you just traded for him." My dad was born and raised in Cleveland, and I said, "Just remember this deal, because Vizquel is going to play a big part if there is a resurgence in the Cleveland Indians. He will play a big part in it because defensively, there are not too many guys around who play like that."

Ozzie Smith is another guy who was phenomenal. But bear in mind that Ozzie played his home games on the artificial surface, which is a little bit easier to do than playing on the natural surface. He was a magnificent shortstop, a Hall of Famer, and he got much better as a hitter. At first, you could absolutely knock the bat out of the hands of both Smith and Vizquel. But they both went on to not only be great defensively—that goes without saying—but also to make a difference as far as swinging the bat is concerned. They each became decent offensive players.

But let's go back to the fundamentals of the game as played at shortstop. Although Derek Jeter, the captain of the New York Yankees, has slowed down a step or two, I look at him as probably the smartest player on the field in every game he plays.

Jeter never seems to be out of position, is fearless as far as going after pop-ups as much as going into the stands to go get them. He's just very, very solid in all aspects of the game and richly deserves to be called the captain of the Yankees.

A shortstop has one asset that's almost irreplaceable, and that's arm strength. Many young shortstops arrive at the major league level with strong arms, but the best I've seen on a daily basis for arm strength was Shawon Dunston when he came up with the Chicago Cubs. Unfortunately, he was terribly inaccurate. Mark Grace saved him a ton of errors, except when Dunston threw it over his head. Some fans along the right side at Wrigley Field had to consider wearing batting helmets because of Dunston's erratic throws.

Shortstops also must have a certain amount of range, and everyone's range differs. But the shortstop must possess a strong enough arm to get the throw across, and he must have the same amount of range to his right, which is in the hole at shortstop, as he has to his left. That's because many pitchers aren't particularly good defenders. Generally the biggest hole on the infield is up the middle.

I have talked about the pitcher being the fifth infielder after he throws the baseball. But the Jim Kaats of the world, the Greg Madduxes of the world, and the case now—the Mark Buehrles of the world—these guys are few and far between as far as taking care of that hole up the middle. More times than not, you'll find that ball gets by pitchers because on their follow-through, they're not in position to field that ball hit through the middle.

Being the cutoff man is just one of many duties the shortstop must perform. The shortstop will be the cutoff man on a ball into left-center field. If the shortstop has a much stronger arm than the second baseman, the shortstop will run out to take the relay throw from whoever digs the ball from the wall in right-center field. Some teams do this but not quite as often as they perhaps should.

Sometimes there is so much of a disparity between the arm of the shortstop and the arm of the second baseman that they'll send the shortstop out there to make the relay throw. Again, it's up to the advance scouting, the coaches, and the manager to know to send that shortstop into that cutoff position. If they do that, the opponent will know not to take that extra base because they'll know the shortstop is going to have a very good arm.

Now, in the case of Ozzie Smith or Omar Vizquel or Cal Ripken, to a certain extent, positioning is the name of the game. As Vizquel and Smith got older, they learned how to get rid of the ball more quickly because they just didn't have enough on the throw. Maybe the guy who was nicknamed "Justin Nuff" typified the shortstop who doesn't have the overpowering arm. That was David Eckstein, who has played on two world championship teams.

Yet he fielded a ball at shortstop, and there was a little hump in the throw to first base. He did this for a long time. But he always seemed to get it there—one half-step or one step in front of the runner. He didn't have a strong arm, but he had a very quick release and made up for a lack of arm strength with positioning and the ability to get rid of the ball quickly.

I've seen Ozzie Smith conduct warm-ups differently than most shortstops. Smith would have one of his coaches hit him intentional high choppers. He'd charge in on a high chopper toward home plate, barehand the ball, and throw to first base. I saw Ozzie do that a lot. During practice, he would have whoever was hitting him ground balls also hit pop-ups to him where he had to go straight-out with his back to the infield and make the catch. I haven't seen many shortstops warm up like that. The time and diligence it took for Ozzie Smith to do this on a daily basis was a testament to why he was one of the greats of all time.

• • •

When fielding a grounder, shortstops must pick their own hop, especially because they have a very long throw. Also, a shortstop will get a number of baseballs hit his way with a lot of different spin. If he plays on an artificial surface, he's going to get a certain amount of spin as it comes off the artificial surface to the dirt. For other shortstops, they're going to get completely different hops, depending on the infield grass. That's very important.

That's one of the reasons you'll see shortstops taking ground balls during batting practice. For instance, in Texas they have very short grass and very hard dirt. You can judge your hop on the hardness of the dirt and the length of the infield grass. Depending on the length of the grass and the speed of the base runner, that shortstop will have to charge certain ground balls.

The shortstop absolutely must know the speed of every hitter, even pinch-hitters. We have copious defensive charts on just exactly where guys hit the ball. So they line up a certain way, depending on their length of service in the major leagues and how much they know the hitter. If the shortstop is smart, he'll know how his pitcher is going to attack a certain batter and then move accordingly. However, you don't want to shift drastically immediately before the pitch because you can tip off the pitch doing that.

If a shortstop wants to shift on a given hitter, he'll take a couple steps straight forward and then maybe smooth out the dirt, which is a normal routine to clean up some cleat marks. But when he goes back to his normal shortstop position, he will go back to a place that's two feet to the right of where he was setting up before. That little trick will fool a hitter into thinking he was in the same spot he was before and consequently he won't know which pitch is coming.

When it comes to the double play, the shortstop has an advantage over the second baseman. The reason is, the shortstop always has the play in front of him. The toughest part for a shortstop is actually when he's asked to make a severe shift, as they do with David Ortiz with the Red Sox or Jim Thome with Minnesota. In this situation, the shortstop is on the first-base side of second, or right over the second-base bag, and he's being used as the pivot man on a throw from third. This is so difficult because he's not used to looking to his right and getting that throw coming in at that angle to the bag, then having to get the throw off. Some do it better than others, but it's not a comfortable play.

The biggest mistake that young shortstops will make involves their anxiety on double plays. It happened with Shawon Dunston on the north side of Chicago when he was young and with Alexei Ramirez coming out of Cuba and playing for the White Sox, where he moved to shortstop from second base. These two guys were so anxious that they got to the bag very quickly and consequently took themselves into the paths of the runner. They were coming across the bag too fast.

The art of playing shortstop is to come to the bag under control. Then the shortstop has a few ways to take care of the base runner. One is by stepping across to the second-base bag and moving well wide of the bag so that if the runner does come at the shortstop, it is interference. In other ways, the shortstop is just like the second baseman from the other side. He moves across to get that throw from the second baseman and can see that base runner all the way and see exactly where he is. If the shortstop comes down and makes that throw occasionally from the side or he looks straight in the eyes of that base runner as he throws it right over his helmet, the runner will get down. That's what a shortstop has to do—make sure that base runner that is going to slide into you gets down as early as possible.

As far as pop-ups, the same holds true with the guys with good range, the guys with good speed, and the guys who are fearless. They want every pop-up. They go out and take anything until they hear the voice of the center fielder, the voice of the left fielder, or the voice of the third baseman calling them off. But that play in foul territory over the third baseman's head where he's running with his back to the infield, the shortstop is running straight across. His back will be to the infield somewhat, but he has a much better angle on that ball. That's why it's a lot easier for him to make that play.

One thing teams must remember when they go and make that play is, if the third baseman and the shortstop are out trying to field a pop-up, then that catcher better be covering third base. If the ball is in foul territory, it doesn't matter as much, but if it's in fair territory, sometimes the only one left to cover is the pitcher or the catcher, and that's if they're alert.

Of the many responsibilities a shortstop has, one is to signal the third baseman. Not all of the guys do this, but some will give the third baseman a sign when a left-hander is on the mound with a right-handed hitter and a breaking ball is coming, to tip the third baseman to maybe move toward the line. There's a pretty good chance that on a breaking ball, the right-handed hitter is going to pull it. The last thing you want to do is see the ball hit between the third baseman and the bag, because invariably that hit is going to be a double. If the ball is going to be hit to the left of the third baseman, well, it's usually going to be a single.

So the teams that take advantage of details will have a shortstop signaling to the third baseman or to the left fielder on a breaking ball or a slow breaking ball. This is one of the things we used to employ when I was with the Baltimore Orioles, although a lot of teams have since forgotten, for one reason or another.

The shortstop must also have the ability to make a pickoff, and most of the pickoffs from shortstop are of the daylight variety. That is when a shortstop gets as close to the base runner as he possibly can because that shortens up his move to second base. If he's 15 feet behind the base runner, then it's a longer run to second base. But if he gets close enough behind the base runner where the base runner can't feel his breath on his neck but he knows he's there, then all he has to do is put his glove out. If the pitcher sees the glove between the base runner and the bag, then he turns around and throws, the shortstop breaks to the bag, and he tries to pick the guy off second base.

The shortstop has responsibilities on the wheel play in a bunt situation as well. We talked a little bit about this earlier, and there are a few variations on this play. From a shortstop's standpoint, he'll have one duty where he's got to maybe jockey that runner back to second base, maybe just move in behind him, darting to the bag a little bit. Then as the pitcher gets ready to make a throw, the shortstop will run to cover third base while the third baseman charges straight in. The pitcher will charge straight in, the first baseman will charge straight in, and they're all thinking about getting that out at third base, with the shortstop going there to receive the throw.

The next incarnation of the play is when the third baseman holds his ground, the pitcher will move toward the line to take away that bunt at third base, and the shortstop will look for a couple of different things because he knows on a bunt, if the first baseman is charging, the second baseman is going to cover first base and the shortstop has to cover second base.

But sometimes you'll see this with guys who don't run very well at second base. The bunter will bunt through the ball, the shortstop will go straight to the bag at second, and the catcher will throw through to second. The reason for that is that runner at second, getting a good secondary lead and anticipating the guy is going to get the bunt down, is vulnerable for being picked off.

There's also a form of the wheel play where the shortstop will assume his position, then break to third base. The second baseman then sneaks behind the base runner, and they try to pick him off that way. With the third baseman charging and the shortstop moving to third, the base runner may believe he can get an extra jump. That enables the second baseman to break to the second-base bag to attempt the pickoff.

That sets up yet another incarnation of the wheel play. I know that a lot of people don't understand this particular play or know that there are this many options for the team that's defending, but there are several plays. In this variation, the third baseman comes straight in, the shortstop fakes going to third, and then he goes behind the base runner, and they try a pickoff play before they throw to the hitter. This is one of those plays that's designed to shorten the runner's lead at second base so you can eventually try to cut him down at third or else prevent him from getting to third.

A shortstop has to assume he'll be involved in all of the plays, including rundowns. Many people don't understand that on rundowns, you have to follow the baseball. In other words, when you throw the ball, you have to follow the baseball and clear the path of the base runner so that you don't run into him. Good base runners are going to look for a guy who has just unloaded the baseball, and they will try to come back the other way and get a piece of you. If they can do that, they will be awarded a base on interference.

But the good shortstops that use the rundown make sure the rundown is going to take that base runner back to the base he came from and make sure that ball is held right next to his head. That's so the infielder the shortstop is throwing the ball to can see where the ball is coming from.

The last thing you want to do in a rundown is have the man who is going to catch it guess where it's coming from.

Let's take an example of a shortstop involved in a rundown in which he sneaks behind the base runner at second as the batter bunts through the ball, prompting the catcher to throw to second base, and the runner knows he's dead. The runner cannot get back to second, so you have a rundown. You also have a runner at first base, so that rundown is going to consist initially of the shortstop and third baseman.

If the pitcher, who has no other responsibilities, is smart, he's going to position himself behind the guy at third base. The catcher is going to stay home on this particular play. If the man starts running as fast as he can toward the third baseman, the shortstop will throw the ball to the third baseman with about three steps to spare.

The third baseman, who receives the ball, should always be moving forward. The base runner has to put on the brakes and go back to the base where he came from. The ideal rundown will take one throw. Normally, since the third baseman has momentum, he should be able to tag the runner out. Or the second baseman, having filled the void of the departed shortstop, who has made the first throw on the rundown, is available to take the throw from the third baseman.

If the rundown is conducted quickly enough, the runner at first base stays there. But if you don't do it quickly enough, the next possible scenario is you get that man out, running him back to second, and then you'll have two men on second base and be able to tag one of them. But normally you want a one-throw rundown, where the infielder is moving toward the base runner as he's ready to take the throw. That's because if the infielder has any momentum moving forward, he should be able to run down that base runner who has to stop and head in the other direction.

• • •

It helps if your shortstop has good range and a strong arm. But it also helps if he is very good on pop-ups. Of course, you love the spectacular play. But a winning shortstop has to make the routine play as well. We've seen a lot of guys come into this league with great arms. You see a lot of guys enter the league who can make the spectacular plays that you want. But on the routine play, more times than not, they don't make it in key situations. Those are the guys who don't last long.

Just about every manager will tell you he wants his shortstop to get all the outs he should get, a few of the outs that he shouldn't get, and just a couple of the outs that are impossible to get. That makes a good shortstop. If he has a strong arm, it's even better—assuming he can harness it and get it there in time. Watching the maturation of young shortstops as they come to prominence in the major leagues is one of the great joys because of the many responsibilities that they have.

If your shortstop is very good at what he does, he'll also know how to talk to that pitcher and settle him down in key situations so the pitching coach or manager can save a trip to the mound.

When I was pitching, I had the greatest respect for shortstops. They saved games for me a number of times. I had Mark Belanger when I joined Baltimore. He was state of the art for a lot of years. Like all great shortstops, he saved me many runs.

Belanger had an ability that most shortstops don't have. First, every shortstop has a different interpretation of what he should do as far as preventing the ball from getting through the infield. Most shortstops will tell you that with a man at second base on a potential base hit, a shortstop must dive to make sure that ball stays in the infield and prevent the runner at second from scoring.

Belanger was quite the contrary. When he visited me in spring training he told me, "Hey, I know you're new to the ballclub, but let me tell you a little bit about what I do at shortstop. Don't expect me to dive for anything, because I don't. If I can't get to it standing up, it shouldn't be gotten to."

So that was his philosophy about the play. I know most pitchers appreciate a shortstop diving with a man at second base to keep the ball in the infield, but it wasn't Belanger's style. But what he did better than just about anybody was stay in front of the ball and always keep his glove down. That's a lesson for any infielder. You keep your glove down, you come up with the hop. If your glove is riding high and the ball flattens out, it's very difficult to go down and get the baseball. Mark was a master at that, keeping his glove down.

Many times, Belanger was like a catcher blocking low pitches, where a catcher doesn't try to catch the ball but has it hit off his chest protector or part of his anatomy and keeps the ball in front of him so the runner can't advance. Several times Belanger would keep the ball in front of him on bad hops, and I saw this on a number of highlight films.

Belanger was so quick and stayed in front of just about everything. What might look like a routine hop would take a bad bounce, but he would field it cleanly and throw to first base to nail the runner by plenty. To all who watched it live, it looked like he caught the ball in his glove, just like most shortstops do, and threw the ball. If you were to slow down the videotape, however, you'd see that the ball actually bounced up right into Belanger's chest area as he went down for the baseball. He kept his arms in, went down for the baseball with his glove. The ball took a bad hop and hit him just below the chest, but Mark was so quick with his hands that he was able to pick the ball off his body and throw to first base in the same motion.

When I got to Baltimore, Cal Ripken Jr. was tearing up the minor leagues, and they brought him to the major leagues as a third baseman. Earl Weaver was the first guy to say, "This guy is pretty athletic. I think he can play shortstop."

You've got to understand that Cal was a very big guy, 6'4" or so, and he was about 225 pounds and not the prototypical shortstop. But he was a guy who could give the offense another power bat, and Earl, above all else, loved home runs.

So we know how that worked out. Cal is in the Hall of Fame, set a record for most consecutive games played, and did several things very well. Cal threw the ball in a fairly unorthodox way for a shortstop, but he got it there in plenty of time and it was positioning by Cal that made him the shortstop that he was.

Now here's a story involving a shortstop, Earl Weaver, and general manager Hank Peters. This happened in the mid-1970s, before I got to the Orioles, but it was told to me as being very accurate, and I'm sure it is, because I've seen Earl do this with other guys.

Peters had a rule with Weaver that, "Don't tell me specifically what player you want because I might not be able to get him, and then you're going to get aggravated and mad at me, and then I'm going to get mad at you, and it's not going to work out well. So give me a type of player that you want, and then I'll go out and see if I can get that type of player."

So Weaver went to Peters one day and said, "Look, do we have anyone in our system who can catch a ground ball? Anybody at all who can catch a ground ball at shortstop?"

Peters said, "Yes, as a matter of fact, we do."

So Weaver said, "Good, I want you to bring him up. I'm going to pinch hit for Belanger, usually in the seventh inning or later, every day, and I need a guy to come in and catch the ball after I take Belanger out of the game. He doesn't ever have to get a hit. He just has to catch the ball."

Hank replied, "We got a guy like that. We'll bring him up tomorrow."

So they brought up a kid by the name of Tim Nordbrook, who was a good kid. In fact, I had run into him earlier with the Chicago White Sox. But this was after his stint with the Baltimore Orioles. So, true to his word, when Earl wanted somebody on the big-league team because he was going to do something, he usually did it that first day. That's what he did when Nordbrook got there: he pinch hit for Belanger and told Nordbrook, "Okay, you're in there."

Nordbrook entered the game in the eighth inning and it was a very close game. Baltimore didn't score many runs, but they had excellent pitching, usually spectacular defense, and they held just about every team to a fairly low score. The games were usually very close. So Nordbrook goes to shortstop, where he might be facing the first ground ball he's going to field in the major leagues for the Baltimore Orioles.

Sure enough, in his first inning with one out, there's a ground ball hit to him. It literally clangs off his glove and bounces away, and the batter reaches base safely.

At the end of the inning, as the story was told to me, Weaver wouldn't even let him get in the dugout. Nordbrook was on the top step of the dugout because he missed the one ball that had been hit to him and Weaver just reamed him.

"Hey, let me tell you something, kid," Earl said in a very raspy voice. "Our general manager told me that you can't hit very well, but you're supposed to be a great fielder. So I said, 'Well, if he's a great fielder, bring him up. Because I'm going to hit for Belanger, and I'm going to need a great fielder for the last couple innings.'

"And then I'm taking a look, and the first ball hit to you clangs off your glove. You don't look like a great fielder to me. Let me tell you something: I got you up here for one reason. That reason is to catch the baseball in the late innings. They tell me you can do that. So far, you haven't shown me you can. So let's put it this way: you better never miss another baseball while you're here. You miss another ground ball, you're going to be gone, because I need someone to catch the ball late in games.

"That's why you're here. I'm going to go to the playoffs. This team is going to go to the playoffs, and I'm not going to let you stand in the way of me going to the playoffs because you can't do the one thing that you're supposed to be able to do, which is why you're here in the first place. I don't care if you never get a hit. Odds are you're not going to get an at-bat. But you got to catch the ball. I never want to see you miss another baseball the rest of this season."

Well, this was Weaver's way of finding out if this guy was tough enough to actually play for him in a pennant race. Nordbrook, of course, was absolutely scared to death because here's a Hall of Fame manager, Earl Weaver, berating him on the top step of the dugout, and he's only played one inning as an Oriole.

So Weaver gives him a couple days off to think about it, then puts him in a second time. And the first ball hit to him goes right through his legs and into left field.

Needless to say, Tim Nordbook's career with the Baltimore Orioles was very short and very unproductive.

CHAPTER 7

The Outfield

Of the three outfield positions, the center fielder, by far, is the most important. Here's an overview of the outfield.

You would like to have your strongest arm in right field because that's the longest throw as far as home plate is concerned, and it's the longest throw to third base in the case of a base runner going from first to third. You'd like your right fielder to have an accurate arm. Also, you'd always like your right fielder, whether he's a left-hander or a right-hander, to throw over the top.

The advance scouts and the coaches of every team have a very good idea about which outfielders—especially right fielders—have a tail on their throw. For a right-hand-throwing right fielder, that means the ball kind of moves left to right, and in that case you're going to be off-target with it unless you account for it. The throw doesn't arrive as quickly when outfielders don't throw over the top. The best right fielders charge in, have the right footwork, throw over the top, and don't have any tail on it. Those are the ones who usually throw people out.

For the most part, throwing people out from the outfield has become a rarity. But you see it coming back to the game in some areas, just like a lot of different aspects of offense and defense as far as execution is concerned. With the performance-enhancing drugs outlawed, that's going to put more of the emphasis on small ball, execution on offense and defense, and that will include occasionally throwing out base runners.

But probably the most important thing to understand is hitting the cutoff man. That's because on certain plays for your outfielders, hitting the cutoff man is the only way you're going to get the out.

This points to the importance of the center fielder. One of the things you need more than anything else in center field—which is certainly a value but not essential in your corner outfielders—is speed. You can't do without speed in center field, especially with some of the bigger outfields that have come into existence. For instance, look at Petco Park in San Diego, AT&T Park in San Francisco, and Comerica Park in Detroit. Center field at Tropicana Field in St. Petersburg is very big. Coors Field's center field is also very spacious. I could go on and on as far as some of the very big center fields in baseball.

In that position, there is no substitute for speed: getting a jump on the ball, understanding that the toughest ball for any center fielder to field is the ball hit right at him, because he really doesn't know where that ball is going. He can't tell if it's going to take off, if it's going to sink, what it's going to do, because it's coming right over his head or dropping in front of him. It's a tough ball to play. You would be surprised by the sound of the bat and what that really does for an outfielder. Particularly with the ash bats, if a guy made strong contact, that sounds very different from if he hit it off the end of the bat or got jammed with it.

Believe me, the outfielders can hear that sound. Certainly pitchers can. Being a former pitcher, I know the sound of a ball that was hit well. I know the sound of a ball that's going out of the ballpark. But we're talking about center fielders, and with the preponderance of maple bats today, you're going to get that crisp sound regardless of how hard the ball is hit. That makes it a little more difficult from a sound aspect to tell if that ball is going to land in front of you or go over your head. The advantage, if you have a great executing staff, is that when the pitching coach, the pitcher, and the catcher go over the scouting reports, they will coordinate that with how the defense is going to line up.

When the center fielder has that and knows that his pitching staff can execute, then he'll be able to shift on the counts. There are many teams that do that. For instance, on the first pitch of an at-bat, it could very well be that the center fielder plays the guy as an off-field hitter, meaning a right-handed hitter to right center, a left-handed hitter to left center. However, if the pitcher falls behind 2–0, that's likely to be an aggressive swing by the hitter. Then the center fielder might want to cheat by a step into the hitter's power. So against a right-handed hitter, the center fielder might want to cheat toward left center, and into right center, with a left-handed hitter.

Some teams have a philosophy about moving with the counts. Some teams don't move very much at all because sometimes the pitchers aren't capable of executing. The center fielder can't see what the catcher is calling unless he has terrific eyes. Some pitchers are fully capable of throwing it 90 percent of the time to where the catcher is setting up, thus giving the center fielder a good step ahead when a guy takes his swing. Sometimes the great center fielders make it look like they're actually moving before the ball is hit. It's just great anticipation and understanding of where the ball is being thrown and consequently adjusting to that. That's one of the real big factors in playing center field.

So with speed being a nonnegotiable factor in most of the ballparks today, then you have to look at throwing. The most difficult throw for a center fielder is the throw going away from the play.

Let's say a center fielder goes to his left. The play is going to be at second base, and he's catching the ball in right-center field on a hop or whatever the case may be. The ball is about ready to get by him, but he closes ground quickly and realizes the base runner is thinking two bases right out of the box, challenging the center fielder.

If you're a right-handed center fielder going to your left, then you're going away from the throw. That means catching the ball and doing a 360-degree spin or trying to right your footwork and round off your approach to the baseball in order to get that throw into second base. That becomes a difficult play. The same would hold true for a left-handed center fielder and an aggressive base runner who hits the ball into left-center field. He is going away from his throw, away from the second-base bag, and again, he's either righting himself or performing a 360-degree spin to get it there.

But the most difficult throw for a center fielder is trying to cut down that runner at the plate. The reason for that is the pitcher's mound. People don't consider it very much, but it's 10 inches high, you have the pitching rubber there, the rosin bag is somewhere in the middle of it, and you have to make sure of a few things. First, if you're close enough and charging the ball aggressively enough, then you can probably try to make that throw exactly right on the money on the fly. Then you don't have to worry where the ball is going to bounce because there is no bounce, and if you throw it well enough, you're going to be in very good shape.

Also, you really want to have that ball thrown low enough so that the catcher doesn't catch it on the short hop. By low enough, I mean you want to throw it so it goes over the mound and lands on the grass—not on the downside of the pitching rubber. This is why many center fielders have a hard time throwing out base runners. If you hit the back of the pitcher's mound, that ball will bounce straight up. If you hit the front of the pitcher's mound, that ball is going to flatten out and skid toward the catcher. You want to keep your throw low enough so that it doesn't take that high hop. Interestingly, sometimes the cut of the grass, just exactly which way the grass is mowed, has a lot to do with whether the ball takes a high hop or a low hop, just one more thing for the outfielder to consider.

Several managers, including Buck Showalter, talked about the way they were cutting the grass at one of his stops. I will not mention which one it was, but he said because of the way the grass was mowed, when throws came in from the outfield, the ball took a little higher hop, making it more difficult for his outfielders to throw out base runners, and he was going to work on it and suggest a way to cut it.

Other managers don't concern themselves with that. But the mound is the single reason why center fielders have trouble throwing out base runners at home plate. You have to carry the mound if you're going to throw it on a hop and make sure that throw stays low enough so that someone can get to it.

At other times you have to hit the cutoff man. You must always bear in mind that you want to give that cutoff man a throw that is high enough that it won't one-hop the cutoff man. Whether you're going to the left-center or right-center alley, you're probably going to play it off the wall. You're going to hope to get a good carom off that wall, and that has to do with the way the ball hits the wall and the spin with which it hits it.

When you see the ball is headed for that alley, you want to position yourself so you're not too close to the wall. If you get too close to the wall, the ball will carom by you. If it does that, you're going to play a double into a triple. But on balls that hit the wall on a couple bounces and bounce back to you, when you do get to it, you want to make sure you hit the cutoff man. Make sure the throw hits him above the waist so he doesn't have to bend down and pick it on a short hop, doesn't have to go behind him; and always throw to his glove side. The cutoff man should have the best opportunity to make a very good relay throw. That's of critical importance for center fielders.

Managers and center fielders should know the speed of every base runner, and that should be in the scouting reports. A center fielder should take notice of the idiosyncrasies of every one of the base runners, especially if a runner at second is known for taking wide turns. That is something that comes with experience. It comes with observation.

Many managers, including Hall of Famer Earl Weaver, will stress that if the outfielder isn't 100 percent sure of making a play at the plate on the tying or winning run, he better make sure to throw the ball to second base, especially with no outs or one out.

The reason is that by doing so, you keep the double play in order. That was one of the mantras of the great Earl Weaver, as well as other great managers: stay out of the big inning. They kept preaching that, and that means making sure the throws are able to be cut off. Make sure they're at the proper height because a good, solid base runner who is thinking two bases out of the box, especially on the hit, is going to take a look at the angle of the throw. That's an advantage you want to take away from them.

• • •

Whether a player is a right fielder or left fielder, the guys in the corners must remember the ball is always going to hook or slice toward the line.

Once you realize that, you can adjust accordingly. That means your best arm is in right field. In left field, many times you have your big run producer, your home run hitter, your big RBI leader. That goes hand in hand with the philosophy of having power at the corners—first and third, left and right—those are your power positions. Many teams feel that if you're strong up the middle and you've got power at the corners, you're going to be in pretty good shape. If you get some power out of your middle infield, that's a plus. I'm thinking of Jeff Kent at second base. He had six consecutive seasons with the San Francisco Giants driving in more than 100 runs. He holds the all-time record for home runs by a second baseman. He was always known as an offensive second baseman.

If you get power from that unlikely power spot, just as the Cubs did with Ryne Sandberg, then maybe you don't need as much power on the corners. But for the most part, the outfield is not made up of guys who are the best fielders around, but guys who can really hit. Some of the notables are guys like Matt Holliday and Adam Dunn, who played left field. Those guys, for the most part, are asked to get the ball from the outfield to second base on a base hit. They want to make sure the double play is always in order. They're most likely not the speed burners, although you have some fast left fielders.

In the case of Boston, Carl Crawford is one of those guys who is going to steal as many bases as he wants to and is also a tremendous defender in left field. Crawford is not a power guy but a speed guy. I remember Vince Coleman was the same way with the St. Louis Cardinals, where they put a team together on the artificial surface under Whitey Herzog that had one beast and the rest fleas.

With one beast, Jack Clark, in the middle and all of the fleas around, that team was able to score in unconventional ways. Tommy Herr didn't even get to double figures in home runs, but he drove in 110 runs because he had a lot of guys at each position who could run, including Coleman in left field.

With the White Sox of 2010, you have Juan Pierre, a leadoff hitter who plays left. It's very rare to have a leadoff-hitting left fielder, but he's a guy who can steal a lot of bases. At last count, he had more than 500 career stolen bases. By the time you read this, he'll have more than 520 stolen bases. He's in league with Rickey Henderson—probably the greatest leadoff hitter in history. Henderson combined power with exceptional defense and great, great, great speed.

Guys like Henderson come around very rarely. He was a game changer. He was a left fielder who, when he got on base, could make you completely change your philosophy. He had 81 leadoff home runs. Henderson was the type of left fielder that you dream about but not one that shows up all that often.

In the National League, you want to have your bangers at the corners. In the NL, that's more important, while in the American League you can make up for it with the designated hitter. If you want to, you can have another cleanup-type hitter in your lineup. You also can have another speed guy in your lineup. Or, with a right-handed starter, you can have another left-handed hitter who might not be that speed guy or that power guy, but just another left-handed hitter to balance your lineup. Same thing with a right-handed hitter against a left-handed pitcher. That's the AL, and it's a different style of baseball. That's why putting together a team in the National League is a little more difficult: you can't use that designated hitter to fill in the gaps.

It's of much more importance to have a balanced lineup in the National League because you don't have the designated hitter to help you with that balance. If you're going to be a National League GM, you must be more aware of how you put your lineup together.

It's very difficult to just go out and sign defensive players and put them on your team, because if they can't hit, then you have a hole in your lineup. In the National League, when you look at most lineups, the seventh, eighth, and ninth hitters just don't contribute a great deal. If they do, then you have a very decent lineup and you end up in good shape.

But if you look down through the history of baseball, there are very few postseason appearances won with just an overwhelming offense. (Although one of Bill Veeck's great lines was that if you're going to err, err on the side of offense because it's a more entertaining game.)

Well, if you can hit the baseball, hit it out of the park, and score six or seven runs a game, that's pretty exciting. The fans do get into it. But for an overall rule and philosophy in baseball, the game is won or lost because of pitching and defense. That's what can keep you respectable on a game-to-game, year-to-year basis. Yet, as easy as it sounds, it can be very difficult to pull off because you might find certain positions where you're willing to give up defense in order to get offense, as is often the case with left and right field.

But more times than not in the course of a game, the ball is going to find your weakest defenders. It always does. And when it does, if they don't make the play, then your pitcher has to throw many more pitches.

If you have good pitching but weak defense, maybe at the four-and-a-half-month mark, that pitching is going to start to tire. If your starting pitcher doesn't go deep enough into the game, eventually that great bullpen will start to dissolve. As pitchers get into the 45-appearance range, and when the bullpen dissolves, so do your chances of winning.

It revolves around the simplicity of picking up the baseball. In building a baseball team, if you think pitching and defense first, then you can add hitters. If you draft good pitching, and you have defenders who can field and pick up the baseball on routine plays (and whatever they make on the spectacular variety is just a bonus), you're going to find yourself legitimate.

Many teams that have a great pitching staff also have great defense. That will be the inner defense in the infield, but most certainly it will be outfield defense as well, and it starts with the center fielder. That's what it means to be strong up the middle—the catcher, second baseman, shortstop, and center fielder.

If that's the defensive strength of your club, and you have adequate defense in the outfield on either corner as well as pretty good defense on the corners in the infield, that can be one of the greatest assets of your pitching staff.

These days, stadiums have walls that are a little bit lower than they used to be, and outfielders are able to go over the walls. When you take a look on a daily basis at the highlights, you watch the outfielders making circus catches, going over the wall to get hits. I'm thinking of Colorado's Coors Field and Minneapolis' Target Field. White Sox center fielder Alex Rios took a home run away from Minnesota's Michael Cuddyer that I thought was completely out of the ballpark, but Rios went up high, took the ball literally out of the bullpen, and made just a spectacular catch.

Baltimore has a low fence. Guys can go over that. The fence at Dodger Stadium is fairly low. A number of parks have those low fences that invite the circus catch.

I like the lower fences because it leads to more spectacular plays. That brings into play the great timing of some of these tremendous athletes in the outfield. It would help if you were a little taller to go up over the wall. But obviously that's not the greatest prerequisite for your outfield positions.

• • •

For all players, but for outfielders especially, knowing the different ballparks throughout the league is a huge advantage. There's so much information you can gather just by looking around, knowing your surroundings, and finding out what you're up against.

Just as there is a tremendous home-field advantage for most teams, depending on how the grounds crew maintains the fields, you must know, as a visiting team, how each and every field plays. For instance, at U.S. Cellular Field, the home team seems to know that if a bunt, especially on the third-base side, gets on the dirt or rolls from the grass to the dirt, that ball won't roll foul. That ball is going to stay in the field of play and roll back toward the grass instead of letting the spin take it into foul territory. Knowing that ahead of time is a tremendous advantage for the home team. That's where it comes into play with the coaches of a visiting team. If not the coaches, then the third and first basemen must find this out when they come to a ballpark, because they don't know exactly what the grounds crew are going to do with it. Thus, they must work out early, roll the balls down the foul lines, and figure out what the ball is going to do. Sometimes they have to roll it from the grass to see if it's going to roll foul once it hits the dirt, or they have to roll it down the line on the dirt to see which way the ball is going to break.

Obviously, if you have a fast team, with a few players who tend to bunt, you're going to have that foul line where the ball rolls into the field of play. But a lot of teams don't really do that type of investigating, and because of that, they don't have a particular advantage going into a new park.

You must also have a good idea about how lively the fence or wall is going to be. That's why, in a new park, you should have guys working out and maybe hitting a baseball into the corner to see how it's going to carom off the wall. Is it going to get caught in the drainage area or under the padding if the padding doesn't stop a foot off the field? That happens sometimes. You'll see the ball get stuck in there, and the outfielder, waiting to get that carom, doesn't get it. This is an advantage for the home team because they know exactly what's going to happen. The visiting team has to be prepared for that.

If it's a wall all the way around, you have to know how the ball is going to come off the wall. However, in some parks, you have a wall and then a chain-link fence where the bullpen sits behind so the players can see through that fence. Then you must know that a line drive off the fence is going to act completely different from a line drive off the wall. Again, that's part of understanding a visiting ballpark, the advantage of a home team and the disadvantage of the visiting team, unless the road team is prepared for each and every ballpark.

Many times different outfields play differently. For instance, at Wrigley Field, which is one of the most unusual of the parks, you have the ivy covering brick. Consequently, when you play a carom off the wall, you have to know which way it's going to go. You also have a different configuration. You have what's known as the well at Wrigley Field. The well is an area that comes out at a little angle where the bleachers are, from left center to right center. The bleachers are a little closer than that wall, and if a ball hits in the well, it can actually go back farther. Where, if it were in left center or right center, it would be a home run, if it hits into the well, you can go back and make a catch.

The most important part of understanding the curvature of that part of the ballpark as a visiting player at Wrigley Field is knowing the ball is going to hit off that corner occasionally and take an unusual bounce. In one instance, Kevin Millar—a very slow base runner but a good hitter—hit an inside-the-park home run on a ball he hit to right field. It happened to catch the angle perfectly in the well in right field, and when the right fielder ran over, that ball hit off the corner of the well and caromed all the way to the corner in right field. Millar, amazingly enough, ran out the inside-the-park home run. He probably needed some oxygen when he got there, but because of that crazy carom and because of the configuration, he was able to hit that inside-the-park home run.

I'm not sure how many of those Millar had during his career, but at the most it was two. Most likely, it was one. But that was the one I remember, and that's because of the idiosyncrasies of that ballpark.

Another feature at Wrigley Field that most parks don't have is the basket that's put out there to prevent fans from rolling from the bleachers to the field if they get a little vociferous during the course of some celebrations.

Some of the advantages the Cubs had back in the day when Ron Cey and Larry Bowa played the left side of the infield was that they had the highest infield grass I've ever seen. Frank Robinson, the Hall of Famer, was managing the San Francisco Giants during a visit to Wrigley. He came over and asked me if they cut the grass with a helicopter.

I said no, but if you had Cey and Bowa on the left side, you'd want that grass as high as you could possibly have it.

To illustrate just how high the grass was, there was a case where Jody Davis caught the last pitch, and a left-handed reliever by the name of Al Holland was coming in from the bullpen for Philadelphia. Jody rolled the ball toward the third-base side. Fortunately, Ozzie Virgil, the catcher, had a pretty good idea about where Jody rolled, it because when Holland came in, he stood on the mound, took a look around, and couldn't find the baseball.

It's almost inconceivable that you could lose a baseball in the infield grass, but that's exactly what happened.

Finally, after Holland looked around a bit for the ball, Virgil came out about three-quarters of the way toward third base, found the ball, and tossed it to Holland so he could warm up.

Depending on your infield and its ability, you're going to have that infield grass and dirt a different way than most teams. That holds true for every team, and that's why you must take stock of what that field looks like when you visit other parks. Sometimes it changes during the course of the year, too, depending on the heat and the amount of rain they get.

There's another aspect of the various ballparks that you have to know, and that is exactly where the openings to the dugouts are. Normally you'll have an opening toward home plate, an opening up the middle, and an opening toward the other end heading toward the bullpens. Those openings come into play when you're trying to catch a foul ball. If you're the visiting team, you have to know just exactly where you can fall in, which you're going to do if you happen to be a little too close to the dugout. As the visiting team, you're not going to get any help from the home team.

You also must know where the tarp is. In many ballparks, it's on the third-base side. If you're a first or third baseman, you have to know that. You see many guys get tangled up, and some will try to go up and over it. Some will try to step on top of it. It's something that people don't often think about, but knowing where that tarp is can either get you an out or cost you an out.

The infielders, particularly the shortstop and second baseman, must be familiar with the railings. That's essential on pop-ups, and it's much easier for them than the third baseman or first baseman because of the angle. They must have a good idea about where that wall and the railings are.

For the outfielders, it helps to know the depth of the warning track and to know exactly how many steps you have. That also depends on the size of the outfielder. A small outfielder with small strides might have another step on the warning track before he gets to that wall. That's important to know because there are many instances where you are running as hard as you can after a ball, and you suddenly find yourself running out of room.

So you must have a good idea of how many steps you can take before you hit that wall. It certainly helps to know that at Wrigley Field, because behind that lush-looking ivy are the bricks. And going into that wall is a very difficult situation for a lot of outfielders. They either shy away from it or go headlong into it, and they usually come in second.

I know Pittsburgh has a Bermuda Triangle in left-center field where a ball will get hung up on occasion. They also have a 21-foot-high wall in commemoration of Roberto Clemente. Or you go to the Green Monster in Boston, where you have crazy caroms off that 37-foot wall, depending on if it hits on one of the ball marks that happen to be on that wall or perhaps hits off the scoreboard. There have been some great left fielders in Boston who played that wall like they would play a concert violin, and there are others who play it like they've never seen a baseball before.

If you're going to be a defender in left field, you must know all the caroms. Left fielders usually perform a great deal of work on that to hold many would-be extra-base hits to singles, and that happens a lot.

Historically, you have young and fast infielders, so you'll want a fairly fast infield grass. That could also mean a fairly hard infield dirt. Sometimes the dirt gets a little too hard, and the grass gets a little too fast, and you have the Texas infield. That's one of the fastest infields of the non–artificial turf surface variety because of the great baking of the sun, the tremendous heat, the ability to keep the grass short enough so the ball shoots through. It's a tremendous advantage for the hitters, and a great disadvantage for the infielders.

• • •

I think the era of small ball is on the horizon, and to a certain extent it's already here. Because of the testing for performance-enhancing drugs, slug ball is slowly beginning to recede. You will have guys hit 50 home runs, but you just won't have many of them. Many home run leaders will hit in the 30s and 40s—the way it used to be—as opposed to the 50s, 60s, and 70s they hit in the steroid era. But as small ball comes into vogue, there has to be a greater emphasis on being able to put down a bunt. This is for the National League. And some guys will have to learn it quicker because of the interleague play.

If you're in the American League, it never hurts a pitcher to gain more knowledge and learn how to bunt. For nonpitchers, you have to learn how to bunt for a hit. It helps if you can push bunt and drag bunt. A left-handed hitter can push bunt to the third baseman and lay down a drag bunt to the first-base side. A right-handed hitter can push bunt to the first-base side and drag bunt to the third-base side.

If you can't bunt for a hit or bunt for a sacrifice when called to execute, there's a very good chance that failed execution will cost your team the game. If that's the case, then quite obviously your teammates and your manager are not going to be particularly happy with you, because you're not a complete player. I think you're going to see more players being asked to be complete players as small ball plays a more prominent role.

Many players come up through the minor leagues and don't have that big power because they arrive at the major league level sooner. They might develop power in the major leagues, but you never know.

Hank Aaron was a line-drive hitter who also hit to the opposite field. We all know that Hank finished with 755 home runs. Don Baylor, another prolific home run hitter, was a line-drive hitter and an opposite-field hitter as he came up through the Orioles system. He became a proficient slugger when he signed as a free agent with the California Angels.

Ryne Sandberg came up as a No. 2 hitter with the Chicago Cubs from the Philadelphia organization. As a No. 2 hitter batting behind Bobby Dernier, Sandberg would hit the ball to the right side. He would hit-and-run a lot. He was a line-drive hitter who hit 19 triples in 1984, when he won the National League Most Valuable Player Award. Well, suddenly he began to pull the ball a little more. He became more comfortable. He got a little older. He understood what pitches he could hit out. He understood what pitchers were going to do with him. But he developed that in the major leagues.

We can still develop our players in the major leagues to be a little more powerful. But in the meantime, learning how to bunt is something we've lost. It's coming back, and it's certainly something we have to work on. Hopefully, organizations will work on that in their minor leagues, because having a pitcher work on his bunting, and then having a coach throwing 65 mph doesn't teach you how to bunt.

You can talk about the fundamentals of getting up in the box. Some pitchers prefer feet absolutely parallel to one another. Some prefer having the back foot in back, and the front foot toward the front of the box. It's important to get as far up in the box as you can. However, you have to face some live pitching because you're going to be facing live pitching in a game.

That's one of the mistakes that a lot of organizations make: having a coach throw bunting practice to various guys. You're never going to see that coach in a game. Maybe you can bunt at 65 or 70 mph, but where are you going to find that guy in the game? You won't. He'll be throwing 90 to 95 mph with nasty curves and sliders, throwing a lot of high fastballs, and doing everything he can to stop you from bunting. You've got to see that in bunting practice.

Base running is kind of a dying art in baseball today, and I'm not talking about just stealing a base or any of the other things that go into scoring from second. I'm talking about every aspect of base running: how to cut the bases, where to take your shortest turn so you don't swing out and lose a couple of extra steps around third base trying to score, when to dive headfirst into first base (which, by the way, is never good unless you're trying to avoid a tag).

To me, the mistakes I see on the base paths are unbelievable. Very observant middle infielders might keep the glove on the leg of runners who use pop-up slides in case they miss the tag the first time. A veteran infielder will keep the glove on him, and the runner will be called out. Those are baserunning mistakes you can't really afford to have happen because they take you out of baseball games.

But in this good baserunner aspect, I want to address the art of reading the relay throw and taking the extra base. As soon as a good base runner gets a hit and starts running around first base, he will read that relay throw coming in from the outfield. If the runner sees a rainbow-like hump in that throw, he'll realize that throw can't be cut off and will take off for second base.

It's worth repeating here that one of the great managers I had was Earl Weaver, who felt you had to throw to second base to keep the trailing runner from going to second base and keep the double play in order. His mantra was "Stay out of the big inning," and I think that's great advice.

CH AT E R

Managing

Managers come in all shapes, sizes, and dispositions; and each has his place. In fact, when you look at the hirings of managers, you'll find it's fairly cyclical. With the exclusion of Bobby Cox, who has retired, there are very few managers who leave on their own terms.

If you've hired a laid-back manager, you have a manager who has that "live and let live" attitude, what some would describe as a players' manager. That manager will let his players do whatever they want to do as long as they follow a couple of simple rules and get the job done.

If you ultimately fire a laid-back manager, odds are overwhelming that the next manager you hire is a fiery-type manager. When that fiery manager starts to wear thin on some of the players after a few years, you will likely hire a more laid-back manager.

If you hire a manager with very little experience, there's a good chance the next manager will have lots of experience, and vice versa. There are different qualifications for managers. You would like them to have some experience, preferably on the bench in the major leagues, before you hire them. There are some managers, however, who didn't have that experience but turned out to be pretty good.

There isn't any one criterion for being a manager. The personalities vary with each person as far as how they want to run their team. Maybe the best example of different philosophies of managers occurred when I went to the Arizona Fall League, where I look at the six best prospects from all of the 30 teams each year.

I was sitting with Bobby Cox as he took a look at one of his players. I mentioned to Bobby that Lou Piniella, one of Bobby's contemporaries who had wonderful success in the game before ending his career with the Chicago Cubs, once said to me that he didn't believe you could manage guys today the same way you managed them in the early 1990s.

I related this philosophy to Cox, to which he responded, "Well, that's a bunch of crap. You can manage today exactly like you could manage back then. You can take the '70s, the '80s, the '90s, or the 2000s—whenever you want. You lay down a set of rules. If the team or the individual players don't adhere to those rules, well, then there are consequences."

Bobby did say that the Major League Baseball Players Association wasn't going to allow managers to assess stiff fines from the players. But the manager does have the power of the pencil, which is taking playing time away from these various guys.

Here's an example:

We were broadcasting a game between the Cubs and the Braves, who had a young center fielder named Andruw Jones. There was a ball that fell in front of Jones for which he gave less than 100 percent effort. It was around the sixth inning, and Cox came out and asked the umpire for time, which was granted.

Bobby took a couple of steps from the dugout and pointed to center field—right at Jones. Bobby used his finger to motion Jones to come in. He just waited there. He didn't even have the replacement ready. He just motioned for Jones to come in—in the middle of an inning. Everyone was waiting around as Andruw jogged in.

I never asked Bobby what he said, but it was the equivalent of "Apparently, you don't want to play. Come in and take off the uniform." Only after that long run from the outfield, and only after Jones disappeared into the tunnel leading to the locker room did Bobby allow his center-field replacement to go to that position.

That clearly hit home with Jones, who went on to become one of the great center fielders in the history of the game. But Bobby was laying down some rules that he wanted everyone to adhere to. Granted, that was years ago, but the point was that he had a set of rules that he didn't deviate from. And he never has.

Ron Gardenhire is very similar to that in Minnesota. Alexi Casilla, a youngster having a good year, once didn't hustle on a play to first base. He received a chat from Gardenhire, who explained what he expected of his players.

A couple of days later, Casilla laid down a bunt and carried his bat to first base in a half-jog as he sacrificed the runner to second. The next day, Casilla—as talented as he was—was demoted to the minors. That particular lesson hit home, and I think since then Casilla has hustled and become a productive player for the Twins.

Notably, Gardy told me he had a couple of guys on his team who helped him out so that he or his coaches didn't have to deal with those kinds of situations. Coaches can deal with these problems before the manager. As Gardenhire told me, if first-base coach Jerry White or third-base coach Scott Ullger talks to somebody about it, then Gardy doesn't have to get involved.

As Gardy put it, when a manager gets involved, it becomes a big production. But if the coaches talk to the players, then it's less scrutinized. Gardy also noted that he has the luxury of having a few players on his team who will just come walking by and say, "I'll take this one, Skip" if they see something that isn't Twins baseball. Those players are Justin Morneau and Michael Cuddyer, and Joe Mauer is getting much better at this.

It helps that those are three of the stars of the team and are homegrown players. The old Houston teams had Billy Wagner, Craig Biggio, and Jeff Bagwell doing some of the policing. If there are leaders on the team, they can take care of themselves. The manager doesn't have to get involved, and if that's the case, everyone is a whole lot better off.

You need different kinds of managers for different teams. You might want a specific manager for an also-ran team and another for a team that's going to finish up the trek. Perhaps it's a rebuilding year, and you just don't have the talent. You need a manager who can handle that situation.

On the flip side, if you have a team you believe is going to be in contention and a team that has several veteran players, you will want a manager who's been through that a few times and can manage accordingly. Sometimes it will be a guy who was a bench coach for a certain team or perhaps a hitting coach for a certain team who then ascends to manager.

Mike Scioscia knows the game inside and out and brings a great deal of intensity to the park on a daily basis. I think his teams reflect that. He has very good ideas about player development, and I think Mike has a great say in personnel matters as far as whom to acquire, perhaps whom not to acquire, whom to move, when to move him, etc.... The smart general managers take that kind of input from their managers. I believe the manager should have some input in player personnel moves, only because he's in that locker room every day, and the general manager isn't.

Although the GM would like to think he knows everything that's going on, there are times when he really doesn't have a good feel for various guys at various times and what they're going through. Managers, on the other hand, tend to know when it's time to allow a guy to move on via trade or free agency with the idea that it's always a little better to trade a guy one year too soon than one year too late. That is one of the standard truisms of baseball and always will be.

But that's how a good manager can help his GM and say, "Look, I don't know what you're seeing up there, but I can tell you what I'm seeing down here." That happens a lot.

• • •

Many baseball folks have wondered what the toughest spot is in the batting order. A lot of people will say the leadoff position is toughest because of the demands on the batter. Managers would like him to be a table setter and see him steal bases. Others say batting second is toughest, since the batter has to hit down in the count, take some pitches to allow a base stealer to steal, and possess the ability to bunt and hit to the right side.

But for my money's worth, the most difficult place in the batting order to hit is the eighth spot in the National League, ahead of a pitcher who usually doesn't hit very well. That's why it's imperative, especially on a very good team, that you use a veteran in that No. 8 spot if you have the luxury of doing that. Many first-year players don't have the plate discipline you're looking for, and they might have a nose-to-toes strike zone. And if they're put into that eighth spot, you're going to find out very quickly that they will draw a few more walks than they normally draw in another area of the batting order. However, they're not going to be pitched to all that often, because if they don't show any plate discipline, it's pretty easy for pitchers to pitch around them with the pitcher coming up next.

So when you see a manager putting a youngster into the eighth spot, that player better have pretty good plate discipline, because he's going to be pitched around a lot. If he doesn't, he'll probably take a few walks at first and then get so anxious he'll expand his strike zone.

• • •

It's a little more difficult to manage in the National League. In the NL, you must double-switch and make sure you don't burn out your bullpen by pinch-hitting for your pitcher, depending on the score. American League managers don't have to be so careful about burning out their starters because they never have to worry about pinch-hitting for them. You probably don't need as many relievers in the AL, although it's become fashionable to go with 12 pitchers, and some go with 13. If you have 13 pitchers, you generally don't have a good bullpen. If you have 12 pitchers, you usually have an adequate bullpen. If you have 11 pitchers, you have a very good bullpen.

Most teams feel it's a gamble to go with five starters and six relievers. But if you can do that, that actually gives your manager one more move to make off the bench because then he has another position player to deal with. If you go with five starters and seven relievers, then you have 13 position players and one less move to make off your bench.

The better managers will try to manage their players into the matchup they are looking for. They will spend seven, sometimes eight innings making various changes to corner you into that matchup they're looking for, which might be in the eighth inning. It could be a certain pinch-hitter he holds back to face a certain setup man that he knows his pinch-hitter has had very good luck against. He's going to manage that game around that eventuality to keep that guy ready to help win a baseball game.

In my estimation, that's why it's of critical importance in both leagues that a manager have at least one, and preferably two, quality left-handed veteran pinch-hitters. Show me a bench loaded with youngsters, loaded with guys waiting for their turn to play in the major leagues, loaded with guys who have been everyday guys in the minor leagues and are now part-time players in the majors, and I'll show you a team that probably will not win.

Your bench should be guys who have had experience, played every day somewhere, and now have accepted the role of a pinch-hitter. It helps when pinch-hitters who don't get regular at-bats have short swings. It's of critical importance to have that left-handed pinch-hitter. Obviously, you'd like to have a good right-handed pinch-hitter as well. But the good left-handers are even more critical.

Many times, constructing a bench is directly proportionate to what kind of payroll you have. The low-revenue, low-payroll teams find it a little harder to assemble a bench, and they will assemble a bench with a lot of kids on it. You can tell two things about teams from the type of bench they have. First, you can tell how much payroll they're spending. You don't have to look at any sheets. Second, you can tell if they're going to be a contending team or if they're going to be an also-ran. Obviously, the more money you have, the deeper your team and deeper your bench can be. But look for those elite left-handed pinch-hitters. They're worth their weight in gold. The reason is that most top-of-the-line closers are right-handed.

How many top-of-the-line closers are right-handed? Take a look at the 2010 Chicago White Sox. Closer Bobby Jenks is right-handed; J.J. Putz, who was used when Jenks was unavailable, is right-handed; Sergio Santos, perhaps the Sox's closer of the future, is right-handed. Matt Thornton is one of the great left-handed setup men in all of baseball, and the Sox have been hesitant to move him from that role.

The Cubs have closer Carlos Marmol, who is right-handed. His primary set-up man has been Sean Marshall, a left-hander. But if you're facing a right-handed closer at the end and have that left-handed hitter sitting on the bench waiting for that right-handed closer to enter the game, that's the matchup you're waiting for.

When I played for the Orioles, we had two left-handed pinch-hitters. One was Jim Dwyer. The other was Terry Crowley, who could turn on anyone's fastball. When we would play the Yankees, Earl Weaver would sit there and would not put in Crowley until Goose Gossage came into the game to either win it or tie.

Now, look around at some of the other closers in 2010. The ultimate reliever, the ultimate closer—Mariano Rivera—is right-handed. San Diego closer Heath Bell is right-handed and dominant. Boston has the right-handed twosome of setup man Daniel Bard and closer Jonathan Papelbon. Texas has hard-throwing Neftali Feliz, Cincinnati has Francisco Cordero, and Milwaukee has rookie John Axford, who took over for Trevor Hoffman. All these pitchers are right-handed.

After Minnesota lost closer Joe Nathan in the spring of 2010, the Twins opted for Jon Rauch as their closer before acquiring Matt Capps from Washington. All three pitchers are right-handed, which brings up the essential aspect that every good team must have a quality veteran short-stroke-type left-handed pinch-hitter.

Occasionally, you'll find left-handed specialists that managers will use in various spots. But I'm talking about that reliever who starts the eighth. More times than not, that reliever is going to be a right-hander. You can bring in the situational left-hander, but he's not the primary setup man most of the time.

Every manager would love to field a lineup in which he can stagger the right-handers and left-handers, since he knows the matchups are that much tougher for the other manager late in the game. You can't just bring in a right-hander because you're scheduled to face four consecutive right-handed batters.

I always felt consistency in a manager was very important. You want to see a manager who doesn't get too high after some wins or too low after some losses. The oddity of Earl Weaver, a screamer in his own right, was that when we were struggling badly and the team was in a slump (which didn't happen too often in Baltimore in the late 1970s and early 1980s),

Weaver was at his quietest. He didn't have to tell us that we were playing poorly. He would start to go on rants after we had won four or five in a row, then threw in a terrible game and made some mental mistakes.

Confidence is essential for a manager, too. When I look at managers and the people they choose to have around them, it's similar to any business. If you're a secure leader, you're going to surround yourself with the best people available because they can only make you look better.

The insecure leaders are always going to surround themselves with more of the inferior people because they don't want to look worse. They want to look better than the people they're hiring, and you see that quite a lot. Take a look at the coaching staffs. It's difficult for the average fan to assess how good the various coaches are because the broadcasters and others who follow the team want to give the coaches the benefit of the doubt. It behooves the broadcasters to play up the coaches.

If you are a great manager, quite often you'll have very good players too. As an illustration of that, I use the philosophy of Sparky Anderson. Sparky was a genius with the Big Red Machine when he could write in the names of all those stars in the lineup. You had Rose, Morgan, Bench, Perez, Dan Driessen, Davey Concepcion, Cesar Geronimo. It was an outstanding team.

From Cincinnati, Sparky went to Detroit. Well, he didn't get dumb on the plane ride from Cincinnati to Detroit. He just didn't have the horses. He finished fifth that first year. Five years later, in 1984, when he did have the horses, he won the World Series. There were several star players, including Kirk Gibson, Jack Morris, Alan Trammell, and Lou Whitaker. Obviously, you're not going to win it without good pitching and defense, and the Tigers had all of that. That was the year the Tigers went 35–5 to start the season, and won it in a landslide. Again, you must have the horses.

Managers must also be organized on a daily basis and have a game plan. A game plan consists of, "What are we going to do today to try to get ourselves in position to win this game?" The good managers think about this from the time they go home from the park at night until the morning of the next game, considering different lineups in their heads and knowing exactly who they're going to face.

The ones who are observant have the advantage. For instance, if the other team has used its closer three consecutive days, there's a very good chance the manager is going to pitch around that closer. Consequently, instead of making a move in the eighth inning, a manager might wait until the ninth inning to make that move, knowing the opposing manager has to close with someone else.

Good managers keep track of just exactly who works before and who doesn't in the days preceding when that team comes to town. Some of the other managers might miss that. That's something that separates the men from the boys as far as management is concerned.

Another factor would be just exactly how they want to keep their bullpen fresh. That's critical because most of the very good managers will say that when it comes to the middle of August, it's the healthiest staff—not the best staff—that usually wins it.

With that in mind, they don't want to burn that staff out too early. When you start to get into the late 40s and early 50s in number of appearances, that's when some guys who were getting batters out earlier are going to have tired arms. That surfaces especially in the pennant race of August, as you move into September. It depends on just how many times you use these guys, under what situations you go to them, knowing when a pitcher needs an inning of work (regardless of what the score is) and knowing when he needs a day off. To do that, a lot of managers trust their pitching coaches to monitor times that the pitcher gets up to warm up even though he may not be used in the game.

Managers take into consideration how many times a reliever was asked to loosen up. Although he hasn't appeared in any games for a couple days, he might need the next day off because he might have warmed up three or four times in the past couple of games. He might have pitched the day before, warmed three or four times in the course of a couple of days, and then he needs a day off.

• • •

Many organizations spend a great deal of time developing their young players at positions in the batting order that they'll never see in the big leagues.

Some guys, like Aaron and Baylor, developed after they reached the major leagues, and that's all well and good. But for the most part, you see guys you know are going to grow into hitters and some who will be in the 3-4-5 spots in the major leagues, and other guys just aren't.

You can look at the smaller guys and say, "Maybe there's a chance." However, you have to teach these guys who hit 3-4-5 in the batting order in amateur baseball or in the minor leagues how to play a small man's game. In the majors, they aren't likely to be hitting 3-4-5, and they have to be able to adjust. There are also some taller guys who must play a small man's game because they don't have that power. They don't have the ability to do that, but they run particularly well.

The No. 3 hitters in the major leagues are the guys who can really hit. First, they should be the best hitter on your team. When you look at Philadelphia, you see Chase Utley. When you look at the New York Yankees when they're entirely healthy, which is a tough thing to do, you might see Mark Teixeira with Alex Rodriguez in back of him. These are guys who you can just tell are going to be a No. 3 hitter.

When I see fast guys, see guys who have no chance of hitting 3-4-5, I think many organizations start to develop them and forget about how to play the small man's game. This guy was developed to hit in the middle of the lineup, and now he's hitting in the American League either 1, 2, 8, or 9; in the National League, he's hitting either 1, 2, or 8. It's going to be a difficult adjustment.

First, you must teach these guys plate discipline. That's harder to do with some than others. Second, you must teach them how to bunt. You must teach them the techniques of stealing bases. You must talk about when to steal and when not to. You have to talk to them about hitting behind base runners. You must talk to them about hitting behind in the count, because if a player is going to be a No. 2 hitter, that's what he must learn how to do, especially if that guy is a base stealer.

Developing guys in spots other than where they're going to be used in the major leagues is not wise. I don't mind flexibility. I don't mind guys who can hit in various parts in the order. But realistically, you know there are certain players who are never going to have the run-production capabilities that you need in spots 3-4-5. When you see that, you have to prepare them for small ball.

If you draft a guy who you believe is going to be a No. 1 or No. 2 hitter and he grows into a middle-of-the-order hitter, that's terrific. You can always put him there.

As a guy develops his power, it really doesn't matter if he develops his power as a No. 1 hitter or as a No. 2 hitter or No. 6 or No. 4 hitter. For instance, Grady Sizemore was always thought of as a leadoff hitter. But as soon as he got better, he started hitting the ball out of the ballpark. Now Sizemore stays mostly in the No. 2 spot.

But no matter who you have, you must spend a lot of time understanding where that player is going to wind up and how best to develop him.

• • •

Some managers absolutely love to bunt. When Don Baylor managed the Colorado Rockies and the Chicago Cubs, he perennially would lead the league in sacrifice bunts, which was kind of strange because Don was a ter- rific hitting coach and a wonderful hitter. Yet, for whatever reason, he felt that the sacrifice was the key.

On the other side of the coin, you have Earl Weaver, who absolutely hated to give away an out. It was something he couldn't stand doing. He would wait for somebody to hit the ball, and maybe use the occasional hit- and-run. That depends on your personnel, understanding you don't need a lot of speed in a base runner to use the hit-and-run. Usually, if you have a great deal of speed and you don't choose to steal, you're trying to use that hit-and-run, or run-and-hit as some people call it, to stay out of the double play. That happens quite a bit.

Some of the better managers in the league are not so well known. That includes Bruce Bochy, who was with the San Diego Padres for a long time. He's currently with the San Francisco Giants, with whom he won the 2010 World Series. Bruce doesn't get the acclaim that some managers do, but I always found him to be solid. He has a good understanding of the game and is another ex-catcher who has taken over the managerial reins and managed for a long time. He's done this without a great deal of national recognition, but to the people in baseball who have watched him manage a game, use his pitching staff, manipulate his bullpen, and get players in and out of the game, Bruce is one of the better ones.

Joe Maddon is a young manager even though he's not a young man. He's done a terrific job in Tampa Bay with some young, talented players, and he has taken that team to the World Series.

There's an older manager who just keeps winning but doesn't get a lot of credit. Maybe it's his personality and the fact that there are several people who listen to that Southern drawl. They wonder what it is that makes Charlie Manuel tick.

Yet, he's done a great job with the Philadelphia Phillies. Charlie knows how to run a baseball game, and he knows how to get the most out of his players.

One of the things that's an art for a manager is knowing when a player who is in a slump needs to be out there on a daily basis so he can work his way out of it. Conversely, a manager must know when it's time to sit him down and maybe take a day or two off or maybe not use him on a certain day involving a matchup that is not favorable to him. That works better with younger players than older players, but there is still the art of knowing how to get guys in and out of the lineup, when they do need some time to reflect and work with the hitting coach, getting extra batting practice and going over certain situations and trying to make a little adjustment in the swing, for example.

Gordon Beckham is a prime example of how to use this tactic to great advantage. When Gordon first came to the White Sox in June 2009, he drilled the ball to right-center field. That was his strong point, and he did it very well. He burst onto the scene and certainly was a candidate for the AL Rookie of the Year. He wound up not winning the award, but he was successful hitting to the opposite field.

The following year, the advance scouts made an adjustment. Opponents started throwing Gordon face-high fastballs and inviting him to try to go that way. It's very difficult on a face-high fastball to drive the ball the other way. There are very few who can do that. A recent Hall of Fame inductee, Andre Dawson, could take a face-high fastball, get on top of it, and hit line-drive rockets, some out of the park. Most normal people can't do that, so when the league adjusted to Gordon and he started swinging at all those high pitches, he really went into a severe slump.

When he stopped swinging at high pitches, they switched to throwing breaking balls, low and away. In the case of left-handers, they threw breaking balls low and in and out of the strike zone. Then Gordon started to swing at those.

Gordon was a good enough athlete and a good enough player to be able to come out the other side. As of this writing, Gordon is starting to hit the baseball like he can. He's still a very young player who had a limited run in the minor leagues, and I see him eventually becoming an excellent major league player. Although he's batting ninth, I believe he will become a run producer in the major leagues, and the way he has been managed has a lot to do with that.

• • •

Managers have different backgrounds as well as different styles. I remember when Tony La Russa first came to the majors as a coach with the Chicago White Sox. He wasn't a particularly good player. In fact, that's very common among very good managers. I think one of the reasons why mediocre, adequate players and sometimes good players make better managers than great players is that they must be more observant to reach the majors and stay there. Just look at the all-time great players and those in the Hall of Fame. They very rarely made great managers when they even attempted to manage. The reason is that one of the many things they did was seemingly routine for them. They were the typical multitooled players—whether it was hitting, pitching, or defensive work that went into being the great players.

Those physical gifts are hard to impart to people who lack those great skills. This is also why many of the great pitchers don't make particularly great pitching coaches. For example, the best pitching coach I ever had was Ray Miller, when I pitched for Baltimore, and he didn't have a sterling major league career.

Whitey Herzog was a great manager, one of the greatest evaluators of talent, who was inducted into the Hall of Fame in 2010. As a talent evaluator when he was a general manager, there were very few who were his equal. But I don't think anyone would tell you that Whitey belongs in the pantheon of great players.

Another example is Rudy Jaramillo. For 15 years Rudy has been acclaimed as one of the finest hitting coaches in the game. Take a look back over Rudy's career and see where he learned to do it.

Jeff Pentland worked for years with Sammy Sosa as his hitting coach. I'm not going to get into enhancement aspects that have been rumored for a long time; I'm just talking about the physical aspect of hitting. Pentland was able to take Sosa and make him into a .300 hitter. Before Pentland started working with Sosa, Pentland had worked with Barry Bonds at Arizona State. Bonds said that Pentland was the best he had ever worked with.

For a long time Sosa couldn't hit a high fastball. He struggled against Dave Burba, a high-fastball pitcher who held him to a .128 batting average (5-for-39 with 16 strikeouts). But Pentland began to work with Sosa, and Sosa began to kill high fastballs. It was just a technical adjustment that Pentland knew how to get across to Sammy, and it worked wonders for him. But when you look at Jeff Pentland's career, there's not too much to write home about.

Many of the great pitching coaches were catchers; many pitching coaches were just adequate pitchers. Mike Maddux, in this day and age, comes to mind as a very good pitching coach. He did wonders for the Milwaukee Brewers before being lured away by the Texas Rangers, and now he's making that Rangers staff a whole lot better than what it was. He was a guy who pitched in the majors but was known more as Greg Maddux's older brother than as a great pitcher himself.

The same holds true for managers. One of the exceptions is Mike Scioscia, who had a solid major league career. He was one of the better players who turned into a top-of-the-line manager. But you also look at Jim Leyland, who has experienced a successful career at Pittsburgh, Florida, and Detroit. As far as a major league player, Leyland was a perennial minor league player.

Another who fits in that category is Joe Maddon, who has led Tampa Bay to the playoffs in two of the past three seasons but didn't possess great playing credentials.

Ozzie Guillen has done a terrific job. He has a 2005 World Series championship under his belt. Ozzie wasn't a Hall of Fame–quality player, but he was a good player. Ron Gardenhire was a decent player who turned into a great manager with Minnesota. Joe Girardi had a lengthy career and has become a very good manager with the New York Yankees. Terry Francona was a pretty decent hitter, but not a star by any means. Nevertheless, Terry manages very well.

Gene Mauch was always considered one of the greatest managers around despite the fact he never went to the World Series, and he managed a game very well.

Joe Torre presents an interesting case. He paid his dues at a lot of places, managing the first three teams he played for—the St. Louis Cardinals, the Atlanta Braves, and the New York Mets. The irony was that he managed the three teams he played for with limited success, before he managed four World Series championships with the New York Yankees, then the Dodgers for three years, including two division titles.

I remember Joe saying something to me one day as he was running by me in the outfield, and I think it's very poignant. I was playing for the Cubs and Joe was playing for the Mets, who were managed by Joe Frazier at the time. The platoon system was becoming more of a factor, and Joe wasn't going to be playing that day. Joe had led the National League in hitting in 1971 with a .363 average and was a very strong hitter. (In fact, back when Joe was with St. Louis and I was with the Giants, I actually hit him once. But the next time I was up, Bob Gibson threw one *behind* my head. That pitch left an indelible impression that has lasted to this day.) He had made the conversion from catcher to third baseman to first baseman fairly well. But it was toward the end of his career at that point, and he was always thought of as a middle-of-the-road guy.

Joe came running by and said to me, "Can you believe I'm not playing today? That guy [Joe Frazier] has decided I can't hit right-handers. I have more than 2,300 hits. You think some of them were against right-handers?"

I said, "I know you're pretty tough on me, Joe."

He said, "This is getting ridiculous. I can't play against right-handers. Right-handed hitters can always hit right-handed pitchers. We see them 80 to 85 percent of the time."

He was right about that, and it really showed me the downside to the platoon system. Unfortunately, in a straight platoon system used by most managers, it's the right-handed hitter who really takes the short straw, since most of the pitchers are right-handed. That means the left-handed counterpart in a platoon system will get somewhere between 70 and 75 percent of the at-bats.

If the veteran is a left-handed hitter, and the young kid or rookie is right-handed, it could cause some problems. The reason is the veteran hitter batting left-handed is going to get 70 to 75 percent of the at-bats. The right-hander, if he's a rookie, will get only 30 and sometimes 25 percent of the at-bats. That will stunt the rookie's development. You would be much better off with the veteran right-handed hitter and the rookie left-handed hitter because the left-handed rookie would get most of the at-bats, which is how he's going to hone his skills.

After Joe managed his first two teams with the Mets and Atlanta, he got a chance to broadcast games for the Angels, who were the California Angels at that time. He came back to manage St. Louis and later the New York Yankees, where he had a tremendous amount of talent. Joe's genius always was dealing with owner George Steinbrenner and the press in New York. He was a master at that, as well as handling egos. One of the major factors for any manager is the ability to deal with the egos of major league players. Joe could do it very well. As far as the Xs and Os and inner workings, I'm not sure Joe is going to be considered with the all-time greats.

Many of the great managers don't exactly fall into that category of managing the game particularly well. What they do is manage the egos and personalities. They understand what it takes to get the best out of their 25 guys, whom to give a kick in the butt, whom to put their arm around, who needs a little special treatment because he's a tender-psyche guy. It's also about knowing which guys you can leave alone when they're doing well, which guys you have to leave alone when they're doing poorly, and knowing the difference between those certain players.

You can leave enough up to your coaches. But if a manager calls a player in to have a talk when that player isn't doing so well, then he must have a game plan, a good feeling about that guy as a person and know some off-the-field activities, such as family problems or any of the things that players deal with on a day-to-day basis. Managers must know a lot about their guys and how to deal with them and get the most out of them.

But for Joe, after five and a half seasons in the booth with the Angels, he said he had a different view when he went into the dugout to manage again. The announcing experience gave him a much different perspective by observing from a high view when watching the players.

It is a unique perspective when you're in the booth. You take a look at the players and you can see the angles that various outfielders get on a ball. You can see how quick the break is that they get. You can see it much better from the booth than you can from any dugout. In fact, the dugout might be the worst seat you can actually have.

Billy Martin is another player-turned-manager who got a lot more attention as manager. I remember him very well. He had an up-and-down playing career, but he was a great manager. The Yankees kept bringing him in and taking him out. Owner George Steinbrenner was behind that, but Billy was a terrific manager. He would come in and turn your whole program around. Throughout his career, wherever he went, that's exactly what happened.

However, Billy was often a destroyer of pitching staffs. I remember when he was manager of the Oakland Athletics in 1980, they threw 94 complete games. That was the year that Mike Norris finished second to me in the American League Cy Young Award voting. But most of those pitchers—Brian Kingman, Norris, Rick Langford, Steve McCatty, and Matt Keough—didn't go on to have much of any kind of career after that. Some guys had decent years, but they weren't long. The reason is four out of five of those pitchers that year—and this is an amazing number—under Billy Martin threw 14 innings in at least one game. The exception was Brian Kingman, who, nevertheless, threw 211⅓ innings despite losing 20 games.

163

I can understand maybe not paying attention to some pitch counts, but Billy knew the bullpen wasn't all that good and his starting rotation was, so he managed around that. Nevertheless, Billy went far and beyond what he should have done.

Billy was the ultimate quick-fix guy as a manager. You brought him in, and he got you to respectability. In many instances, he brought you a winner. But when he left, your organization was in a shambles, and you had to rebuild it with someone else.

When Tony La Russa came to the White Sox as a coach, he was very smart and very observant. That's one of the things I look for when I watch managers. I watch whether they're watching a game or observing a game. That's two different things. You can watch a game and take it all in, and you can certainly see what's happening. But when you're observing certain aspects of the game, whether you're a coach or a manager, you have to pay particular attention to it.

I did this as a player, primarily because I wasn't all that good for most of my career. I was pretty decent some of my career. I was exceptional for a short period of time. But overall, I wasn't given the great skills, especially after I hurt my arm in my second year. But I would sit there and observe the game, observe various pitchers and various players and what they did, how they hit, and observe guys I was going to face and what they did to make an adjustment.

Managers do the same thing. I noticed that Tony La Russa seems to observe things more closely than most. I once asked him about some of his managerial philosophies, but even before he managed in the major leagues he was very guarded about his secrets regarding the way he was going to manage. I do remember that I thought this was strange for a coach, and I had a feeling he'd be a good major league manager.

I remember finally pestering him enough until he said to me, "Okay, I'm going to tell you one thing, but this is the only thing I'm going to tell you, and it's what I'm going to use. I don't want to tell you too much about what I'm going to use because maybe you'll be involved in a team that's going to play against me."

So even then, at that early stage, Tony La Russa was thinking way ahead about any way I could have a little bit of an edge against him in some capacity.

Which I thought was very Tony, but very unusual.

But he did tell me that he will get every one of his teams prepared to play the seventh, eighth, and ninth innings, because the seventh, eighth, and ninth innings in any game are special. He's going to do whatever he can to get to a situation where he is in the game in the seventh, eighth, or ninth inning and prepare his team for that particular aspect of the game. He was focused on reaching that final third of the game.

There are some good managers who will break the game down into thirds. The first three innings you handle things a certain way; for example, you might be a little more adventuresome on the base paths because you have a long way to go. Some managers will take it down to 27 outs. So you go nine outs for the first three innings, nine outs for the second three innings, and nine outs for the final three innings. Those outs get more precious as you move along. But there are many managers who will gamble, and they'll gamble early.

As a former pitcher, one of the things that I really liked—especially when I had Rick Dempsey behind the plate in Baltimore—was that if I walked the first guy or gave up a hit, I didn't mind him running even if he was a good base stealer. I felt Dempsey could throw him out. Plus, the less time I spent in the stretch, especially in the first inning, the better I liked it because I started in the windup like most pitchers. That first inning and sometimes the second inning were the most uncomfortable for me.

The good managers that I've seen love to see that pitcher go into the stretch early. One of the reasons is you never really know with any given pitcher just exactly what percentage of warm-up throws from the mound before the game he's going to take from a stretch as opposed to a windup.

The better pitchers understand this. Let's break this down with runners per game. If a team is batting .250 against you, that's nine hits, 27 outs, 36 batters faced. That means one-quarter of the time you're giving up a hit.

Obviously, some pitchers give up a few more hits than innings pitched. Let's say that you give up 10 hits per nine innings pitched, and you average four walks per nine innings. That means in a nine-inning game, you're going to have 14 base runners. Then assume there's going to be an error, depending on how good your team is. So that's going to be 15 base runners on 10 hits, four walks, and one error in nine innings.

Depending on how many 1-2-3 innings you have, you'll be throwing overwhelmingly more pitches from the stretch. The average pitcher will throw more pitches from the stretch than the windup. Yet most pitchers will throw many more pitches from the windup than the stretch during their warm-ups.

That's another reason why you'll see a pitcher sailing along. He'll throw three or four perfect innings. The first time you put a man on, you put him in the stretch. All of a sudden, he walks the next guy or gives up a hit and gives up a couple runs in that inning because it's the first time he's moved into a stretch position.

The average pitcher will deliver the baseball to the catcher from a stretch position in 1.3 seconds. The major league average for a catcher catching the ball and throwing to second base—what they call "leather-to-leather"—is two seconds.

From the time the pitcher settles to a set position in his stretch, to the time he throws home, to the time the ball is thrown to the shortstop or second baseman, the major league average is 3.3 seconds. If you have a pretty decent base runner, and the time is below 3.3 seconds, it's going to be tough with a good throw to steal second base. If it's over 3.3 seconds, the average base stealer probably is going to be safe at second—even with a good throw.

Then you factor in throws that aren't particularly good, and you can run on this guy. So pitchers will vary their times with a slide step and other various ways, such as holding a baseball. That's why a good manager wants to see that pitcher in the stretch as much as possible. Of course, it has to play into the character of the team, whether he uses straight steals or hit-and-runs.

• • •

You must know the tendencies of each manager before you go into a game against him. There are certain managers who truly love to use the suicide squeeze. Many times it depends on the personnel. It takes a lot of great coordination because when you have a right-handed pitcher on the mound, the timing has to be perfect. You don't want that man at third base to leave too soon, because with a left-handed bunter up, it's very easy to throw a pitch over the right-handed batter's box. With a right-handed hitter up, it's very easy to throw a pitch right at his head and back him out of there, if the pitcher can pick up that the runner from third is going.

David Eckstein is one of the best at the suicide squeeze because you know he's going to get the bat on the ball more times than not and be successful doing it. Tony La Russa is one of the managers who really likes the suicide squeeze.

Other managers love to use the hit-and-run. That tendency comes from advance scouting. They like to use a hit-and-run play on certain counts with certain players. Managers will use hit-and-runs not only with faster players, because many times with a very good base stealer, you're doing yourself a disservice if you use the hit-and-run. But if you have a proficient base stealer, it doesn't make a great deal of sense to use the hit-and-run with him. It would much more preferable to have him steal second, then use a bunt or hit behind the runner to get him to third.

Many times managers will use a hit-and-run play with a slower base runner because people aren't thinking about it with a very slow guy on base. But it really depends on the personnel you have and the ability of a batter to make contact.

Some of the best hit-and-run men have an inside-out stroke, meaning they can take a fastball inside if they're a right-handed hitter, and they can hit it through that hole on the right side. That is the biggest hole on the infield when you have a first baseman holding the runner close and a second baseman that perhaps might be covering on the play.

When watching a manager closely, you can pick up his tendencies. Because everything is quantified today, it makes it a little easier to defend against those certain situations. It makes all the difference. As I said before, games are won or lost 90 feet at a time, whether you take that 90 feet or give up that 90 feet. That's what wins close games more times than not.

Many times, the good managers hold down or are able to expand their repertoire because of the ability of the personnel they have. That's why there is no substitute for talent, but you don't have to have great talent. You don't have to be a great player to be a great executor of the hit-and-run or the suicide squeeze. That's why guys like Derek Jeter, Placido Polanco, and David Eckstein stand out.

All Eckstein does is help you win. The opposing pitcher constantly has Eckstein on his mind with a runner at third because Eckstein can execute the suicide squeeze exceptionally well.

The main thing a manager needs to understand is the strengths and weaknesses of all 25 guys and try not to put guys in a position where their chances of success are very slim. Earl Weaver was probably as good as any manager around at understanding what his players could and couldn't do. Very rarely, if ever, did he put players in a position where they couldn't succeed.

For example, if you have a guy who can't catch up to a very good fastball, then you can't bat him against Justin Verlander. You really shouldn't bat him against Stephen Strasburg. These guys throw fastballs in the upper 90s or even into triple digits. You're asking a guy to do something he can't do, and you can't put him in a lineup hoping that one time that pitcher is going to miss the pitch. Instead, you try to find your better fastball hitters and maybe play them against those guys. That helps out a great deal. It helps you be more successful, and good managers seem to know that innately.

When you look around the league, often you'll find there is a great deal of recycling in baseball. You'll see managers who get a job because they've been managers before. You'll find someone who gets a general manager's job just because he has been a GM before. Very few people who I've found in this game have any desire to think outside of the box. This is a generalization, but for the most part this game is so conservative that it's almost reactionary. What's been done before, it seems to be repeated and done again and again and again. And when one team is successful because they're doing something a little different, then other teams copy it.

I've tried to buy three different baseball teams, had a few different ideas as far as how to finance the purchase, and have worked with a number of alternative groups. In going through this process, one day I was talking to an executive of a baseball team who shall remain nameless for several reasons. I can tell you that this executive worked for an also-ran team that had not even won a division title since the playoff format was expanded in 1995. This executive told me that if a particular idea was any good, it would have been used already. He added that any perceived new idea already would have been done by someone else, so that idea can't be any good.

My question to him was, "So what you're saying, basically, is that there are no new ideas in the world? No one in baseball is willing to take on something that hasn't been done before because there are no ideas in baseball that haven't been done before?" It's a circular argument but that is essentially what this executive was telling me: "If this idea, which has never been done before, was any good, it would have been done."

Well, that's kind of the attitude that a lot of baseball people take. They are completely unwilling to think out of the box until their backs are absolutely stapled to the wall with failures of one sort or another, and then they might have an idea. "Hey, we haven't tried this before. Why don't we try this?" But until that point, it's very difficult to convince anyone to try something new.

• • •

There are many classic stories from the Earl Weaver–Jim Palmer interactions throughout the years when Earl managed and Jim pitched for Baltimore. One of the classic encounters took place during a trip to the mound, which Weaver would occasionally make when he wanted to say something and didn't want to convey it through the pitching coach. Palmer was often annoyed to see Earl out there.

On one of these trips to the mound, Weaver arrived only to hear Palmer say, "Hey, Earl, look. Go back to the bench. Because the only thing you know about pitching is that you couldn't hit it. So what are you going to tell me?"

Of course, Weaver sputtered, turned around, and walked back to the bench. That was about all the advice he could give Mr. Palmer about the art of pitching, which he knew exceptionally well.

I remember Jim Frey, then the general manager of the Chicago Cubs, decided one off-season he was going to get rid of Lloyd McClendon and Gary Varsho, two quality bench players.

The Cubs, at that point, were between winning. They had won in 1989, but they were destined not to get to the playoffs until 1998.

Jim Leyland recognized the value of these guys. Varsho could run-and-hit well, even though he couldn't field or throw particularly well. But he was a very valuable left-handed pinch-hitter on occasion who could spell one of your outfielders, and he was a good man to have on your bench.

McClendon was one of those rare players who could catch and play a number of different positions. He could bring four or five gloves to the park every day and use any one of them equally well. He was another guy who didn't complain at all. Varsho and McClendon could have been frustrated by not playing every day. But they realistically accepted the fact they were bench players.

I remember that Varsho was one of Leyland's favorites. But I remember that every time the Pittsburgh general manager came down to the field, Leyland would walk over to Varsho and say, "Hey, look. Don't go out on the field. You've got to hide someplace, because if the GM sees you, he's going to remember you're on the team, and then he's going to release you. So make sure he doesn't see you."

I remember Varsho being a very valuable member of the division-winning Pittsburgh Pirates who could not quite get it done and get to the World Series under Leyland. Of course, that team was absolutely loaded, with Barry Bonds, Bobby Bonilla, and Andy Van Slyke in the outfield. You had a very strong Pittsburgh team who unfortunately found a way not to get to the World Series three consecutive times under Jim. But Jim was later to get his world championship with Florida and be acclaimed as one of the better managers around.

General managers must be very careful when choosing managers, depending on the size of the media market and the media scrutiny that a manager will be under. You could have a certain type of manager who could manage quite well in places like Pittsburgh, Kansas City, Arizona, Milwaukee, or even Cincinnati. But that same manager might find a lot of frustration if he's in a bigger market, and many times it becomes very difficult and he has a hard time handling it. If you're going to manage in Philadelphia, New York, Boston, or Chicago and can't understand exactly how to deal with the media—which is a big part of managing today—then you have a problem. And that problem is not going to evaporate, because those media markets aren't going to change.

The press is intrusive. They fight for stories. They ask questions you might not want to answer. You're conducting pre- and postgame interviews. You're having tremendous demands on your time to do a number of things as they pertain to the club. They certainly want to understand the personal aspect of what you're doing. Every decision is dissected. Every move is viewed from 15 different angles under a microscope, and this goes on from the start of spring training to the end of whatever postseason run you might have when you're in some of those bigger markets.

We talked about Joe Torre and the art of handling owner George Steinbrenner when he was there, but Joe also handled the New York media. Joe Girardi has done a good job of this as well. Also, when you have a player from the Pacific Rim—especially if he's a very good player—you will have an increase in media scrutiny because you have the Asian media following their star players around in addition to the U.S. media.

In New York, you had Hideki Matsui. In Seattle, which is a fairly small-market team, you have Ichiro. In Boston, you have Daisuke Matsuzaka and Hideki Okajima. Manager Terry Francona, who has a couple of world championships with Boston, has a large press contingent from the Pacific Rim to go along with the stress and strain of the local media.

Terry might be as underrated as any manager in the game, maybe because of his personality and just because of the guy he is. But he's done a great job handling all the pressures that come to bear in Boston. Which are many. That's a tough place to manage.

Chicago can be very tough. I remember Dusty Baker and even Lou Piniella, who managed in New York, getting frustrated with the media with some of the questions being asked. Lou viewed some of the inquiries as not being the smartest questions around or too intrusive, and he sometimes challenged the reporters by saying, "What kind of team do you want this to be? What would you do?" and that sort of thing.

Of course, that's not the objective of the reporters. They don't know what they would do. They want to know why you did what you did. The manager must understand the reporters are just doing their jobs. Sometimes, especially when you're losing, it becomes more frustrating than at other times. You must deal with that if you're going to manage. Even in Los Angeles, which is a little more laid-back than most, it's still a big city with big-city media.

If you're going to rate them, probably the toughest of all is New York, with Boston and Philadelphia running 2 and 2A. Chicago is right behind as far as scrutiny is concerned. Then I would rate Los Angeles behind them with the size of the market. Those are probably the toughest places to manage because of all the other things you have to do away from the actual playing of the game.

As GM, you must take these things into consideration when you're making a decision as to who is going to manage your team. It becomes very difficult, and the people who manage at these places understand all too well once they start. They must know how to do this on a daily basis. You have a press conference before the game. You have some media people coming into your office. This is something you never can really get away from. It's very difficult to have a lot of time to yourself, especially when you come to the ballpark. That's why most managers get there very early—to get their work done before the media can come in and consume all their time.

After you lose, things are even more dissected. Also, you have to worry about injury problems and talking about what you might or might not do. It could very well be that you haven't discussed it with the general manager yet. Or, as a manager, you don't have much power at that point and don't have much authority to say who is going to come up to fill a void. You haven't received medical reports, which the trainers review with the managers and general managers on a daily basis. So there are a number of things you must go through to get yourself prepared to put certain people in certain places to be successful. At times, explaining this to the media becomes very difficult.

Peter Gammons, a member of the Hall of Fame, is a sportswriter who is very good at what he does. He was one of the pioneers as far as a print reporter moving to the electronic media. You have some great reporters in Tim Kurkjian, Jayson Stark, Buster Olney, and Tom Verducci. You also have some other excellent reporters that must get their information, too. And who is the best guy to get it from? The manager.

As a manager, if you participate with the reporters, they can make you look a little better. If you don't participate or try to lead them astray too often, then consequently, if they get a shot, they're likely not going to make you look as good. I think most major league GMs understand that they have to participate with the reporters and give them as straight a story as they possibly can. But when you are a major league manager or a major league general manager, sometimes you really can't tell them the truth because that's not something you're prepared to do. There are certain things that you have to hold inside. Even at times when you'd like to be truthful, you'd like to tell certain guys this is why a player is doing what he's doing, realistically you can't. With injuries, this is complicated by the HIPAA (Health Insurance Portability and Accountability Act) laws, which prohibit certain officials from speaking publicly about specific injuries. You must be very careful about what you choose to put into the public domain.

As a media personality myself, I've always respected the managers, and I try to see every one of them in their office, before the games to get what I can from them. From a broadcast standpoint, I want to bring to my listeners something they can't get out of the newspapers, something they can't get out of the media guide, or something that they haven't seen on television.

One way to do that is to talk to the opposing manager, whether it is Ron Gardenhire or Joe Girardi or Joe Maddon or Terry Francona, if they'll give me 15 minutes in their office. Mike Scioscia is terrific at accommodating me. He's one of the guys who really understands the media and my job. I certainly respect the jobs they do. I appreciate the ones who respect the job I do, and I will go in and talk with them.

Some are more guarded than others. Some will give you a more Pollyanna approach with what's going on with their team, and other guys are more straightforward. I truly respect the on-the-record, off-the-record policy. That is one of the things I have built over the course of my three decades as a sports broadcaster: the trust that I have with just about every manager in the game. When people tell me something is off the record, they will never see it coming from me in the public domain. They know I'll protect them. If they tell me it's on the record, well, then I'll use it.

Although some people feel there is no such thing as on and off the record, I'm not one of those guys. I truly believe that when a manager is giving you something on background to help you understand a little bit more, you're not going to burn that guy. Also, you're going to give him the benefit of the doubt. All we ask for—and I'll use "we" as being a representative of the media—is not to be misled. I don't mind when I guy tells me, "I can't tell you that."

I do mind when a guy tells me something that isn't true. When a guy does that and has a habit of doing that, you lose a great deal of respect for him, and you will not give him the benefit of the doubt. There are many ways to call a baseball game, and there are many ways to look at all the decisions that are made during the course of a game. It's just human nature. If the guys are good to you and participate with you and help you do your job, you're going to give them the benefit of the doubt.

As far as evaluating the very good managers, there are some guys who I think are terrific who I don't particularly care for and never have. There are others guys who I think are just adequate, but who are good to me so I might have a tendency to rate them a little higher. But when I go down and tell you the guys I truly respect, the better young managers, the better old managers, the guys who have a chance to be a whole lot better who are going to mature and get better at what they do—that is personality aside. I'm going strictly by ability. The same thing is true with players.

When I'm evaluating players, I might not particularly care for a guy, but I'm going to evaluate him to the best of my ability. Obviously, you're right sometimes. You're wrong sometimes, like everyone else. But you have to be very careful in what you do if you're evaluating. You can't let personality color your evaluation, depending on what position you're in. If you're assembling a baseball team, you want to make sure this guy fits in with the plan you're trying to establish, and all managers have visions for the team they want to assemble.

CHA**P**TER **9**

The Front Office

You could write an entire book on organizational charts, detailing what responsibilities each person has within the organization. I'll just take a cursory look to show you how a major league team is constructed, what the organizational charts look like, who is in charge of what areas, and how things work in getting your favorite team's players on the field on a yearly basis. At times it can be very complex, but I'll try to make it as easy as possible.

Let's start person who is customarily the No. 1 guy—the general manager.

The GM is at the top of an organizational flow chart for the baseball department. There's also a business department, which employs people who work very hard to market the team and develop revenues inside and outside the walls. The business department usually has a distinct group of people who work exclusively for that department.

Many years ago, the GM occasionally had the tag of president/general manager. But as the game has grown, as revenues have increased, and as the challenges of the business of baseball has become more difficult, we find that they have split the responsibilities of the business and baseball sides.

On the baseball side, we'll examine the GM and who reports directly to him. The assistant GM reports directly to the GM. Some organizations have an executive vice president of baseball operations that sits above the GM, and the GM reports to the executive vice president of baseball operations before he reports to the owner.

In some organizations, they find this desirable, but most want the GM to report directly to the owner to explain to him why they're making specific moves. The assistant GM also deals with plenty of information that comes from other departments and the field staff. A lot of assistant GMs are strong at negotiating, and they negotiate a lot of contracts.

Sometimes they don't negotiate the big free agent contracts—such as maybe a CC Sabathia or a Mark Teixeira—but many assistant GMs learn the skills of negotiating by dealing with the agents. That frees up the GM to make other decisions. So the assistant GM is very important.

The baseball department can be divided into various sections, such as player development, domestic scouting (including the scouting of high school, junior college and university players in preparation for the amateur draft), international scouting, and professional scouting.

Many teams have international scouts who handle the Pacific Rim, which is being scouted more these days and has resulted in the signing of players from South Korea, Taiwan, and Japan (which involves amateur and pro players).

Of course, there's also the Dominican Republic, where most teams have their own academies.

In professional scouting, you're looking at other teams and other organizations and finding out what they have so you can write reports and be well-prepared when you're ready to make a trade so you know who to ask for. You have advance scouts within the ranks of professional scouting that write the reports of the next opponent for the next series. They're very valuable, and the good ones are worth their weight in gold because they can tell you a player and manager's tendencies.

From an advanced scouting report, you will receive the rating of the arms of the outfield and tendencies of managers (when they like to run, the counts they like to run on, who will bunt on that team, who push bunts, who drag bunts, when they like to use the hit-and-run, and other tendencies). You document the various arm strengths of every infielder. The good advance scouts will tell you which outfielders throw the ball that travels straight, who makes a throw that tails into the infield, which of the outfielders you can challenge, which of the outfielders always hit the cutoff man, which outfielders sail the ball over the head of the cutoff man, and that's where you might want to gamble.

Also, those advance scouts can tell you who the hottest player is at any given time, because that changes throughout the year. You might catch a team when a star player is just swinging at everything and has lost his rhythm. The advance scout will inform you. The advance scout will check times and tell you how long it takes a pitcher to deliver the ball to home plate, as well as the time on the catcher throwing to second base, and that will tell you who you can run on and who you can't. The advance scout will tell you the pickoff move of each pitcher. It's a fairly entailed breakdown, and sometimes he'll follow a team for two series, depending on how often he's seen the team before. That all comes under the purview of professional scouting.

Some organizations have a director of player personnel who oversees those areas. It depends on how much money each organization wants to devote to that side of the operation, and how much talent they have in terms of the ability of their scouts. Terrific major league scouts are invaluable, but the lifeblood of an organization is still the amateur draft and the Rule 5 draft (taking players from other teams that are left unprotected). These are things that can make an organization look good or look very bad.

The GM, the assistant GM, the player development people, and other staffers are responsible for the execution of these duties. Obviously, there is no substitute for good scouting. Your scouting director comes under considerable scrutiny. I could tell you all of the wonderful scouting directors, but all you have to do is look at the talent that each organization brings to the major leagues. You can get a pretty good idea about the scouting director and how good a job they've done. Look at the Cubs. They have Tim Wilken as their scouting director. I hold him in a great deal of esteem because I think he's one of the best.

Some scouting directors advance to the GM position or another job in the organization. Others last longer as scouting directors. The White Sox's scouting director is Doug Laumann, who took over shortly after the 2007 draft. Although the organization is considered in the lower third as far as minor league talent is concerned, it seems to be getting better.

The Cubs, however, are probably a little above the middle, as Tim Wilken has tried to restock an organization that was almost devoid of talent for years. Wilken has done a tremendous job, and I think the White Sox are hoping that Doug Laumann will do similarly. Their international scouting director is Jerry Krause, whom you might be familiar with from his days with the Bulls. But very few of you will remember that Jerry was a baseball scout. The White Sox also have Dan Fabian, who, along with assistant GM Rick Hahn, runs the scouting element.

The Cubs' international scouts include Steve Wilson, who is terrific, and takes care of many players from Korea and Taiwan. Paul Weaver also handles similar duties in the Pacific Rim. If you can bring some players from there, it helps you round out your organization and adds depth.

Under your scouting director are national crosschecker scouts. Depending on the organizations and what they want to pay, you can have from two to four national crosscheckers. Their duties could be divided by region or type of player. Some crosscheckers are specialists in evaluating hitters. Some specialize in evaluating pitchers.

If your crosscheckers work by region, then you have a certain amount of territory. If you elect to employ crosscheckers who scout everywhere, you can have one for pitchers and one for hitters.

It depends on organizational preference. There is no right or wrong way. Simply ask if the manner in which you're developing players is creating a good, solid organization. If the answer is yes, then you have the right amount of crosscheckers.

Under the crosscheckers are supervisors who essentially carve out sections of the country. They will give their recommendations, and the crosscheckers can be sent out to take a look at guys recommended by those supervisors.

The area scouts are very important because of their connection to the crosscheckers and the scouting director. The area scouts are people who perform exactly what their title says. You might have at least two in states like California, Florida, and Texas. But most likely one guy can cover a state. It becomes a question of economics and if you're doing a good job of scouting, you don't need double coverage in those areas. But the country will be divided up. The responsibility will be divided into those areas. Your California scouts, for instance, would report to a West Coast supervisor. The area scouts on the other side of the country would report to an East Coast supervisor.

This funnels to the scouting director, who has to filter a tremendous amount of information. This is where computers come in handy. The reports are sent by area scouts from all regions and compiled by the scouting director.

Each area scout will have part-time scouts who are called "bird dogs." They might not scout all the time because they have other jobs. Bird dog scouts are invaluable, especially if they're able to lock in on certain baseball tournaments or high school games or junior college games.

I was first seen by a bird dog scout who signed only one player in his career. His recommendation from 17 years as being a bird dog scout for the San Francisco Giants was me. I was the one player who the Giants felt was worthy enough on a recommendation from Jerry Gaun, who has since passed. In 17 years, he was batting 1.000 and obviously not as productive as you would like because I was the only player he recommended. But I wound up making the major leagues, so that worked out well.

You must divide the international scouting duties. You have scouts in charge of the Dominican Republic, Venezuela and the Far East. They also compile and submit reports to the scouting director.

The scouting director has a difficult job that is all encompassing. They spend a lot of time assembling these reports and sifting through information that sometimes comes to fruition but sometimes doesn't.

You're not going to have one person that's in charge of Latin America and the Far East. You must have different contacts, and it's an all-encompassing situation. It helps if you have a few people in charge of the scouting and development of those players in Latin America where you have academies, as opposed to the Far East.

In the Far East, chances are that you will get players who are more advanced. Some organizations will choose not to spend large sums of money on the Japanese free agents because of the posting fees. For instance, the Boston Red Sox spent $53 million in posting fees just for the right to negotiate with pitcher Daisuke Matsuzaka. The posting fee allows major league teams in Japan to receive large amounts of financial compensation for losing the player. Of course, the major league team has to cut a deal with that player. Matsuzaka cost Boston about $105 million in the contract and posting fees.

Those organizations not willing to spend that kind of money on posting feels won't look at the Japanese major leagues with the same intensity as others. Those organizations will get videotapes and information from other resources. They just don't want to waste time and money sending a person over there to scout them individually. The same thing occasionally holds true for some of the organizations that do scout international players.

The New York Yankees got a tremendous player in Hideki Matsui. They got one of the best clutch players in baseball, and they got him out of Japan, just as the Cubs got Kosuke Fukudome.

Kosuke was reported to be a guy who was between both Matsuis— We call them "Big Matsui" and "Little Matsui." The little Matsui—Kazuo Matsui—being more of a punch hitter. Big Matsui turned into a great player. Little Matsui was just fair, and Kosuke Fukudome is somewhere in the middle. The one thing where the Cubs were led astray was they believed they needed a left-handed bat. So did the White Sox, who still are in search of difference-making left-handed bats. But Fukudome was never a run producer. He never has been, and probably never will be.

The Cubs gave Fukudome $48 million over four years. Don't get me wrong, Fukudome is a terrific right fielder. The White Sox wanted Fukudome and actually bid a little higher for him. But they wanted him as a leadoff hitter and center fielder. Kosuke doesn't play center field very well. He plays right very well. That's his natural position. But as a corner outfielder in the National League, you'd like a guy with a little more power. Kosuke is an on-base percentage guy who has a good arm and is a good fielder. But the Cubs overpaid, as happens so often.

When you're evaluating players like that, you have a tendency to overpay. That's especially the case with major leaguers from Japan or many times on guys that defect from Cuba. Some work out well.

Aroldis Chapman received $30 million from the Cincinnati Reds, and he has a chance to be very special. However, he still has to develop, and the jury is out on whether he will or not. For years, outside of Orlando "El Duque" Hernandez or his half-brother Livan Hernandez, those guys didn't work out very well. But there are other guys, like Rene Arocha, Ariel Prieto, Osvaldo Fernandez, who were adequate, at best. Yet they were paid premier dollars because they either pitched well in international baseball or did other things well to get them that big money.

Many times we value players from afar much more than we value players on our doorstep. Look at Korea, where the White Sox haven't done much. The cost is much lower when you bring players from Korea, but many Korean players, especially the better ones, will go to Japan. If that's the case, you won't be able to acquire them for a while because they must spend a significant length of time in the Japanese leagues because the Japanese team owns you and that you must pay a posting fee for the right to negotiate with the player.

The Korean players, of course, will usually choose to go to Japan because they can reach the majors more quickly, and there's bigger money for them. That's one of the reasons why the Koreans go to Japan instead of going to the minor leagues in the United States.

• • •

One of the developments in the past few years is advance scouting that is augmented by video work. Each team has a video department that is so comprehensive that you can literally break it down so you can see as many as your 100 at-bats against a certain pitcher. You can see exactly how that guy gets you out, and you can look at flaws.

Also, there are many pitchers who tip their pitches. Through the video department, scouring each tidbit and reviewing advance scouting reports, you can look for tips. You can look for base runners. We've talked about tells. You can see if a baserunner changes a pitcher. When you have extensive video departments, it does really help. It's one of the major advances of the last 10 to 15 years. You have more information and it's certainly just an outstanding way of getting another layer of coverage.

Combining these resources provides a tremendous asset for your team. There is a need for these people who break down the film and identify tendencies. They're just like scouts—some are good, some are bad. But all the information is available on video. There's a service called Dartfish that several teams use.

Manager Mike Scioscia of the Los Angeles Angels told me they get film of the final 15 pitches from every pitcher in their organization. They can tell from these final 15 pitches exactly what kind of stuff the pitcher has left by the time he's ending his performance. It doesn't matter when those last 15 pitches are. They can be the last 15 pitches from a reliever or the last 15 pitches from a starter. They take a look at the velocity, the movement on the pitches, break on the curve or slider, and determine if a guy has started to deteriorate, or if the velocity and late movement holds up through the final 15 pitches.

Dartfish is a wonderful tool in evaluating which pitchers might be destined to become full-time relievers or starters in the major leagues. If you find a guy who runs out of velocity or movement on a slider or curve, you know this guy is going to be a reliever for you. It doesn't matter if he's a right-hander or left-hander. Some teams try to determine this on their own, but Dartfish is an exceptional service.

Scioscia raised a strong point about limiting the innings of young pitchers. Some organizations will put 175-inning limits on their young pitchers, some even as low as 150 innings. It's personal preference, and it depends if you have a young pitcher out of high school or if you have a pitcher who played in college and is more developed, older and stronger.

There should be some caution if you shut down pitchers consistently at 185 innings, and you have a 100-to-105 pitch limit. If you reach the playoffs and have a pitcher who consistently tops out at 185 innings, you'll be challenged to get that pitcher to provide you with 230 innings.

Much of this depends on how in-depth your scouting may be, but many organizations make mistakes. Take a look at postseason pitching. There are guys that pitch well during the regular season, but they flame out and people say, "He can't pitch in big games."

Well, it's not really a question of that. They're just not prepared to go that extra 35 to 45 innings, depending on how far you advance in the postseason. They don't have the strength and endurance built over the course of that time. You must be very careful in your evaluation. You must know what pitchers can take you to the promised land and what guys can't, because the last 30 or 40 innings on any pitcher beyond what he usually reaches tend to make the pitcher more vulnerable. That's a big factor when evaluating your pitching staff.

• • •

There are different ways to scout the other 29 clubs. Two common methods are horizontal and vertical scouting. The White Sox subscribe to a horizontal scouting system in which scouts are assigned to specific leagues, such as the Southern League, the Florida State League, and the Eastern League. Scouts who have these assignments write their reports on each team in these leagues.

Vertical scouting means that scouts are in charge of a specific organization. If you are scouting the Florida Marlins organization, it means that you're responsible for every player in their organization. Consequently, there will be more traveling, because their minor league teams will be spread out. But it's a matter of personal preference for each organization.

If you decide you want to scout vertically, you'll break up the other 29 teams. Sometimes you'll chop it into six or seven scouts, and you might have four teams per scout, and one of the scouts will have five teams. That scout will write a report on every player in their system by going to every one of their minor league teams. You must see them more than once because players change over the course of a season.

There is an advantage to horizontal coverage. Because scouts are assigned to specific leagues or regional coverage, it's much easier as far as travel is concerned and more cost-effective. You have one guy traveling through one league instead of having four guys who have to scout the same league because they're scouting the different teams in that league. Some organizations will have six to 10 scouts, depending on their resources and how much they want to scout the minor leagues in a horizontal or vertical manner.

But there are advantages to the vertical system. For instance, if you want to make a trade with the Atlanta Braves, you get to talk to two to four scouts who cover the Braves on a daily basis. You have that organization completely broken down from top to bottom, and you have several scouts watching these players numerous times. They might have seen a player in up to 15 games and have a really good idea of what they can and can't do. You might have seen players over parts of two to four seasons and watched them develop.

If a scout is assigned to the Braves' organization, he might have seen a specific player since Rookie League and later at Low-A, High-A, Double-A, and Triple-A before making a trade. Obviously, you'd like to see him by the time you get to the Arizona Fall League, which ideally has six of the best players from every organization. Also, you want to see players from the Instructional League. That league usually starts in September, and you get a chance to see these guys at the very early stages of their career and get an idea of how they play and what they can do.

It just comes down to a matter of cost. Also, it's much more difficult on the scout when you do it vertically because he's got to travel to every one of these leagues. It depends on your scouts and your philosophy. Every organization has a different one. I'd say most organizations use the horizontal method, as opposed to the vertical, for the reasons of cost and efficiency.

It's also very important than an organization scouts their own scouts. I've always said it's imperative that when scouts write their reports, they take a stance on just how good a player is now, how good he's going to be, where you see his ceiling, and then you review these categories.

It takes a healthy amount of time, but it's of critical importance for an amateur scout or pro scout to understand their strengths and weaknesses. Some scouts are better at scouting hitters. Some are much better at scouting pitchers. There are some scouts who do a great job at the top part of the draft—where you find more developed players there. Some scouts are exceptional at identifying players in the middle rounds.

Then there are scouts who can find the diamonds in the rough, players who are overlooked because of certain deficiencies at the time of their selection that a scout truly believes can either be eradicated or, just through growth, will naturally be eliminated. Also, an organization may have the resources to fix a problem once the player is signed.

That could involve a player selected in the 25th round. He might not have been selected higher because he has a lack of power or arm strength. You look at his body frame and his delivery. You should know the size of his parents so you can project where his development might come.

Knowing baseball acumen is very important. Amateur scouts who identify this in a player are worth their weight in gold because they can get you low-round picks that you have to spend more time with, but those guys will eventually turn into gold.

I look at Mark Buehrle, who was drafted in the 38th round. I look at Mark Grace, who was drafted in the 24th round. Those guys went on to have great careers. Originally, I was drafted in the 16th round by the Indians, but wasn't signed. At that time, they had a winter draft in which I was selected in the fourth round. That sounds better than what it really was because they drafted only five players that winter. The winter draft has since evaporated.

So maybe the 16th round is where I belonged. But there was a certain competitive nature that you couldn't really tell unless you had scouted me. As far as scouting tools, I was a 5-foot-9¾ right-handed starting pitcher, which even at that time was not exactly valued as far as the major leagues are concerned.

It's valued even less now. Teams like their right-handers big. They'll take left-handers with any size. They obviously look for the fastball, and that's very important. They look for intangibles and how guys can dig a little bit better. They could find players that might not be a first-division All-Star player or a first-division regular player, such as from the Big Ten or Pacifc-10 Conference or other places that develop very good players. But these guys slide down for any number of reasons. You have to decide if a certain player is going to be a backup. Can he make the major leagues? What kind of player is he going to be?

But the scouting of the scouts is essential because you'll find which guys will consistently get those diamond in the rough-type players, and which guys can really help you. The traditional scouting system is on a 20-to-80 scale. So when you hear that a guy has a 60 arm, that's a pretty good arm. An 80 arm is the best arm you could possibly have. When you hear that a player has a 70 speed, that tells you that he's very fast. Obviously, 80 speed is saved for the fastest of the fast.

That doesn't really tell you if he's going to be a good base runner. Is he a good base runner? Does he understand good base running? All it tells you is his natural speed. Obviously, teaching speed is impossible. It's like teaching velocity. Once a pitcher grows into how big and strong he's going to be, velocity is something he either has or doesn't have. He can maybe tweak it by a couple miles an hour, but once he's fully developed, he either has it or you don't.

You can't scout all positions as if they're the same, because if you're scouting catchers, you're looking at arm strength—as well as delivery and footwork. We talked about it in the catching section, but I'm talking about it from a scouting standpoint. You're looking at different things than you would for a shortstop or a second baseman. You can take a shortstop, look at him and say, "OK, this guy has very good baseball aptitude," but then you'll put a tag on him and say, "He's not going to play a major league shortstop. His arm is not strong enough to consistently play that position."

Those are the players you envision maybe sliding over to play second base. Or if the guy is big and strong enough and has a strong bat, you can project him as a major league third baseman. But the report will state he's not going to be good enough to play shortstop. You rate the player based on your projection of him. There are certain players who believe they can play a specific position or project to be a certain hitter. But when it comes times to play in the major leagues, they're not going to be that player.

In recent vintage, Gordon Beckham was a top-of-the-line, quality college shortstop at Georgia. He hit 28 home runs, tied for the national lead in his junior year, and he helped lead his team to a College World Series appearance. But the White Sox had a hole at third base, and Gordon filled that vacancy when he was promoted to the majors in 2009.

Eventually, he became a very credible third baseman, only to shift to second base for the 2010 season. As the reports read now, can he play short? Yes, he can. But can he play major league shortstop as well as their current shortstop—Alexei Ramirez? He might not have the arm for it, and the second base position seems to be the one he'll settle in to.

Baseball is a projection business. From an organizational standpoint, the scouts who project players better are the scouts that you covet.

A good scout is a guy who will make suggestions as far as upgrades and development are concerned. He might even talk about how the organization can best unlock the potential that's within a player. If a guy is already performing at that level, can he actually get any better than that? Or, has he maximized his development? Those are some of the keys that a good scout will look for. If he has a technical flaw in one aspect of his game, a good scout will mention this in his report and say how he feels the player can overcome that. Or, if he feels they can't overcome that, then he will suggest this is a guy to stay away from.

That's how guys who seemingly appear to be drafted higher eventually slip, to the surprise of a number of people. That doesn't mean that somebody can't unlock that door. It just means that your particular set of scouts don't believe it's going to happen. So you pass on him and turn your attention to someone else.

Many organizations like to apply their scouting in five-game bursts. You watch a guy for five games, many times in the first part of the year. Sometimes you want to watch him for five games in the second half of the year. If this guy has a tremendous amount of potential, you might send one of your national crosscheckers who can take another look on a follow-up for another five games.

So you might see this guy 15 times, depending on where he's going to fall in the draft, and depending on just exactly what information you have with each guy, where you might want to pick them, and the reports that you have on this guy. This is very important if a player looks one way the first half, only to look completely different in the second half—especially if the latter half shows much more improvement. Or maybe the player fixes a few flaws. Maybe the player's high school or college coach is very good, and he's recognized this flaw and was able to fix it. You want to know that.

It's obviously tougher to get that much of a read on a pitcher than it is a position player because you can probably succeed if you want to see a position player up to 15 times. But as far as a relief pitcher is concerned, you might sit there for 15 games and see that reliever only a couple times, and you still have to write your report. You'll have to be better at evaluating because you won't be able to see this guy all that much.

Many organizations are copycat organizations in that if they find a system that works for another organization, they'll try to implement that system into theirs. The Minnesota Twins are probably the standard that most everyone uses, and former manager Tom Kelly is one of those guys who sits with each minor league manager during the course of the season and talks about exactly what they're doing in relation to what the major league team does. He'll do that at every level for four or five games with the manager and talk about what to do in certain situations and how to train his players to do what they do in the major leagues. They run through it in spring training, in Rookie League, Low-A, and every stop along the way. Some organizations are much better at it than others, such as Atlanta, St. Louis, and Baltimore (until the Orioles got away from it). That's the structure you're looking for within the framework of your organization.

Buddy Bell is the White Sox's farm director, and he coordinates the entire staff and is in charge of teaching just exactly how it's going to be with the players as they get to the major leagues. If your organization isn't very good either in scouting or development, you won't bring that many players to the major leagues.

You can teach them all you want, but if you can't get them to the major leagues, it really doesn't matter. They'll eventually go to another organization, who will teach them exactly what they want. It's a situation where you find players doing better, depending on their own baseball acumen.

You can help them along by showing them exactly what you want them to do. The Minnesota Twins tell their pitchers at an early stage, regardless of what kind of stuff they have, to throw strikes and be around the plate. Keep your walks to a minimum. That sounds easy. In reality, it is much more difficult because you find guys with great stuff—especially in the minor leagues, still young with great arms—who're very wild. But in Minnesota, the Twins simply tell them, "You can throw as hard as you want to and have stuff as good as you want, but if you intend to pitch for the major league team, you're going to get the ball over the plate. If you don't, you'll either get sent to the minor leagues or you'll never get to the Twins in the first place."

That's an organization that has won six division titles in the past nine years under Ron Gardenhire. But that system has been put in place for a long time with people like former general manager Terry Ryan, former manager Tom Kelly, and now Gardenhire. Many people remain with the organization and still work hard to make sure it's as good an organization as it possibly could be to maximize the talent they have because, for years, they couldn't spend a great deal of money. It helped to develop their own—which helps in any organization.

Most very good minor league organizations will have one pitching coordinator and one hitting coordinator, and under them are instructors that move around their minor league affiliates. They'll extol the virtues of whatever system you decide to implement. Much of it depends on your pitching coach in the major leagues and what he believes in, along with your general manager. In my opinion, you get to a situation where you sit down and write out the mission for each player at every level.

Obviously, different pitching coaches at every level will bring their expertise to it. But the overriding goal is to get guys a certain amount of uniformity by the time they get to the major leagues.

My feeling is always that you must have a uniform organizational philosophy and go within the framework of the talent you have at hand. White Sox pitching coach Don Cooper has proven many times that he can get the most out of pitchers after their original organizations have given up on them for one reason or another. Then you can go back down and have an organizational philosophy. The Sox have not been the best in developing and bringing up their pitchers to the major leagues and continually stocking their organization. Just take a look at the 2010 starting rotation.

Freddy Garcia was originally from Houston and learned how to pitch in Seattle following a trade involving Randy Johnson. Gavin Floyd was a first-round pick of the Philadelphia Phillies. He came over in a deal for Garcia. John Danks was a first-round pick of the Texas Rangers who came over in a trade involving Brandon McCarthy. Mark Buehrle was a low pick of the Chicago White Sox who ascended through the system and has done a terrific job. Edwin Jackson originally started with the Los Angeles Dodgers and was with a number of teams before he came to Don Cooper, whose adjustments have him throwing the ball very well. That's the starting rotation.

Jake Peavy, who is recovering from shoulder surgery, was developed by the San Diego Padres. The Sox are an organization that has spent a great deal of money and has made some pretty good trades and acquired some very talented guys from other organizations and then put them in hands of Don Cooper and gotten the most out of them. That's in the major leagues.

Had you possessed these guys in your minor leagues system, it's much cheaper. You don't have to pay for anyone else's development system. You have pitching coaches at every level. You have a roving base running coach. You have a roving bunting coach. You have roving outfield, infield and catching coaches who will go from spot to spot, teaching what they teach to all of the players that you have. Hopefully these guys are very well connected to a philosophy that you developed with your major league hitting coach and your instructors who handle bunting and running in the minor leagues. You teach them a uniformed way. All this falls on the shoulders of the guy who is in charge of the minor leagues, which is your farm director.

He has to implement what you have and decide at every level if you're teaching what you're instructed to teach and examine the reports. You can assume your scouting director and farm director are fairly equal as far as the thought process in most good organizations. The scouting director will explain to the farm director why you drafted a kid and what they see in this kid. From there, it's up to the farm director and his staff to develop those drafted players and make the necessary adjustments.

Of course, the player has to be coachable. He has to take that next stride, and there are some guys that come into professional baseball with a world of skills that just flame out. For one reason or another, they can't attain that. The strong organizations with good scouting and good player development run into that less often than others.

It would help for each organization to possess a tremendous amount of patience early, because that's where you run into some difficulties. Every organization is completely different. By showing patience early, you scout a guy, you draft a guy, he enters your organization, and then you turn him over to the development people.

But you don't really have to change things you perceive as flaws early in a guy's development process because you never really know if he's going to grow out of some of the things you don't like, or what he could develop into. It's best just to stay away from these people for a while. It doesn't matter if he's a hitter or a pitcher. Just start to let him develop into what he can do. Keep a close eye on him. See if what he does is good. See if what he does is bad. But you still don't go change him until you see just exactly if it's going to be projectable as far as his future growth as a player is concerned.

But to do that, you must have a certain amount of patience with guys. Unfortunately, patience is something that a lot of organizations are short on, which is why they decide to trade players slightly before their time because they see something that they might think is irreconcilable as far as their organization is concerned. So they trade him, only to see him come to stardom with a second or third organization. Sometimes, it takes a while. You have to understand that these players coming into your organization must find out what it is to be professionals. It's very difficult. The life is different. The routine is different. Everything is different.

Then you send him to spring training. The player will work with instructors that possess the highest level of knowledge that he has dealt with. The player will be talked to in terms they probably have never heard before. You have to watch these guys and see how they adjust to pro ball. Check their performance on a day-to-day basis and see how they cope with the highs and lows. See exactly how can a guy bring out his best on a daily basis when he doesn't have his best. How is he going to play? Then you

191

must decide if he can maximize what he has. You must figure out if what he's doing is or is not going to work out.

Then, within the framework of each player, you have to create a plan for the best way to develop them, and that takes time. It takes a lot of communication in your organization, on the part of your farm director and your managers and coaches at every level, about how these players are going to perform. Obviously when you deal with a lot of Latin players, you develop them in a different way because of the cultural adjustments that the American players don't have to deal with. They try to address these adjustments at their Dominican academies.

Many teams have pulled out of their Venezuelan academies because of the political situation down there. Teams used to have multiple academies and various players. I remember when I first started closely evaluating how organizations plan, the Houston Astros were doing a great job out of their Venezuelan academy. I remember Richard Hidalgo, Bobby Abreu, and Freddy Garcia coming out of there. There was a wealth of talent coming out of Venezuela.

Ozzie Guillen, of course, is among the top players who came out of Venezuela. You have plenty of talent out of Venezuela, but most organizations aren't investing as much there. Changes in federal law in Venezuela make it very tough to run academies down there right now. It becomes cost prohibitive to build a complex down there.

Also, it's a smaller place. It might swing back at one point. We don't know what's going to exactly happen now. But in recent years, most clubs have concentrated on the development of the Dominican academies and the talent that comes out of there.

Some scouts will look at Curacao. Andruw Jones is one of the great players to come out of there, and Randall Simon is a product of that territory. Panama produced Mariano Rivera. Those areas fall under the Latin arm of international scouting. But you don't take nearly as much time because you don't have that many players to look at. We're going to see some scouts taking a look at Brazil, which obviously is a soccer-crazy country.

Whether that means we're going to find a great deal of Brazilians baseball players, I don't know. But that's just one of the areas that teams are going to look at. My estimation always has been that China eventually is going to be a very big place as they start to develop more players. That's probably a logical plan in talking with Commissioner Bud Selig and eventually opening an office there.

There are some complications in a Major League Baseball agreement with the Chinese federation. The relations between the United States and Chinese governments also comes into place. So there are a few more difficulties when you talk about the development of Chinese players. Right now, sending extensive scouting and development people are not what clubs are looking at. But one day it will happen.

The minimum age for a player signed out of the Dominican Republic is 16, and everyone has an academy there. They must have a provable birth certificate, the verification of which is taken much more seriously than it used to be. The date is July 2 where guys who turn 16 in recent months are eligible to be signed. July 2 is where you see many signings because they've been waiting for these guys to turn 16, sometimes from five to eight months. When you do get a kid at that age, they most likely will go to the academy. Some of the kids there are 17 and 18. It depends on just how large of a bonus these kids have received. You might keep them in your academy for two to three years.

Ideally, they will develop to the point where they will arrive in this country around the age of a freshman in college. If you give a 16-year-old a large bonus, he has a very good chance of coming to this country in two years. That's like drafting a high school kid. Hopefully, those two years in your academy will be used very well by the time the kid gets here. He will be more advanced—baseball-wise—than your average 18-year-old. But he will have a lot to contend with moving to a completely different culture. That's done very well by the White Sox, and many teams are getting better at this.

Most of the Dominican baseball academies are close to Santo Domingo. You want them to be close to the airport and in the densest popular areas. The White Sox have their academy in Moca.

Buscones play large roles in Latin America. They control where certain players are seen. Economics play a big part in this. You want your academy located where you can see as many players as possible.

They're like agents for very young people. There's always going to be a bidding war that the *buscones* hope to control. There have been a lot of improprieties involving buscones. Many times *buscones* get 30 percent of a player's bonus. Many times they try to get the player as ready as they can before they show him to you. The *buscone* is an agent, but a different type.

Once a *buscone* gets a player signed, his duties are done, and the player joins your organization.

A *buscone* can be several things. The good *buscones* serve many roles. Finding a good buscone is of critical importance. Not only is a *buscone* an agent, but, in many instances, he's the player's personal trainer and family adviser in terms of nutrition and instruction. There really isn't a comparable high school or college league for these players to play in because they're so young. There are several tryouts, and the *buscones* take kids sometimes 15 years old and younger and spend years developing them to perform well at tryouts.

There's plenty of room for chicanery when it comes to the *buscones*, but I think we're getting a little better. I know Sandy Alderson went down to the Dominican Republic to try to oversee what has been going on there for many years. Some *buscones* have trained "workout warriors" who were prepared exactly for these tryouts.

It's almost like cramming for a test where you know exactly what's going to be tested, but you don't have a great idea of the subject matter except you test exceptionally well. That's what happens in many instances to these *buscones* who are trying to put their kids in the best light possible.

They train these players to throw, run and field in the outfield. They train them to perform many skills in which scouts will examine their tools closely. The scout might say, "OK, this guy is going to be terrific." But the problem is the players don't know a great deal about how to play baseball because they were so young when the *buscones* started to control them. But the *buscones* get them ready to perform very well in all those areas scouted by the major league teams.

These players have great tools, but that's it. They don't even know the rudimentary aspect of how to play the game of baseball. When you sign tools, you have to make them baseball players, and that takes a long time. You can get fooled very easily by spending a lot of money unless you recognize which players were developed solely to test well. Some perform well at these development workouts, only for the scouts to find out these players know nothing about how to play the game of baseball.

• • •

Scouting players away from the field and learning their habits is very important in the major leagues. It depends on the city you live in and who you're scouting for. It's much easier for amateur scouts to do that. Many amateur scouts have seen players coming up for several years, and they can get a little closer to the player.

To excel at scouting players in the major leagues, you must probe into the backgrounds of these guys to really understand what they do away from the field. You must dig to find out which players are going to hurt themselves away from the field, which guys will help themselves, which guys run the streets at night, and which guys take their profession seriously. It's all part of scouting, and these are some of the most difficult parts of what a scout has to do.

Professional scouts must dig deeper. They must count on some of their scouting contacts in the community—former players, broadcasters, or people who actually know these guys—before you plunk down a great deal of money or you trade many players for a specific player, only to find out the player you acquired never comes in at night. That becomes a big problem because he probably isn't going to help you, depending on the city he's in.

Because I'm a Chicago person, I know there are areas where businesses have 4:00 AM liquor licenses, and in a couple of instances, 5:00 AM liquor licenses are available to certain establishments. You must find out which guys avail themselves of that. It becomes especially important with the Cubs and their 51 day games a year, for them to understand who they're bringing to their organization. The same thing with the White Sox. It's still

Chicago. The same thing with teams in New York. They don't call it the City that Never Sleeps for no reason. You must hope the player you're acquiring doesn't subscribe to that phrase. Because if he does, it's going to be a very difficult place to play.

You must learn from your scouting department which kids are actually bad kids and which kids that did a couple of bad things early have overcome those mistakes and grown up. You're going to do things when you're young that you don't do when you get older. You're going to get involved in situations that you won't get involved in when you're older. You must figure out which guys have been able to overcome some of those things, and which guys have not.

Sometimes you pass on a guy because you think he's a bad guy and it turns out he really isn't. He just did some things that you take a look at and you hear about. It would help if you heard about them from multiple folks and figure out which are the kids that have started to take it seriously. There are several players who are passed on by organizations because they might have done something wrong, such as failed a drug test—whether it's marijuana or another illegal substance—and as they've gotten older, they've gotten away from those things and have started to take the game seriously.

Some organizations pass on these guys for any type of infraction. Other organizations give second chances, and that depends on each case. It's a very difficult thing to do. It's not an exact science. You can tell that some players were very good in cities like Kansas City and Pittsburgh, but you put them in major cities and you discover they don't thrive as much.

To sum up a section that has been long and, in some cases, fairly intricate, let's just break it down in terms of the most simplistic approach— attempting to bring players of all different types to your organization.

Players with great skills. Players with wonderful tools. The prototypical five-tool player. Sometimes you won't find five tools. In fact, in most instances, you won't. Sometimes you'll get a five-tool player that you won't be able to develop. It depends on the quality of your organization. You would just assume you run a standardized organization from top to bottom, from getting a player into your organization, to teaching them how you're going to play in the major leagues from the time they arrive in the organization.

You get players at different ages. Some are signed from Latin America at 16. In this country, you sign players who graduated from high school at 17. You also acquire junior college and college players. You get players of different ages and skill sets. You take a look at them, you evaluate them. The better organizations wind up trading players that look terrific. It's just like buying that car that might have been in an accident—only you don't know it. You buy the car, and the car turns out to be a lemon. It's a beautiful car on the outside, but it really isn't that good of a car.

When it works very well, you trade away that player that looks terrific, but you know he has a couple of fatal flaws that you didn't pick up when you drafted him, or you couldn't fix once you had him. The other guys that you feel will be wonderful for your organization, you keep them and try to develop them. No organization is 100 percent at this because this is never going to be an exact science. Some organizations will always do it better than others.

• • •

Computers are extremely valuable when it comes to evaluating every nuance of a player in every situation. We're at the point now where every organization has a complete computer system and computer department, where guys sit and evaluate just about everything. They integrate their own scouting with computer evaluation, and every team does it.

Some teams do it better than others, but every team has a number of computer personnel working on breaking down various players, their idiosyncrasies, when they get their hits, where they get their hits, a pitcher's sequence and how many fastballs he throws, and much more. It's all computerized. You can look it up, and then they give their reports within the framework of the baseball side of everyone's operation.

However, computers have their weaknesses. For instance, there are players who have played on non-contending teams for their entire career. Adam Dunn hasn't played on a true contender. In fact, he's been on some very bad teams. He's been on some very mediocre teams. He started with Cincinnati, which wasn't a very good team, then went to Arizona in a midseason trade, and that wasn't a good team either. He went to Washington, and that speaks for itself. He's put up some pretty good numbers, but can a computer figure out what he's going to do in the middle of a pennant race in August and September when he's never gotten that far in the past? I don't believe it can.

I'd also like to find a computer that has a very good idea of every competitor's heart or the size of his stones. It's very hard to figure that out. That's why you must send some excellent scouts. The teams with the excellent scouts usually have older scouts. Those teams might use their older scouts to teach younger scouts exactly what they're seeing because two or three or four scouts can be looking at the same thing, but one of the guys is going to see something that the other three don't. They see things a computer can't.

Although I see the value in computer work, I prefer the experienced eyes on the great baseball evaluators to help the computer people evaluate the players, whether it's someone they're trying to acquire or someone they might trade away. The front offices have to know as quickly as possible which players are going to be there for the team when it's the middle of August and September, as well as which players are going to fold up the tent. It goes beyond statistics.

But some organizations evaluate players much better than others. I certainly remember the Baltimore Orioles with their super scout Jimmy Russo. He took me from teams that were in the race for a good four and a half months, like the South Side Hitmen in 1977. I led the staff with 15 victories. But for the most part, I was on teams that weren't great that might have been in the race only through June.

I was very young in my first year when the San Francisco Giants won the National League West in 1971, so I didn't know what that pennant push was like. They used me as a reliever in September, then sent me down because I hurt my arm. They brought me back, but I made it by Jimmy Russo's inspection of talking to scouts and various players who had seen me in various places. Jim asked them what kind of teammate I was, what my nightlife like was, and a number of other things that this super scout would check into before you were even signed by Baltimore.

Once you were signed by the Orioles, Earl Weaver would try to intimidate you as soon as he possibly could. It was all part of the player evaluation.

Evaluating your own player is important. I was traded a number of times, so my own organization didn't think I was going to amount to much. The San Francisco Giants traded me to the White Sox, and the White Sox traded me after one year to the Cubs. The Cubs held me for three years and then lost me in the first free-agent draft. Then I chose to go to Baltimore, and everything went very well. What I was able to experience while I was with the Baltimore Orioles was very valuable to me.

• • •

Organizations that can't or don't evaluate their own talent exceptionally well are going to lose players in the Rule 5 draft and waiver claims. They will make bad trades because they don't see their players as well as a very aware scout from another organization does, and they don't know the players who are coming into their organizations.

The Rule 5 draft involves players who aren't protected on the 40-man roster, who signed their first professional contract at age 19 or older and have played professionally for four years, or signed at age 18 or younger and have at least five years of professional experience.

Because you have only 40 spots, you have to make a decision. There have been a few great Rule 5 drafts. Two of the best Rule 5 draft selections in history were Roberto Clemente by Pittsburgh (from the Brooklyn Dodgers) and Johan Santana by Minnesota (via trade through Houston). Clemente and Santana were left unprotected and other teams were able to draft them.

But I'm much more familiar with the situation with the Arizona Diamondbacks in December of 2005. It came down to a couple of guys who are still playing, and the administration at the time was discussing who would be the 40th man they wanted to protect.

The 40th man came down between a second baseman who had some power but not a whole lot of defensive skills, and a catcher who was a switch-hitter. Usually in that situation, catchers might be a little more valuable. But I knew the scouting director of the Diamondbacks at the time—Mike Rizzo—who now is the general manager of the Washington Nationals. Rizzo was battling for the second baseman because it's unusual to find a run producer at second base. Jeff Kent, Ryne Sandberg , and Joe Morgan were exceptional. In the case of Sandberg and Morgan, they had some speed. In the case of Kent, he's the all-time home run leader among second basemen.

So Rizzo argued for the power-hitting second baseman, as opposed to the catcher, to be protected on the 40-man roster. The organization went with the catcher. The catcher was Koyie Hill, who at least through this season plays with the Chicago Cubs.

The second baseman is Dan Uggla, who got to 100 home runs faster than any other second baseman in the history of the sport for the Florida Marlins, and he was a Rule 5 draft pick. He was not protected by the Diamondbacks. He was put on the Triple-A roster, left off the 40-man roster, drafted by Florida Marlins in the major league phase for the $50,000 price.

If Uggla didn't make that Marlins team, before they could send him to the minor leagues, they would have been forced to offer him to the Diamondbacks for $25,000. Uggla, of course, made the major leagues, and the rest is history as Uggla became a force in the middle of the Marlins' lineup, before being traded to the Braves.

But organizations are getting much better at evaluating their own talent. They employ many evaluators to take a look at their own club. It used to be where they would spend much of their time evaluating everyone else's organization and not doing a great deal with theirs. Ask yourself how many great players or how many simply good players has Atlanta lost or traded away in the past 15 years? Now sometimes if they think they can win a championship, like when they brought in Mark Teixeira from the Texas Rangers, they will be forced to give up some pretty good players—in this case, Elvis Andrus, Neftali Feliz, Matt Harrison, and Jarrod Saltalamacchia.

But in the normal Braves trade, they usually do a good job of evaluating their own and not trading away the good guys. For instance, in the past 20 years, the Braves have traded the Cubs at least 12 pitchers. The names Andy Pratt, Kevin Coffman, Kevin Blankenship, Ruben Quevedo, Micah Bowie, Todd Blackford, Angelo Burrows, Jose Ascanio, Joey Nation, Robinson Lopez, Tyrelle Harris, and Jeffrey Lorick come to mind. The jury is still out on the latter three pitchers.

But most of the others spent a short amount of time with the Cubs, and none of them achieved the potential that was forecast for them by the Cubs. My feeling was if the Braves call, hang up the phone because they always seem to know more than you do. They're easy to deal with. When they want somebody, you ask them what they want in return. Sometimes they say yes, sometimes they say no. If they say yes, then I think you must go back and reevaluate and find out why they're saying yes, because they've been very good at evaluating their own talent.

• • •

In the end, if you look at organizations that perpetuate competitive baseball teams, you'll see certain things that absolutely stand out. First, it's continuity of personnel. Second, it's the quality of the instructors. Third, it's the amount of money you spend in the development process as opposed to the amount of money you spend on free agency because the development process is a cheaper way to do it in the grand scheme of things. Yet, there are organizations who want to polish up the major league product because that's where they believe the revenue comes from. It does, to a certain extent. However, they don't understand when you consistently develop your own players, it's cheaper in the end, and it costs your major league team less to put a very good product on the field. You wind up spending less money and the teams that go out and consistently do it via the free agent market are, to a certain extent, penny-wise and pound-foolish.

If you've built a wonderful structure and a strong farm system that provides you with home-grown talent on a consistent basis, then the expenditures in the major leagues are much less. When you must spend money consistently on other teams' development systems, then you run into trouble and run into the great expense that is the cost of free agents as they come on the market. Understand that for every CC Sabathia and Mark Teixeira that comes on the open market that's bought by the New York Yankees or any other high-revenue teams, there are a number of others that are a gamble—$30–40 million gambles that absolutely don't pay off.

Consequently, if you had developed your own guy, where you control him in the major leagues for a six-year period, you spend much less money. You build a history, and if he likes what you have to offer, he won't run out for highest bid. He'll stay with you. That's become scarcer as we move along. However, it is still done. Some organizations do it better than others. One of the frightening things is when a very good organization builds a new ballpark and suddenly has money to spend that they didn't spend before.

The Minnesota Twins come to mind because they've been very good for a long time as a small-market, low revenue team that has never lost that idea of developing their own talent. Now they have a new stadium in Target Field, with more revenue coming in, which allows them to spend in excess of $100 million on talent. With that going hand in hand with the homegrown folks that they develop, it becomes very frightening because they're going to be very good.

The Cincinnati Reds are another organization that has a top-of-the-line general manager in Walt Jocketty. They've had very good young talent in recent years. When you look at Joey Votto, Drew Stubbs, Jay Bruce, and some of the younger players that they have developed through their system, and then you realize they had the $30 million to pay Aroldis Chapman. Who knows how well he'll work out? But his left arm, without question, is terrific.

They also developed homegrown pitchers Johnny Cueto and Homer Bailey. That's something that should scare organizations in the National League Central because they have a wonderful general manager who understood how to put together a great team in St. Louis, and now he's with a good, young organization in Cincinnati.

Again, I could point to Jon Daniels and the wonderful organization in Texas, the 2010 AL Champions. It should be frightening for the teams in the American League West because the Rangers always were known as the team that could hit but couldn't pitch. With new ownership led by Nolan Ryan, and with Jon Daniels, who is a tireless worker and a wonderful GM, they look to be a team that can only get better. So in the American League West, you now have an organization that has developed a few of their own players, made some wise trades in trading with the Atlanta Braves and bringing in players like shortstop Elvis Andrus and Neftali Feliz in the Mark Teixeira deal.

They are one of the few teams that were able to get tremendous talent from the Braves because they had something to offer—Mark Teixeira—who the Braves would be able to control for more than a year and were willing to give up some of their talented youngsters for. Other organizations have had a difficult time in getting that type of skill set of players delivered to them by the Atlanta Braves.

But there are organizations, like the Tampa Bay Rays, that have a solid job with their development system and their high No. 1 draft choices after being bad for so long. But suddenly they have become a wonderful team with Andrew Freidman and Daniel Sternberg. They've become a better and more competitive team for a very low amount of money spent. They've developed some very good pitching with David Price and James Shields. Delmon Young, who was a former first round pick, was traded for shortstop Jason Bartlett and workhorse pitcher Matt Garza, who, even though they're gone, we integral to numerous playoff teams. They also have a potential star outfielder in Desmond Jennings.

Again, it should be very frightening to the teams in the American League East even though you have the high-revenue Boston Red Sox and the always free-spending New York Yankees to deal with. But Tampa Bay has turned their team with their young talent and built around it.

So there are great success stories, as far as developing organizations through their scouts, draft choices, and player development. Those organizations are sprinkled throughout the major leagues, and while other organizations may try to copy some method here or there, the truly great organizations build with a unifying philosophy from top to bottom.

CHAPTER **10**

The Commissioner

For the longest time, I felt the best commissioner in Major League Baseball was Kenesaw Mountain Landis because he picked up the game of baseball from the shambles of the 1919 Black Sox Scandal, in which the game lost all its credibility.

Landis brought it back. He certainly did it with an iron hand, and he probably wasn't the most popular man around, but he gave baseball the credibility it desperately needed. Because of what Landis did for the game when it needed it most, I always felt he was No. 1 among commissioners. Bud Selig and I have talked about it a lot.

I'm not sure I'm in the majority here, but it doesn't matter because I've been in the minority a lot. Now I believe that Bud Selig is the best commissioner we've ever had, and I will detail that as we go along.

First, let me explain why the commissioner has such a difficult job to do. It's very simple: because the commissioner is the commissioner of all of baseball. He is the commissioner of all the players. He's the commissioner over the umpires. He's the commissioner over all of the owners. He's the commissioner of everything that goes on—in professional baseball at the major league level and at the minor league level. He certainly has to do a job internationally. He is constantly promoting the game, doing what he can to increase revenues. Because baseball has become an international endeavor, the commissioner's job has expanded. With that, so have the responsibilities.

The commissioner is chosen by the owners, and that creates a difficult situation. The problem is that with the owners choosing the commissioner, the players and umpires have no say in the selection. Then, every time you have a Collective Bargaining Agreement, the players have their own self-interests, and maybe they are suspicious of the commissioner's leanings.

The umpires feel the same way every time their agreement comes up. They have a word in what's going on. It used to be we had the American League umpires and National League umpires working only in their respective leagues. I could make the case to perhaps go back to that. But right now, they're major league umpires, so we don't have those two sets of umpires any longer.

Whether you're talking about the CBA or not, the commissioner will take a lot of heat because he's supposed to be the all-everything as it pertains to the game of baseball. Consequently, he's consistently at odds with all of the folks with different agendas or those who simply don't agree with him.

With the game expanding as rapidly as it has, you have media outlets expanding as rapidly as ever. You have talk radio, and sports talk radio is getting bigger than it's ever been before. You have not only ESPN showing SportsCenter, but you have the Major League Baseball Network running a 24-hour baseball-evaluation process. You have many magazines covering the sport. You have bloggers all over the country. You have websites that are everything you could possibly think of—invasive, intrusive, and trying to get stories. You have rumors, trade sites, and minor league information that's out there. You have *Baseball Prospectus*, you have *Baseball America*. You have a number of services that people can subscribe to if they're playing rotisserie baseball.

There's so much information out there that it becomes something where everybody seems to know everything about the game. Usually that's not the case, because there is a lot of misinformation out there. It gives people the feeling that they can criticize everything the commissioner is doing.

Selig took over the commissioner's post in 1992, and in that time, he has accomplished some of the goals he set out for himself. For instance, in 1992, the revenue of the game was $1.2 billion. It stayed essentially flat for a great deal of time, and it wasn't bad. Bud, who has been gracious to me over the years, told me his major goal when he took over was figuring out how to get to $2 billion in revenue, making the game healthier and as successful as he possibly could make it. Not only did he get to that $2 billion mark in gross revenues, but those gross revenues have zoomed to $7 billion as of this writing. It has been growing and getting stronger. The game is healthier than it's been, even in the very bad economy that we've had over the past few years.

The attendance actually rose in the 2010 season, which is somewhat surprising when we've seen some advertising revenues going down. We've seen some teams that would love to see higher attendance. But overall, the attendance has gone up. As of this writing, the average attendance in Major League Baseball is right around 30,000 fans per game per team.

Obviously, there are some teams that draw substantially less than 30,000 and other teams that simply have problems putting people in their park on a daily basis. The Florida Marlins are one of those teams, but they're getting a new stadium in 2012. Beginning in 1992, many new stadiums were built, and Bud Selig has had a strong hand in that. He was influential in going into the communities and convincing those communities to have revenue generated by the public.

That's to the dismay of some people, but many cities recognize it's in their best interest to use some tax dollars to offset the cost of parks with their teams, and keeping their teams in downtown areas, which in many cases rejuvenates those areas so that they become an asset to many cities.

I came into the professional game in 1969 and reached the major leagues in 1971, when Marvin Miller was the head of the players' union. Marvin's philosophy was, "Never give anything back." Once you have won it in collective bargaining, you never were supposed to give anything back. Donald Fehr, who learned at the knee of Miller, was very similar in his approach.

But eventually times change. Bud is very proud of the fact that heading into the next Collective Bargaining Agreement, which expires after the

2011 season, there will have been 16 years of labor peace. Hopefully the next negotiation will be as successful as the last few.

When I was coming up, there were strikes. 1994 was, of course, an infamous year for baseball. We lost out on a World Series. There were walkouts by players and any number of work stoppages. Every work stoppage has done a little bit to damage the game, and the big one was 1994. That's the one that really hurt baseball.

I know a lot of people feel Bud Selig and the owners turned a blind eye to steroid abuse in an effort get the game back on the right track. But they're only part of the equation. You also have the Major League Baseball Players Association. This isn't a treatise on the steroid issue or what should have happened. All we know is what *did* happen. Eventually, it had to appear before Congress to finally convince Donald Fehr, along with Bud Selig, that they had to tighten up testing.

One of the very proud statements that Bud Selig has made to me is that baseball now has the strongest drug-testing program in all of sports. Right now, they're actually testing for human growth hormone in the minor leagues. Hopefully, it will lead to more stringent testing in the major leagues. But that's a battle to be fought in the next Collective Bargaining Agreement or the one right after that. That's one issue that the commissioner always talks about.

Another thing that Bud is proud of is that the minor league testing program is 10 years old. Many believe the major leagues were a little late to the party, and that the testing should be a little stronger. But understand that you not only have the commissioner's desire to test, but you also need the players' desire. I know some players who would have liked testing a little earlier. The fact is, you can't really blame one person for everything; just because one side wants it doesn't mean it's going to work out that way.

Many years ago Bud talked about the internationalization of baseball. With that in mind, he has come up with the World Baseball Classic. That's something that's been very successful. We've seen a lot of teams that aren't the greatest, but baseball is becoming more important around the globe. In my estimation, China is of critical importance. Maybe not today, but soon. Baseball has opened up an Office of the Commissioner in China. I believe that the Chinese will get better. I believe it's going to be very healthy for the game of baseball if, eventually, we see someone like an Ichiro Suzuki, who comes out of Japan and probably will be in two Halls of Fame. Ichiro is certainly a hero back home in Japan and arguably one of the greatest hitters to ever play the game in the Japanese and U.S. major leagues.

But if they can ever get a baseball player of that magnitude out of China, that will help all the teams as far as revenue is concerned. Bud has brought about Baseball's Advanced Media (BAM). It is something that Bud is very proud of, and they have a fairly substantial revenue stream that will only grow stronger. Combining that with international play would have a huge impact on the game financially.

• • •

While I understand that people believe that football is the most popular game in this country, I also notice that as of this writing, there were 10 opening days for which NFL teams felt they might have to black out the broadcast because they didn't sell out. That's most likely a product of the economy, but it is also a point where we are constantly in competition for the entertainment dollar. It doesn't matter whether it is sports or any other form of entertainment. People must pick and choose exactly where they spend their money.

The Cubs, at this point, are drawing more people on a consistent basis and have for quite some time. However, there is no guarantee that will continue. I played with the Cubs and with the White Sox at various times where the White Sox outdrew the Cubs. It has not happened recently, but that doesn't mean it won't happen down the road.

When I had my conversation with Bud, he talked about life after Bud Selig and when he would choose to retire. I truly believe everything that Bud has done has been in the best interests of the sport, and that will include when he chooses to step down. I know a lot of people would urge him to continue on past 2012. He hasn't made a decision, but it's something he is keenly aware of. He'd probably like to write a book and do other things, but his unabiding love of the game goes unquestioned by anyone who knows him.

For the longest time, I got a kick out of a lot of folks who believed that Bud was a puppet of the owners at various times. It didn't matter if it was Ted Turner, George Steinbrenner, Jerry Reinsdorf, or any of the multitude of very strong owners who came along. A lot of people felt they controlled what Bud Selig did.

Knowing Bud as I do, what a strong personality he is, and his abiding love for the game, I just had to laugh. I remember talking to him about the original idea of the luxury tax and talking about the implementation of that. I asked what Steinbrenner was going to say about that, what his reaction was going to be toward revenue sharing and the luxury tax. Bud told me that it didn't really matter all that much because he had the votes to pass it without Steinbrenner.

When you see the votes these days, they're usually 30–0. That's kind of the way it's been with Bud from the beginning, which people really didn't understand. You're talking about 30 different owners with 30 different agendas, and many times they're pulling in 30 different directions.

You must have someone who is able to get a consensus, bring these very strong and diverse personalities and get them agreeing to what is best for the game. They have to understand that although they might be the owner of the New York Yankees or Boston or the Chicago Cubs or Los Angeles Dodgers or any of the big-market teams, you have to play against Kansas City and Florida. You have to play against some of the small-revenue, small-market teams because you're all in this together.

To get them to be successful, that's when you had to go to revenue sharing, the luxury tax, and other places that made the smaller teams solvent.

Bud already has explored the idea of a true World Series between the champion in the United States and the champion from Japan. I really haven't explored this, but it makes a great deal of sense. It would be of great interest to two countries with very good players. This is something Bud has envisioned.

We might not see it in his tenure as commissioner, but it's something that probably will happen. I think it's something that is probably long past due to happen because we like to call it a World Series. In this country, it's been the World Series for a long time. But as baseball has become an international game, it's lacking some of the world as far as the World Series is concerned.

I've always been very proud to consider Bud a friend of mine. I know he's a friend of many baseball people, a lot of us baseball lifers who have spent our days playing, current players, guys who have spent their lives broadcasting, guys who have spent their time on the periphery of the game but intimately involved in the game. They know Bud, and many of them consider him a friend, as I do.

But being the commissioner is a very difficult job, one in which you're constantly open to criticism. Whoever becomes the next commissioner is going to be as well scrutinized as Bud. Bud always has had his defenders, and he's always had his detractors.

I'll give you one instance that a lot of people felt was a sacrilege: the wildcard. Now look how phenomenally successful the wildcard is. Without it, teams were eliminated in June or the beginning of July, and fans would stop attending games because their team had no chance of getting into the playoffs. Since the wildcard was put in, you have sometimes as many as 22–24 teams with a chance with six weeks to go in the season, maybe a month to go in the season.

Bud took a lot of heat for wanting to implement the wildcard, which was a radical idea. The people who consider themselves baseball purists just were apoplectic at the thought of teams actually getting into the playoffs when they didn't win their division. They worried it would cheapen the game and the game would become much like hockey and basketball, where everyone gets into the playoffs. You have 16 teams in the playoffs with those two sports.

But the fact is the wildcard has been a rousing success and has kept teams in contention. Their fans have been more interested, wildcard teams have won the World Series, and it hasn't diminished the game of baseball in the least.

One incident that Bud took a tremendous amount of heat for was at the All-Star Game in 2002. Bob Brenly, who won the World Series in 2001 with Arizona, was the National League manager, and the New York Yankees'

Joe Torre was managing the American League. The game went into extra innings, and they ran out of pitchers. At that point no one knew what to do.

Understand that we have some of the greatest baseball minds, guys who spent their lives in the game, guys who write about it every day, guys who use talk radio as their forum every day. We have baseball specialists. We have baseball magazine writers. We have baseball bloggers. We have people who just dissect the game on a daily basis from every angle. And yet, I can't remember one person ever saying, "What are we going to do at the All-Star Game if we run out of pitchers?"

Bud took a phenomenal amount of heat when it happened. "How could he possibly not think of that eventuality?" Well, it's very difficult for one man to think of everything, even with a staff like the commissioner has, and it's not something anyone else considered either, as far as I know. But after the fact, everyone had something to say about how it should have been handled.

That's just one of the things that I remember him taking a lot of heat for, but there have been many others over the years, and he has certainly been affected by them. He feels deeply about the game, and nobody likes to be criticized. But I think in his heart of hearts, our commissioner, Bud Selig, feels the game is much healthier than when he took over. He feels it's much healthier than it's ever been.

Are there problems? Of course there are problems. There are always going to be problems. There is always going to be the next labor negotiation. There's always going to be the next Collective Bargaining Agreement, and with it, there's always going to be the prospect of the next work stoppage. That's one of Bud's proudest accomplishments, the fact that through the last 16 years of labor peace, baseball has prospered.

They did learn from 1994, and hopefully they will continue to remember the lessons of the year they canceled the World Series, the year the game was shut down, and no one was helped by that.

So understanding the job of the commissioner, how difficult it is and the strain that he's under, I'm very happy that since 1992 we've had a very strong man at the helm.

I remember living through the work stoppages, the damage it did to the fans, the damage it did to the game of baseball, and the way the Players Association, the owners, and the Commissioner's Office used to be consistently at one another's throats. I think we've come a long way. I believe, obviously, that this is the best game there is. I've given my life to it, and I know the commissioner has given his life to it and will continue to do so, regardless of what capacity he does it in.

They just built a statue of Bud in Milwaukee. The unveiling of it was a very emotional moment for him. It was a beautiful ceremony, and it was well deserved. I couldn't think of a better place to put it than Milwaukee, a team that he helped bring back to the city after they lost the Braves to Atlanta. He brought that team back from Seattle and resurrected what now is a very strong presence in Milwaukee, a very big part of the community. Miller Park is a beautiful facility, and hopefully it thrives there for many years, which I believe it will.

CHAPTER 11

The Future of the Sport

When I look at the future, I base my observations on what's happened in the past and what I anticipate happening as a result of past developments.

The first change I see involves the next Collective Bargaining Agreement (CBA) and the limitation of bonuses for players drafted. Maybe it won't be changed as radically as in the NBA, but it could be something along those lines. The signing bonuses for the first 30 picks can be slotted into groups of five (1–5, 6–10, etc.) where they get a certain amount of money over a three-year period or longer.

You would consider at least a three-year period because of that first year of salary arbitration and buying the player out of his first year. The details would be worked out, and I believe this will be discussed at the next negotiations and that the Major League Baseball Players Association will buy into that.

This change has been a long time coming, and I truly believe it must happen for the health of the game; it probably will happen. Once you have a secured cap on the drafting class of new free agents, you can start thinking about trading draft choices, because that's something that baseball hasn't done. It's something that other sports do particularly well.

The trading of draft picks is one of the reasons why the NFL Draft is so interesting. You know the names of the players being drafted, there are fewer rounds, and there's plenty of justifiable hype in the NFL. The same could be said for the NBA. You know the players by the time they get to draft day.

But baseball is different. You're talking about 50 rounds. You might have heard the names of the players in the first few rounds, but not much beyond that. If you have interest in some local players who might be drafted either out of high school or college in the 12th, 14th, or 24th round, then there's a certain amount of excitement that goes there. For the majority of fans the first round is interesting. After that, it becomes more difficult because people don't know the players, and if they do, they know them because of what they read from some of the scouting services and from *Baseball America*, a fine publication.

It makes a lot of sense for the lower-revenue teams to trade draft picks. There's an object lesson of the Washington Nationals, who paid a $15 million bonus for Stephen Strasburg, a big-bodied pitcher with a strong arm who had proven himself in college. He came into the pros but ended up having Tommy John surgery, causing the Nationals to lose a drawing card and top performer for anywhere from 12 to 18 months, depending on the rehab and how quickly he heals. I'm sure he's a hardworking young man who is going to try to rehabilitate as quickly as possible, but bodies heal at different rates, depending on what type of work ethic you have and how nature takes its course.

Fortunately, the prognosis for Tommy John surgery is excellent these days because the surgical techniques have improved so much over the original surgery performed on Tommy John. Another consideration is the recovery from the surgery.

Rick Reuschel, who went 5–5 with the Chicago Cubs in 1984, had two arthroscopic surgeries. Jim Frey, the general manager of the Cubs at the time, had no conception of the fact that as you move further away from that surgery, you become a better pitcher. You become stronger and regain all you had before. You also take into consideration the phenomenally competitive nature of Reuschel despite how he might have appeared. Not only was he a great athlete, not only could he do just about everything he wanted to do as far as bunting and handling the bat and fielding his position, but as a competitive pitcher, he was about as good as they come.

Even when his stuff wasn't as good as you would have liked it to be, it was still good enough.

Reuschel won 75 games after Jim Frey insisted that Dallas Green not even bring him to spring training in 1986 to take a look at him. Dallas, to his credit, did get Rick a job with Pittsburgh. Rick spent some time in the minor leagues before returning to the majors and helping San Francisco win a 1987 National League West title after a mid-season trade. Reuschel won 17 games in 1989, as well as the fifth and clinching game for the Giants in the NL Championship Series—over the same Cubs franchise that refused to give him a look three years earlier.

In any event, the Strasburg injury is a very tough one. But that's what you risk when you draft free agents, especially high-priced ones. I know Washington isn't second-guessing their pick because Strasburg, by far, was the best pitcher in the draft. They drafted him and paid a bunch of money for him. It was just a question of tough luck that he suffered this injury and will have to sit out for a while. We'll see what happens.

The exception to trading draft picks is the case of the Washington Nationals because they had a premier 1-1—meaning a player you draft in the first round as a first pick. They had a similar situation in 2010 in Bryce Harper. But Strasburg is a big drawing card, and he made Washington a lot of money in the starts he had at home. He becomes a different type of player.

But let's take the normal first-round pick. From the 10th overall pick on down, chances are he's going to be a good player. Sometimes he'll turn into an impact player. Albert Pujols was drafted in the 13th round, and we don't have to question the impact he's made on baseball as well as the St. Louis Cardinals, the National League, and the NL Central.

However, those guys are few and far between. Let's say you have between the 10th and 15th overall selection. There's a player available who another team covets. That player might not mean as much to you as he does to another team. You might get two or three players for trading this draft pick, and the team that acquires the draft pick is guaranteed they won't have to break the bank to sign him. The player won't have any more leverage with you than he does with the other team. It makes it a lot easier to trade the pick. You're able to build your team with a few players you don't have for the promise of a guy that you don't really know if he will develop.

The history of baseball is loaded with first-round draft picks who didn't pan out. It doesn't matter which team it is, whether it's the White Sox or the Cubs in Chicago, the Yankees or the Mets in New York, or Kansas City, Cleveland, or the Los Angeles Dodgers. You see No. 1 picks that you would have expected to be much better players, but they don't pan out, for whatever reason. Sometimes they get hurt. Sometimes they don't develop, in which case you'd be better off with three proven guys or three guys who are young enough to have a better shot at developing.

I see the trading of draft picks happening. I also look at one of the inequities of baseball that seems to be very strange to me and I'm sure is going to be addressed. That involves the signing of a Type A free agent when you pick in the second tier of the first round.

Let's say Adam Dunn elects not to sign with the Washington Nationals and decides to sign a two- or three-year contract with another club that has its first-round pick after the 15th overall selection. That team that signs Dunn is going to lose its first-round draft pick. That's a big loss even though they acquire Dunn. Washington would be happy because they would get two high draft picks, and the Nationals have a pretty good success rate with their picks. The team signing Dunn would be happy with Dunn but fairly unhappy with the fact they lost their No. 1 draft pick.

In this case, that's exactly what happened. Dunn signed a 4-year deal with the White Sox, and the Nationals got their pick, the 23rd of the first round.

The inequity comes from situations like the one involving Boston signing Daisuke Matsuzaka. He cost the Red Sox $51 million just in posting fees (which is when you win a bid to actually negotiate with a team), and another $52 million to sign him to his first contract. That means they expended $103 million to get a guy who is a proven pitcher out of Japan, but they don't lose any draft picks at all for signing him. It makes very little sense to me, in that it smacks of the rich getting richer and the poor getting poorer by losing a draft pick that could otherwise help build their team.

That's why I believe what should happen and what probably will happen, assuming that owners have a taste for it, is a full international draft. If baseball goes back to having a cap on rookie draft choices, they're going to have an international draft. They'll save money on these international academies because these schools could very well produce a feeder system for all of the major leagues to start drafting these guys.

Some teams can't go to the Dominican Republic and sign a 16-year-old pitcher, as Oakland did with Michael Ynoa for more than $4 million. At 16! Ynoa could turn out to be a wonderful pitcher. But more than $4 million for a 16-year-old pitcher? If you want to draft a 16-year-old, that's your prerogative if he's out of the Dominican Republic. Or you can wait until he's 18, when you can get a better picture of what he's going to develop into, and then you can draft him.

But if you use a draft choice on a player like that, then you're going to miss out on a player from this country, Japan, Curacao, or all of the other places where you don't have to draft. I view an international draft as something that's coming or should be coming because it evens the playing field. This would be the latest in a progression of recent changes that has included revenue sharing, the luxury tax, and the draft. Eventually, you're going to look at an international draft.

I know there are some political problems, but one of the great horizons in baseball is the Internet facility that not only will become a tremendous revenue producer in the future but already has grown by leaps and bounds. It's called Baseball Advanced Media (BAM). It's the forum in which proceeds are funneled through Internet marketing. For instance, when you sign up for the baseball package, a certain percentage of that goes through BAM.

Think of the excitement that was generated around Yao Ming from China. There are a couple of other Chinese players in the NBA, too. They became heroes in their homeland. The same thing holds true with the Japanese players. It's evidenced by the Japanese media following Ichiro and Hideki Matsui, and to a certain extent, Kosuke Fukudome, Daisuke Matsuzaka, Hideki Okajima, and a number of Japanese players who have come over here and done a very good job. The San Francisco Giants brought the first player from Japan to the United States in pitcher Masanori Murakami in 1964–65. They've been searching frantically for another Asian player because of the huge Asian community in San Francisco. Given all that, imagine if we could develop a Chinese player or players with the magnitude of Ichiro, Matsui, Matsuzaka, and Hideo Nomo.

All of the sports facilities that were built for the Olympics in Beijing have gradually turned over into training athletes, including baseball players. Even with the political hurdles we would have to jump, eventually we're going to get Chinese players, as evidenced by Chinese players playing in the World Baseball Classic that is held every four years.

I'm talking about something like this happening in 10 to 15 years, maybe sooner. It's hard to predict exactly when these things will happen, but I think it will happen. It will open up the whole world of baseball to a country with nearly 1.5 billion people. One can only guess at the number of computers and the baseball packages they will sell for fans to see their stars.

That was one of the ideas of Bud Selig when he initially started the internationalization of the game of baseball. Yet everyone kind of pooh-poohed what Bud was trying to do when he opened the regular season in Japan and played some games in Mexico and other sites. Bud now is entertaining the idea of playing games in Europe on occasion.

People said the fans would never come back after the strike in 1994, but many fans returned in part because of the home run chase in 1998 with Mark McGwire and Sammy Sosa. Shortly after that, Selig started to consider the internationalization of baseball. That's how you're going to keep the game growing, because, as this book goes to print, the economy in the United States has not bounced back the way everyone hoped it would. Unemployment has stayed astonishingly high. We are seeing all kinds of financial trouble. Baseball, more than ever before, is in the battle for the entertainment dollar.

Looking ahead in baseball, we need to revamp our economic system. Baseball must change with the times. That's why I believe that there are going to be a few economic changes in baseball.

I know the Major League Baseball Players Association always cringes when you start talking about salary caps. I think it's going to be a tremendous fight on the top end of any salary cap, and I don't think you're going to see that for some time. Eventually, maybe they'll get there, but not quite yet. You may see a floor, however, in which teams must spend a certain amount if they're going to be involved in revenue sharing because I don't think any of the owners who pay into revenue sharing want to subsidize any of the other teams. They don't want to see those teams with low payrolls make money because of the revenue they're collecting from the more successful teams. They see those owners receiving the money and saving it instead of putting it into their baseball teams.

The easiest way to avoid that is to have a floor on just exactly what you have to spend if you're going to participate in revenue sharing. It's almost like the idea of an election in taking matching governmental funds, where some politicians, thinking they can raise their own money, don't want to participate in matching funds because they can raise much more money elsewhere.

Same thing with baseball. If you're going to take the large payments made through revenue sharing, then you probably should set a minimum you have to spend on your payroll. That way the owners of the baseball establishment know they're not subsidizing some otherwise wealthy owners who might be in small-market towns with low revenues and not investing the money into producing a more competitive product on the field. Many folks in the Players Association might say it's a slippery slope. But if you do establish a floor, eventually you're going to establish a ceiling. And you're going to have a salary cap.

I don't necessarily view it as one and the same. The MLBPA should be very happy with the establishment of a floor because instead of having a team spending $36 million on their payroll, maybe they could spend $56 million to get the revenues that baseball is going to receive as BAM increases and they set up a system to pay each team. I believe that will help teams become healthier and more competitive, and owners won't put the money into their pockets but into their teams.

There was a tremendous controversy toward the end of the 2010 season about some financial documents that were leaked from some of the lower-revenue teams and just how much money they were making without having to put in a large payroll. Pittsburgh was one of those teams, which must frustrate Pirates fans.

The fans' angst is simple to understand. They're being asked to pay good money to see a product that is getting better with younger players for the first time in a long time. They're able to sign and retain some of these good young players. But at the end of the day, that payroll going into the season was only $36 million. With the financial documents being leaked—much to the dismay of Major League Baseball—they're finding out the Pirates' owners have made money while their team has gone through 18 consecutive losing seasons, which is an all-time record for any professional team in North American sports. So the losing continues, but the owners continue to make money because of revenue sharing. Instituting a salary floor is one way to avoid all of that.

On the medical front, surgical techniques will get much better in the future. If you need proof, look at the surgical techniques from 15 years ago and the surgical techniques today. The fact is, with Tommy John surgery, 75 percent of the pitchers who undergo that surgery come back with the same stuff they had before, and they strengthen the elbow through the reconstructive surgery.

Velocity comes from the shoulder, so as long as the shoulder stays intact through a series of strenuous exercises over a long period of time— from 12 to 18 months—you should not have any drop-off in velocity. That late movement on the ball will come from the elbow, along with the curve and slider, and to a certain extent the splitter, where the torque is on the elbow but the velocity comes from the shoulder.

Most of the pitchers who return from Tommy John surgery throw just as hard as they did before. Eventually the movement on the fastball comes back to them because they can pop their wrist at the end of their delivery and make sure the elbow, in their own mind, is strong enough. After the physical aspect of the injury goes away, the pitcher must cope with the psychological aspect and convince himself the elbow won't fall apart. When that occurs, he can return to pitch. The younger you are, the easier it is to come back and pitch. Young people, in life as well as in the game, view themselves as immortal. Also, you heal better as a youngster.

Also on the medical front, one of the biggest topics in the next Collective Bargaining Agreement, and perhaps the next one after that (depending on how successful they are), will be the athletes' providing blood samples. They will be asked to give blood in order to be tested for human growth hormone and its derivatives. The rumors are that the testing is getting better, but I'm talking specifics. They're already testing minor leaguers for human growth hormone. The MLBPA is going to argue, and maybe in some cases justifiably so, that they don't have a 100 percent effective blood test for human growth hormone. But they probably will have one in the not too distant future.

Then the battle will be over the blood test, because at this point, that's what it takes to test for HGH. It could be as they get better, they might be able to test it through the urine. But for now, that's not an option. These are things I have gleaned from conversations with doctors and specialists in that area.

One problem I see arising out of this comes up when someone else is controlling the blood samples. This is not talked about a lot, but it's something I always think about. Once you possess the blood of any player, and it's controlled by the individual team, what stops that team from doing genetic testing and looking at the various patterns of DNA and looking for predispositions of various diseases? There are a number of ailments that can be detected this way.

Let's say you have a family history of an illness that can be verified by the human genome, which we are learning more about on a yearly basis. With genetic testing of blood, you might find out you're predisposed to a heart condition or rheumatoid arthritis. Those are conditions a team would be interested in, assuming that you're playing and don't know when this particular disease might strike you.

Maybe the player has a predisposition to a certain form of cancer that might strike people in their mid-30s, and you're dealing with a player who is in his early 30s. Your first inclination may be to give this player a five-year contract, but after taking a look at this medical finding, you could make a very strong case for saying, "We're going to offer this guy a three-year contract." The player would never know why he was offered three years. The team would never explain why they were offering three years. But that could be the case.

Again, who knows how far this is going to go. But that probably will be one of the arguments that the MLBPA is going to use. If you have the blood, what's going to stop you from taking a look deeper into that? We've made tremendous strides in genetic engineering, the understanding of the human genome and DNA that make us who we are as human beings. What's to stop various teams from using that information to tailor their contracts, depending on what they find out?

Remember the 104 players who tested positive for performance-enhancing drugs during that random sampling of testing? Those tests were supposed to be anonymous, yet at the end of the day they weren't all anonymous because of some difficulties with seizures at the lab. Not all of the names have become public, but several names have leaked.

The players were aware that mandatory testing would be instituted if more than 5 percent of the samples were positive. But it turned out that 7 percent of the players tested positive. You can only imagine exactly what percentage of players were using steroids before the anonymous testing.

But this goes beyond the testing for HGH. This is simply supposition, but another drug that is on the horizon is what some people say is a combination of steroids and human growth hormone that's water soluble. That means it leaves the body very quickly. It becomes very difficult to test for.

We must also understand that chemists are working all over the world on analog drugs, which mimic drugs except for perhaps taking a couple of molecules out of it. The chemical compound of a legal drug is varied so that you have a chemical compound that would be considered illegal, except that it hasn't been made illegal because nobody has discovered it yet. They will, but they haven't. So you have chemists throughout the world who are simultaneously working on drugs to enhance performance and masking drugs to stop people from finding out who is using those drugs to enhance performance.

Other sports, such as cycling and track and field, have already begun to see this. If it's not already in baseball, which I suspect it is, it probably will be soon. If you don't have tests for it, how can you know if it's there? Understand that as soon as we come up with detection procedures for various drugs and various compounds, chemists all over the world will come up with something new to stay ahead of the detectors.

This game won't be 100 percent clean, but we've made some great strides in that area. However, we're not going to completely eradicate performance-enhancing drugs or performance-enhancing techniques. Blood doping, which was used extensively in the Olympic Games, was something that we never really thought about until it became common practice. Similarly, in the Soviet Union their female gymnasts would use drugs to retard puberty so that they stayed much smaller much longer and performed at the top end of their ability. When they no longer could perform, all of a sudden they stopped these drugs that inhibited puberty. You took a look at some of these girls four years later. They were no longer young girls. They grew well beyond the young girl stage into adulthood almost overnight.

I remember the famous photo of the East German swim team on the blocks from behind. From their calves to their broad shoulders, you realize that they had to be doing something because they were just about twice the size of any other female swimmers around.

We also had a Russian female shot-putter years ago by the name of Tamara Press, who eventually had to stop competing internationally when they started doing inside scrapings of the mouth to find out just exactly if the athletes were females or not. She had taken so much testosterone that she couldn't actually pass as a female, which was one of the reasons why she was able to throw the shot so much farther than any other female in the world.

Those were incidents before the testing became very stringent and before people were caught on a yearly basis. It's in every sport. It's not something that's isolated to track and field or to swimming or cycling or

225

football, basketball, or baseball. It will continue to be in all sports. That's something we'll have to come to grips with. That doesn't mean we should stop looking and stop testing. We should actually increase testing and make sure it's a level playing field.

I have a philosophy about the game since the Black Sox Scandal of 1919 and since Kenesaw Mountain Landis became the most important commissioner for a long time in baseball. Landis enacted a lifetime ban on gambling in the sport. Not gambling for gambling's sake, but because baseball had lost all shreds of credibility as far as the honesty of the game. That's the only thing that baseball has to sell to the fans, those parents and sons and daughters who support the game. People take their sons and daughters to the game so the game perpetuates itself, generation after generation.

What keeps those fans loyal for all those generations is credibility, and that's exactly what we have to sell in baseball.

That's what Landis saw. So did Bart Giamatti, who offered Pete Rose a one-year suspension and told him if he admitted to gambling and took a year off and sought some help, Giamatti would bring him back into baseball after that one-year suspension.

But Rose stubbornly insisted he never gambled on baseball. He insisted he had no problem, which was equally ridiculous. With gambling striking at the heart of the credibility of the game, Pete Rose was not intelligent enough to realize the problem of his contention that he never bet against his own team.

Let me give you a situation where I'm the manager of a major league franchise, and I call a bookie and I bet on my team three consecutive days. But the fourth day I don't bet on them. Yes, I'm not betting against my team. However, what I'm telling my bookie is perhaps my closer is not going to pitch on that fourth day. Perhaps I know something about my starting pitcher that nobody else knows. Perhaps I know I'm giving a rest to somebody before it's actually announced.

So by not betting on my team on that fourth day after betting on them for three consecutive days, I'm telling that guy to go the other way in a bet. That's the credibility of the game. That's why Pete Rose should always be banned from the game of baseball.

I don't care about his numbers. His numbers are spectacular. His ability as a player, his competitiveness, is unquestioned. Without a doubt, he was able to go from team to team and make them better. Every aspect of Pete's game was Hall of Fame worthy. But at the time when Pete broke the rule, there was only one rule in baseball that got you banned: you can't gamble on baseball. It's getting back to the credibility of the game, and that's why we have to keep pushing forward and testing for performance-enhancing drugs. That's why it was so devastating with the Senate hearings and to see guys shake their fingers in front of Congress, like Rafael Palmeiro saying, "I've never taken performance-enhancing drugs," when he already had a positive drug test behind him.

One of the reasons many of these players started on steroids was to recover from injuries. But then it primarily came down to the fact that they wanted to be better, and they did this through chemical enhancement. At the time, baseball had not banned these drugs. They started to go after steroids, but only later did they ban amphetamines, which I consider one of the most important bans.

Now the one thing that seems to be a bit of a problem is medical exemptions. Initially, exemptions for things like attention deficit disorder (ADD) and attention deficit hyperactivity disorder (ADHD) were fairly few and far between. On a yearly basis, somewhere in the neighborhood of 15 players were diagnosed with ADD, and they were allowed to take two drugs—Adderall and Ritalin. For kids who suffer from ADD or other types of learning disorders, these drugs act not as barbiturates but with a calming effect.

In the adult body, however, these drugs actually act as an amphetamine. Amphetamines were banned, but Adderall and Ritalin are still exempt. Amazingly enough, we've had many more people in baseball who have been diagnosed with ADD and ADHD, far beyond the normal percentage of the population. Here's a list of the medical exemptions during one three-year span:

2006—28
2007—103
2008—106

It's almost inconceivable the prevalence could rise that much. But those are the legal amphetamines given to players with exemptions these days. Perhaps we'll have to look into a nonpartisan medical panel to figure out exactly who should take them and who shouldn't, because it's a tremendous advantage to those who can take them. While there are people who need them to be able to function very well in their everyday lives, there are people who will always abuse that particular loophole in the testing system. That's something we'll probably have to look into. That's looking ahead into the future, not only in the new Collective Bargaining Agreement but even beyond that. The testing programs that were implemented in the recent past have been fantastic. They've caught minor leaguers. They've also caught a few major leaguers, including Manny Ramirez and Edinson Volquez, the fine pitcher from the Cincinnati Reds.

That brings up a point that is offensive to me, and that is the differences in how the situations involving Ramirez and Volquez were handled. Ramirez actually served his 50-game suspension and his commensurate loss of pay, which for him was substantial. Ramirez served his suspension during the season, which hurt his numbers and hurt the Los Angeles Dodgers. You should be penalized like this if you are caught taking performance-enhancing drugs.

But the Volquez situation was completely different. Volquez was coming off arm surgery and was not going to be available to the Cincinnati Reds until after the All-Star Game. He wasn't going to be able to pitch in the first half. But for some odd reason, which I believe was absolutely ludicrous, he was allowed to serve his suspension and the ensuing loss in pay, which turned out to be around $139,000, at that time. He served the suspension while he couldn't pitch because of the injury. That doesn't amount to much of a penalty.

With craziness like that, I would hope baseball would consider making a rule—and enforcing it—where a guy can't serve his suspension while he's on the DL. How else is that player going to learn to respect the game?

There's a sliding scale of morality in baseball. This has taken place for as long as I can remember. You might look at one team and say, "Well, they'll accept something that other teams won't, and that's good and that's bad." But it's more complicated than that.

The sliding scale of morality was never more clearly illustrated than back in 1983 when the Kansas City Royals had a drug scandal, and it involved outfielder Jerry Martin, first baseman Willie Mays Aikens, former Cy Young Award winner Vida Blue, and Willie Wilson, who happened to be a great center fielder at the time. The organization quickly jumped on the fact they wouldn't tolerate anything like this and released Martin, Aikens, and Blue. But they said that Wilson was very contrite and as an act of contrition, he was going to serve community service and would stay with the team.

Now I'm sure this decision wasn't colored at all by the fact that Wilson had 230 hits in 1980 while the three other players were well past their prime and wouldn't have much ability much longer. Martin, Aikens and Blue were let go immediately, whereas the one player who was very good was kept around. Is it good? Is it bad? I think it sends the wrong message. But it's also the sliding scale of morality.

This goes hand in hand with some teams' philosophy that the rules apply only to the lesser-talented players. There are very successful teams, however, that have a set of rules that don't vary. Try wearing dreadlocks, long hair or a beard with the New York Yankees. You can't. You won't. You just won't get to the Yankees. And I know there's a sure, first-ballot Hall of Famer in Randy Johnson, who used to sport long, scraggly locks, facial hair, and whatever look he wanted with the various teams he pitched for. He was a great pitcher.

Eventually, he found his way to the New York Yankees and was informed, in no uncertain terms, before he got there, "That hair comes off, pal. We don't enjoy facial hair, either. So if you're going to play for the New York Yankees, you're going to abide by our rules or you're not going to play for the Yankees. It's as simple as that." They really don't veer from that policy.

In the same vein, try not hustling for the Minnesota Twins under manager Ron Gardenhire. If you don't hustle, sometimes you don't play. And if you're young and you don't hustle, they warn you, but if you don't hustle again, well, ask Alexi Casilla just exactly what happens after you're warned and you lay down a bunt and carry your bat to first base. What happens is the next day you're playing in Triple A.

Bobby Cox's Atlanta Braves also have rules that don't bend. There were a couple stories about this, including one involving Walt Weiss, who was a very good shortstop.

Walt came to the Braves after being selected as an All-Star, having excelled with Oakland and Colorado. Early in his Braves career, Weiss got to a ball at shortstop that he could have gotten in front of, but instead, he attempted to backhand it. The ball hit off his glove and went into the outfield. And after their game, coach Pat Corrales went to Weiss and informed him that Cox wanted to see him.

Weiss approached Cox, and it was a very short conversation. Bobby said, "I just wanted to let you know, it doesn't matter where you came from. But here in Atlanta, we get in front of those balls." That was it. Very simple. Right to the point, and Walt got the message.

But even as there are teams that lay down the law, there are certain players who have caused problems wherever they've gone because of one sort or another or different things. And those guys don't end up with the teams who are so strict.

For instance, in the long career of Milton Bradley, have you ever seen him play for the Twins, Yankees, Braves, Cardinals or the Angels? I think the answer is no. And I believe that is in part because of the problems he causes. I believe in second chances, but teams that compromise or loosen up their rules on fifth or sixth chances usually end up with a big and expensive problem.

The White Sox used to have a firm rule regarding hair length. At the start of the 2006 season, shortly after they won the World Series, at least four players were told to trim their hair because it was deemed too long. However, in August of 2010, the Sox—who were looking to add a hitter in hopes of surpassing Minnesota in the AL Central—acquired Manny Ramirez on a waiver claim from the Los Angeles Dodgers. Ramirez's dreadlocks were an obvious issue, but the Sox skirted any controversy by reaching a compromise with Ramirez that wasn't afforded the players in 2006.

Ramirez produced a whopping two extra-base hits and two RBIs in 88 plate appearances, so the White Sox didn't get their money's worth from Ramirez while stretching their rules.

In this day and age where the ability groups are as close as they are, when you have big and expensive problems that take the emphasis away from winning, then you're going to underachieve. That happens much more often than a troubled player coming to an organization and putting them over the top.

The one thing that almost always has held true is that you can't tell that much about a guy when things are going well because when you're playing this game well, it's a pretty easy game to play. But you can certainly tell a whole lot about a guy when he's struggling, when things don't come easy. Does his personality change. Do his work habits change? Is he going to go into a sort of baseball depression? Is he going to keep his head up? Do you know for sure that he will come out of it? Or is he going to have a "woe is me" approach in every at-bat and every situation as he continues to struggle?

Does he continue to bring his bat to the field? Does a guy struggling with the bat not make plays? Or does he not think about certain situations and wind up not only not hitting, but also performing terribly in the field? Conversely when he's hitting, is he doing everything right defensively so you know he has the skills? those are things you have to find out about during the scouting process.

Many organizations comprise a multitude of diverse personalities—players and coaches with differing agendas and differing personal habits and lifestyles. For me, if an organization wants to perpetuate winning, that winning atmosphere has to take hold before the organization can win on a consistent basis. You must take all 25 players on the major league team and blend them into a unit with just one common goal.

This is not an easy thing to do, and at times it seems almost impossible.

By having consistent rules in place, when you don't make exceptions for the star player, you can build a cohesive team, even when you have these 25 personalities and 25 agendas.

• • •

I also think we should look into realignment. This is something I've talked to Bud Selig about. Some people have mentioned having a "have" and "have not" league. The high-payroll teams, such as the New York Yankees, the Boston Red Sox, the Chicago Cubs of recent vintage, the Philadelphia Phillies, the St. Louis Cardinals, and other teams that routinely run player payrolls of about $80 million or more, would play in a league where they played head to head. The lower-revenue, smaller-market teams would play in a league in which they played head to head. Then they'd have a David and Goliath Series.

It's a decent enough idea and something that might be entertained. But I think at the end of the day, it's not going to happen. You don't want to change some of the natural rivalries.

There's also the idea of realigning geographically so that you have teams that play one another more than the six times that you have in interleague play. For instance, if you were in New York, wouldn't it be wonderful to have the Mets and Yankees in the same division? Or to have the Cubs and White Sox in the same division? San Francisco and Oakland? Or Texas and Houston?

Let's look at the National League Central. You have the two Chicago teams—White Sox and Cubs. You can include Minnesota and St. Louis, natural rivals of the White Sox and Cubs, respectively. There's another natural rival for Minnesota and the Cubs in Milwaukee. There you have a division with those five teams. First, it's an impressive division. Also, your in-division games would be phenomenally intense. The same thing holds true with the American League East if you want to go through the American League.

The problem, however, jumps right at you. This is a problem that I have no solution for. I'm just bringing up the possibility because it's been talked about. In a new American League East, you'd keep the New York Yankees and Boston playing together, as well as the Mets. You can add Philadelphia and make one of their rivals Pittsburgh. Pittsburgh isn't very good, but someday they could swing back the other way. You probably would like to put Washington and Baltimore in that division for geographical situations.

So you'd have a pretty strong division. You'd have the Yankees, Boston, Philadelphia, the Mets, and one more team—Pittsburgh or another team. You could do the same with a southern division, where you would have Atlanta, Florida, and Tampa Bay. Those teams don't have as many long-standing rivalries as the AL East, but you can try to find other teams down there.

Again, this is a rough version of a geographical division that would cut down on travel and make the interdivision games more intense. You'd play 18 times against each other, and that would be phenomenal for generating more interest.

You might not have all of the teams that you would want, but certainly the Dodgers and San Francisco would have to play in the same division. The Angels must be included because they're sitting close to Los Angeles. San Diego has improved. Oakland needs to be in the same division with the Giants because the Athletics are sitting right there. You might have to throw in Seattle because all of a sudden you would have a West Coast team and your Western Division. You'd go from there.

I'm not giving all the answers here because I don't have them. But this is something that h,as been mentioned. It seems to be a pretty decent idea competitively and you have the ability to cut travel costs. You would, however, have to resolve the issue of the designated hitter.

Nevertheless, you would have more competitive divisions. You would have more intense rivalries. Eventually, if they're in your division, the rivalries would be commensurate with the success of your teams.

So, I think there may be some type of realignment. It might not be geographical or economic. Adding international teams is well down the road, but these are things we talk about when looking at the future.

• • •

The Oakland Athletics have had some wonderful teams. They were world champions in 1972–74, the first two titles under Dick Williams. They had excellent players then, and they had very good players in the late 1980s.

When Sandy Alderson left the helm as GM in 1997 and turned it over to Billy Beane, Beane became somewhat legendary (1) because of the book *Moneyball*, and (2) because of the fact he's done a pretty decent job with low payrolls in Oakland.

Billy is an interesting character, and personally, I like him. I was part of a group that had a chance to buy the Oakland Athletics, and there were rumors that I was going to take over as general manager and fire everyone, including Billy. I had to call Billy on the phone, person to person, and tell him that was not the case.

I already had a five-year contract as president of the team, with an option to buy 10 points of an equity ownership position in this team. But there was no way in the world that I would enter a situation and fire anybody before one year of full evaluation. It didn't make any sense to me.

Good businesspeople use that first year to evaluate what they have to determine if it's successful. I assured Billy that he would be our general manager while we came in and evaluated for one year. Our criteria was who would be the best man for the job. If the best man for the job was currently in the job, there was no reason to make any substitutions or additions.

Now that usually doesn't happen. They usually take one year and evaluate what you have. If every member of this organization is doing the best job that you believe they can possibly do, then you don't make any changes.

But of course, with a team that doesn't win, that's a bit unrealistic. I don't say you have a policy, but you have to make some changes. When I look at low payroll, small-market teams that don't draw very well, I'm not interested in "Moneyball" with Billy Beane. I want to hear about "BeinfestBall" that you see with the Florida Marlins and Larry Beinfest. They've done a phenomenal job with their talent evaluation, their trades, their player development, and that's what other teams can learn from.

You take a look at the Marlins' players, and they're outstanding on virtually a year-to-year basis. Yet that team, which is building a new stadium set for 2012, doesn't draw many fans. But it hasn't stopped them from being competitive almost each and every year. So I would stop production on Moneyball and go to BeinfestBall.

In *Moneyball* one of the players is an overweight catcher by the name of Jeremy Brown, who was the 35th overall selection in the 2002 draft but was supposedly a value pick because he reached base frequently and had a high on-base percentage. They got him fairly cheaply (a $350,000 signing bonus), and this is what a small-market team has to do.

Well, Mark Teahen was selected by the Athletics four picks later and has experienced varying degrees of success. But the player selected nine picks behind Brown was Joey Votto, the 2010 National League Most Valuable Player with Cincinnati.

As for Brown, he did reach the majors in September of 2006 and was 3-for-10 with Oakland. But he was designated for assignment in May of 2007 and retired from baseball before the 2008 season.

What I've seen from the original team that they were talking about in *Moneyball* is Eric Chavez, who was the best high school hitter in the country when he was drafted in the first round by Oakland in the first round in 1996. That wasn't "Moneyball." I saw Miguel Tejada, who emerged as an American League Most Valuable Player. Tejada was signed out of the Dominican Republic. That wasn't exactly "Moneyball." He swung at everything.

What I did see, however, was a wonderful pitching staff that Billy was able to develop, which was great. But that's not really the essence of "Moneyball" because the Orioles and some of the great teams have been doing that for years. The 1971 Orioles had four 20-game winners in Pat Dobson, Mike Cuellar, Dave McNally, and Jim Palmer. Later on, when I got to the Orioles, we had five Cy Young Awards wrapped up in three guys: Palmer had three, Mike Flanagan won it in 1979, and I won it in 1980. Scott McGregor won 20 games while I was winning my 25.

Not many people heard Scott's name, but he was a terrific pitcher. Dennis Martinez went on to pitch a perfect game, and went on to become a great pitcher. That was a five-man rotation. There was nothing startling, nothing innovative about putting a better man on the mound on a daily basis than the other team has. That, to me, has been Oakland's success under Billy Beane.

They have put together some terrific pitchers, either by trade or by development. I don't knock the Oakland development system, although they haven't won very much. Yes, they're competitive, occasionally getting into the playoffs.

But understand something: they're getting into the playoffs by playing in the American League West. If you're going to pick a division where you're going to get into the playoffs, pick the American League West. It has four teams. Usually, one of those teams is going to stink. That means you have three teams left that are competitive. To at least be eligible for a playoff berth, you have to be better than just one team, and maybe you'll get the wild-card berth. Obviously it behooves whatever team it is to win the division. But out of all the divisions to win in baseball, whether it's the AL or NL, the four-team division is the division to be in because you have to beat fewer teams.

If I'm going to extol a system that is employed by lower-revenue teams in smaller markets, I want it to end with a ring or a World Series appearance. If you get to the World Series and lose it, there's not much you can do because anything can happen in a short series. We've seen teams that win 83 games and win the world championship, like the St. Louis Cardinals in 2006 and Minnesota with 85 wins in 1987. They weren't the best teams in baseball in their respective seasons, but they won the World Series. So in a short series, anyone can win.

Over 162 games, there are no miracles. The best team does win.

I've seen the Arizona Diamondbacks, in their fourth year of existence, win the World Series. I've seen the Florida Marlins, an expansion team, win the World Series twice and stay competitive virtually every year.

Grady Fuson has rejoined the Oakland organization and he could bring a change. Grady was largely responsible for the selections of pitchers Barry Zito, Mark Mulder, and Tim Hudson and third baseman Eric Chavez, which made Oakland a perennial contender in the AL West in the previous decade. Now that Grady is back, maybe the Athletics' fortunes will change for the better.

• • •

Not many players—and this is regardless of position on the field or in the batting order—realize what a symbiotic relationship the media and the players have as it pertains to the fans of our sport, which is directly proportionate to the individual players' salaries. If the fans stop watching on television and stop listening on radio, the advertising revenues will start to go down drastically. If the local and national ratings go down, so will the revenues when the next contract is negotiated with Major League Baseball. You get revenues from local deals as well as national stations, and if the viewership and listeners continue to decline, it's just a matter of time before attendance is affected at the ballparks.

If attendance is affected, the players' salaries are going to go up or down in direct proportion to the revenues that the teams make from those media outlets. Many fans know the favorite players on their teams from the local and national media, whether print or electronic. They don't get a chance to talk to their players, so their knowledge of that player is how he is portrayed by the media people.

That includes the beat writers, the columnists, the reporters on some of the bigger stations—the MLB Network, ESPN, TBS (at times), and many others. There are local outlets, like Comcast and, in Chicago, WGN, which is a superstation. How a player is portrayed by the people who do those jobs and evaluate their performance and handle play-by-play duties during the course of the game can define what fans know or believe aboutwhat a player is or isn't.

The ability of the players is there. It doesn't go away with anything that the media says or does, but the players' relationship to the fans is something that is very fragile and sometimes can be affected by how they treat the media.

Many players are smart and very cooperative when you ask them to help you out with something. Those are the players who respect the job that the media person has. However, there are many players who don't care about the media at all, don't bother talking to them. Not only do they not understand the media's job, but they have no desire to help them do their job because they don't care about their job.

Those guys become very difficult to deal with. But when you become a major league baseball player, if you want to participate in owning a gigantic house or driving a $300,000 car, my feeling is that you have to buy the total package.

That could mean being at a local television station and being regarded in a certain amount of high esteem that you never would have been able to do had you not been a professional player. Everything you do makes a certain amount of news, whether it's good or bad.

I equate those who want it all without cooperating to buying a beautiful house but not purchasing the front door to get in. It's the only beautiful house on beautiful grounds, but you can't get into the house. That's how I see players who want to participate in all of the money and all of the great things that this sport affords them, yet don't feel they have an obligation to the fans. They don't feel they should be heroes. They don't feel they should talk to the media.

Some have the attitude that, "Well, if the media says something bad about me, well, then I'm not going to talk to the media." They're going to boycott. But by not talking to the media, they're not talking to the fans either. Those same players aren't going to talk to each fan individually, and without the media, the fans don't have access to those players.

I know the media can be intrusive. I know they might take a little more time than you want to give them. But for the most part, everyone lives off one another.

The players believe they're the most important thing because without the players, you wouldn't have the game. And that's true; you would have other players, but you wouldn't have the game as we see it now. But what the players have to understand is if there were no money coming from the media outlets, if there weren't these dollars being poured into the game by the fans, the players' salaries wouldn't be close to what they are today.

Epilogue

The reason that the title of this book is leaning toward the fans' game is that, contrary to popular belief, it isn't the players' game. It's not even the owners' game. It's certainly not the various cities' game. At times, it appears to be a whole lot of different people's game. But at the end of the day, it's the fans' game. It always has been. That's why statistics are so important. That's why people can come and watch losing teams as long as they continue their infatuation with the game itself.

The fans, almost without exception, have been very good to me my entire career, and it wasn't only the great years. I had some very good years. I had some very bad years. I had all of the mediocre years in between. Certainly, when you're doing very well, it's easy for the fans to cheer you. When you're doing poorly, it's easy for the fans to boo you. I've had the pleasure of being cheered many, many times. I can honestly tell you that being booed on the road doesn't mean a great deal to you because you're the enemy. Being booed at home is a little more difficult, and I have been booed in my home park several times, especially when I went to Baltimore and they allocated a four-year contract to a sub-.500 pitcher. I was 6–7 in the first half of the season while the team was advancing to 102 wins.

I can't really remember being booed too often in Chicago on either side of town, which is why I've always hung around even when I wasn't working on television after 2004. I went to work for ESPN on television and radio for a few years, did some playoffs for TBS, and then I got a chance to come back to radio and television with the White Sox. But the fans on both sides of town have been phenomenal to me, and that's one of the reasons why I have dedicated this book to the fans. First, because it is the fans' game and because they spend, in many cases, lots of hard-earned money, which has been increasing rapidly in recent years. They're the lifeblood of the game. It's the fact that they go out and pay the ticket prices, the souvenirs, hot dogs, and adult beverages as well as sodas, that keeps the game alive.

Without the fans watching on television, without them listening on radio, without them going to the park as many times as they possibly can, without the fans teaching their sons and daughters about whatever team they happen to be rooting for and passing along this allegiance from generation to generation, baseball wouldn't be able to perpetuate itself, and it has. It has done so through recessions, depressions, World Wars, police action, and everything else we, as a country, have been through. The fans always have been there.

Yes, they got a little disgusted after 1994 when the game was shut down and there was no World Series. Every work stoppage gets blamed on the owners or the players or one individual owner or the head of unions or any of the other multitudes of people that the fans think are culpable.

Whatever the case may be, the Collective Bargaining Agreement (CBA), under Bud Selig for the past 15 years has quelled that acrimony, and a work stoppage has been avoided. Fans have had an opportunity to see baseball every year. That's a diversion from their everyday problems. You can go to the ballpark. You can get away from what's going on in a bad economy, assuming you have the money to pay for the tickets or you have a good friend who decides that he or she can't use his or hers on their given day and you're going to receive his or hers. So you go to the park and forget what's going on in your life, just for a short period of time.

For the fan, baseball has no clock. It ends when one team has more runs than the other team. It ends at whatever pace the game is played. That's one of the great things about the game of baseball as it pertains to the fans. They can go out on a beautiful summer day or a gorgeous summer's eve and watch, for many of them, what is a six-month odyssey. Especially for whatever team they're rooting for.

My old partner Harry Caray felt that the best day of the year was the beginning of spring training, followed closely by Opening Day. At the start of spring training, pitchers and catchers reported, and the fans were allowed to get very close to the players—much closer than they will ever get during the course of a season. To Harry, life was renewing itself. Baseball was back, and the long winter was over because people, in many instances, left their colder climates and would follow their team to Florida or Arizona.

They would see the start of what was going to be their 25-man piece of the puzzle, their baseball team. That, to Harry, was a great day. And the saddest day of the year for Harry was the final day of the season. Whenever that final day was—whether it culminated in a World Series win, a World Series loss, a playoff loss, or a year when you didn't get into the playoffs and went home— that was the saddest day of the year. Because now the stage was turned over to football, basketball, and hockey, and winter was coming. You could certainly feel it in the air. It was time to hibernate until spring training rolled around.

More teams are having a fanfest of sorts. Some call theirs a convention. It's usually in January in their home city. In the case of Chicago, you have the creation by John McDonough of the Cubs' fan extravaganza. The Sox do the same thing. That's really a kickoff to the baseball season, a prelude. Because when you go to these fan conventions, you know that pitchers and catchers report in the not too distant future.

When that happens, then it's time for baseball, and the fans start gearing up and paying more attention to reports coming out of Florida and Arizona. How does this young guy look? How does this veteran look after coming back from surgery? How does this guy acquired in the winter look in the uniform of the team you're rooting for? You can go on and on with just exactly the attraction that people have to this great game.

Because it is the fans' game; they are the people who enable the salaries to be where they are. They are the people who sometimes spur their home team on to great heights because of the cheering and the yelling, the excitement and the electricity in a ballpark that takes place late in the game when the team has a rally, or if you're lucky enough to have a team in the race. Those home games and the feelings that the fans give to the home team are things that can't be duplicated. That's one of the reasons that if you take a look at the disparity between the home wins and road wins, you'll see (without exception) that it's much easier to play at home. The reasons are numerous, but one of the reasons is that the fans will be there to cheer you on, giving you that little bit extra, making you play a little harder, and that's the reason for the name of the book.

At the end of the day, when the fans filter out of that ballpark and head home, many dissect the game, talk about the game, and analyze the game. "Oh, I would have done this when the manager did that." They can't believe that third-base coach held up that base runner. "How in the world did this guy not execute it?"

The beauty of baseball, from a fan's perspective, is that each and every fan believes he or she can manage the team better than the manager. A lot of fans believe they can be the general manager and assemble personnel better. Because there is so very little in the game of baseball that's black and white and so much of the game is varying shades of gray, every fan is entitled to his or her opinion about what's going on.

As I always try to tell our fans, through all of the years I've done talk radio and answered the fans on all of the various blogs and other media that we have today, I say to them, "You are entitled to your opinion." That's one of the things that makes this a great game, that there is so much that's open to interpretation.

Bear in mind something that has held true for a long, long time, and will continue to hold true for as long as our great game is alive. That is, yes, there would be baseball without fans, but these guys would be playing for very little money. Now, they might play anyway, because all of us who played the game growing up played because we loved it. Most of the guys playing in the major leagues today still love it. But the game would be substantially changed were it not for the fans.

Because at the end of the day, regardless of what owners, what players, or what unions or economic circumstances, what wars or tragedies that have happened in the world, the game has lived on.

The game is thriving.

The game has prospered.

And it is all because of the fans.